VENOM AND LAUGHTER

VENOM AND LAUGHTER

A Colleen Copes With Anti-Irish Prejudice
in 19th Century New England

Julia Cooley Altrocchi
and
Paul Hemenway Altrocchi

iUniverse, Inc.
Bloomington

VENOM AND LAUGHTER
A Colleen Copes With Anti-Irish Prejudice

iUniverse books may be ordered through booksellers or by contacting:

iUniverse
1663 Liberty Drive
Bloomington, IN 47403
www.iuniverse.com
1-800-Authors (1-800-288-4677)

ISBN: 978-1-4697-8836-4 (sc)
ISBN: 978-1-4697-8837-1 (hc)
ISBN: 978-1-4697-8835-7 (ebk)

Library of Congress Control Number: 2012903397

Printed in the United States of America

iUniverse rev. date: 04/30/2012

Contents

What stronger breastplate than a heart untainted?
  Thrice is he armed that hath his quarrel just;
  And he but naked, though locked up in steel,
  Whose conscience with injustice is corrupted.

—Shakespeare, *Henry VI, Part 2*, III, ii, 232-235

1961 Dedication

To the memory of my
lovely Irish Grandmother

Julia Adelaide Sweeney Wooster

1830-1908

and her shining life among
hostile Connecticut Yankees.

—Julia Cooley Altrocchi

Portrait of Julia Sweeney Wooster, 1830-1908

DRAMATIS PERSONAE

Julia Sweeney Wooster
Letsome Terrell Wooster—Julia's husband
Alice and Emma Wooster—their daughters
Submit Swayne Chatfield Wooster—Julia's mother-in-law
William Sweeney—Julia's father
Mary Canty Sweeney—Julia's mother
Kevin Sweeney—Julia's brother
Maggie Sweeney—Julia's youngest sister
Chatfield Swayne—Submit Wooster's brother
Amy Goodwin Swayne—Mrs. Chatfield Swayne
George Swayne—son of the Chatfield Swaynes
Sally Goodwin Swayne—daughter of the Chatfield Swaynes
Almira Aurelia Humphreys—third cousin of Submit Wooster
Helena Humphreys—dominated daughter of Almira Humphreys
Gideon Dunlap—neighbor and friend of the Woosters
Elvira Gunn Dunlap—wife of Gideon Dunlap
Gunn Dunlap—son of the Gideon Dunlaps
Annie Dunlap—pleasant, homely daughter of the Gideon Dunlaps
Rev. Epaphroditus Smith—minister of First Methodist Episcopal Church, Seymour
Caresse Monnier Smith—Reverend Smith's wife, of French descent
Father O'Laverty—priest of St. Augustine's Catholic Church, Seymour
Dr. Abiram Stoddard—family physician and neighbor
Dr. Thomas Stoddard—his son, also a family physician
Dr. Fritz Steudel—MD successor to the Drs. Stoddard in Seymour
Mrs. Lydia Kinney—Julia's kindly young neighbor

Llewellyn Kinney—her husband, reported missing in the Mexican War

Mrs. Benajah Johnson (Urania Johnson)—Mayflower descendant

Benny Johnson—her son, involved in tarring and feathering episode

Yelverton Perry—delinquent trouble-maker of Seymour

Minerva Buckingham—one of the "upper crust" of Seymour

Philo Buckingham—her son, involved in tarring and feathering episode

Mrs. Charles Goodyear—"Genteel" lady of the town and aware of it

Mrs. Austin Goodyear Day—ditto

Mrs. Henry K. Beecher—ditto

Anson G. Phelps—wealthy manufacturer

Ann Phelps Stokes—of New York, his daughter

Thomas Hart Seymour—Democratic Governor of Connecticut, 1850-1853

Alexander T. Stewart—wealthy Irish merchant of New York

Judge Robert Munger—of the New Haven Court

Henry Tomlinson—defense attorney, New Haven

Wilphalet Todd—orator; Fourth of July Speaker

William Hull—hired man of the Woosters

Eliza Hull—William Hull's wife who worked as cook for the Woosters

Page Sanford—blacksmith and son of "Pitchfork" Sanford

Marcel Boudreaux—ambulatory peddler from France

Awley O'Neill—manager of the Whittemore Tavern

Maeva O'Neill—his wife

Dennis O'Neill—their son

Moira O'Neill—their daughter

Patrick O'Neill—Awley's father

Crotty Hartigan—owner of saloon at foot of "Knockmedown Hill"
Mary Hartigan—his wife
Whiddy Hartigan—their son; coachman of the Woosters
Claragh, Gavan, Aileen and Heafy—other Hartigan children
Lazarus Jones—half-black, half-white fugitive slave
Tribulation Cumming—old black living on Knockmedown Hill

Portrait of Letsome Terrell Wooster, 1830-1908

2012 PREFACE

The mid-1800s in the United States were years of unrest, foment, tension-inducing rapid social mobility, ethnic and racial prejudice and violent emotions over slavery which soon evolved into civil war. Outwardly quiet and quaint New England towns in seemingly peaceful river valleys were no exception.

Julia Cooley was a witness to this book's saga of powerful Yankee prejudice against the Irish, including considerable negative drama within her own family. She was born in 1893 in Seymour, Connecticut and, although brought up in Chicago, she spent the next fifteen summers visiting her very affectionate grandparents, ended only by their deaths in 1908. She overlapped for five years with her great-grandmother, Submit Swayne Wooster, who perpetrated malignant ethnic prejudice within the family, particularly against her Irish daughter-in-law, Julia Sweeney Wooster.

Julia Cooley had vivid early childhood memories of the prejudice described in this book. Submit died at the age of 92 in 1898 after living in the same home with her son Letsome and his Irish wife, Julia, for forty-eight years, a significant burden for any daughter-in-law even without being the daily target of hostile remarks sustained by mindless intolerance.

Julia Cooley Altrocchi, mother of the present co-author of this book, always regarded those Seymour summers, despite the blatant intolerance, as a major high point of her life, full of laughter and intellectual encouragement from her grandparents. It was Julia Sweeney Wooster who introduced her namesake granddaughter, Julia Cooley, a gifted child-poet beginning at the age of four, to The Enchanted Hill behind their stately home at 28 Pearl Street and who stimulated both her lifelong love of nature's beauty and her poetic talent.

Young Julia Cooley spent long hours on that hill during those memorable summers communing with nature at the urging of her grandmother and writing poems which were assembled into *The Poems of a Child*, published when she was eleven years-old, the first book of poetry by a child in the United States. Here is a sample, written in Seymour when she was a reflective nine year-old:

Youth

When I was young I loved the birds and bees,
I loved the sky, I loved the sighing trees,
I loved the fields, I loved the babbling stream,
And all day long I used to dream and dream
Of all the lovely things I saw and heard—
The hill, the field, the little singing bird.

Young Julia adored her grandmother whom she described as the gentlest of women with a soft lilting voice, great affection for children and infectious laughter at the slightest trigger. There was a somber undertone in the household, however, readily apparent to grandchildren from the youngest age—endless biting sarcasm and denigration of her lovely grandmother by the straight-lipped, cold granite Submit Swayne Chatfield Wooster. Submit considered herself a privileged member of New England's Anglo-Saxon elite which had the God-given right to look down upon and castigate an inferior species.

Julia Sweeney Wooster was Irish, a lowly race looked down upon as crude peasants by the English for centuries. This learned loathing was passed down from generation to generation and even across the seas to New England. Julia's dour, widowed mother-in-law was her ever-present verbal torturer in close confines with Julia for most of Julia's adult life. Submit did not even allow the name "Sweeney" to be spoken in the Wooster household, nor did she permit any mention of Julia's Irish ancestry.

The contamination of supposedly pristine Wooster genes by Irish blood was a point of pervasive shame and embarrassment for the Yankee side of the family. Pollution by the Irish horrified many New England gentry in that era, families whose often-embellished or even fictitious pedigrees were endlessly trumpeted as they sought to climb into empty upper class niches in the New World by hook or by crook, often by blatantly fraudulent pedigree chicanery.

As many historians have pointed out, if all claims of ancestry from Mayflower passengers were correct, the Mayflower, like modern cruise ships, would have held several thousand passengers rather than a mere one hundred pilgrims. The actual Mayflower voyagers were primarily simple tradesmen and craftsmen from lower and lower middle classes fleeing England's restrictive atmosphere to seek religious and social freedom and new economic opportunities. The ship was not jam-packed with England's upper-crust nobility—so often claimed by later eager aspirants for social status and prestige in New England, much easier to achieve fictitiously than by earning it.

Julia Cooley Altrocchi, 1893-1972, was the first child of Helen (Nellie) Wooster Cooley who was the third of four living daughters of Letsome and Julia. Nellie was born in

1865, the final year of the Civil War, nine years after the end of this book.

Julia Cooley was never told in childhood or young adulthood that she was one-fourth Irish. The name "Sweeney" was successfully suppressed and the secret was well kept, breached at last by Nellie when her daughter was forty-five years-old.

This book has been revised by a great-grandson of Julia Sweeney Wooster who inherited his mother's manuscript and whose orange hair derives from the Mac Sweeneys of County Cork. The book is still primarily the work of poet and novelist Julia Cooley Altrocchi.

This story of cruel ethnic prejudice against the Irish is particularly sad because Submit's son, Letsome Wooster, and his Irish wife, Julia, were soul-mates throughout their entire fifty-eight year marriage. They adored each other and were inseparable. When Letsome died on November 27, 1908, Julia died eighteen days later of what her physician diagnosed as a broken heart.

One can still find vivid evidence of the ethnic prejudice within the Wooster household described in this book, all attributable to Submit's malevolent, venomous influence for half a century. When Letsome and Julia died in 1908, they were not buried together under one tomb in Seymour's Trinity Cemetery. Letsome lies under a stately, seven-foot white marble tombstone in the center of the family plot, chiseled with name, birth and death dates, and a tribute to his exemplary life. His shining shamrock wife was buried twenty feet away in a corner of the plot where a simple bronze plaque, corroded green by time, and flush with the earth, states only: Julia Wooster, 1830-1908.

The 2012 author thanks his brother, John Altrocchi, and Pencie McBride Huneke for very helpful advice on editing the inherited manuscript, and artist Dorothy Norton of Bend, Oregon for creating the Irish book cover.

Paul Altrocchi, MD
Kaneohe, Hawaii

CHAPTER 1

YANKEE PERDITION

(September 4, 1850)

The little Naugatuck Railroad train clattered along the new roadbed from Derby to Winsted on the morning of Saturday, September fourth, 1850, like a string of blocks dragged by a playful boy. Paper flowers of female passengers' straw bonnets nodded, demi-veils fluttered, eardrops tinkled and the travelers seemed, in spite of their jiggling spines, to be enjoying the journey. All, that is, except Submit Swayne Wooster who sat coldly plumb, disdaining even to look out the window.

The tall, fair-haired young man in gray broadcloth and gray top-hat who sat next to her resembled her in build, coloring and good looks but not in facial expression for he had a happy countenance. He cast a sidewise glance at her profile and noted her rigid lips and scriggles at eye-corners, the subtleties of which he had learned to read by the age of three.

Letsome smiled as he thought of his soon-to-be wife. He hoped the smile would lure his mother into a more joyful mood. He laid his hand affectionately on her black lace mitted hand. "We're almost there. Waterbury, as you know, is a special town because that is where Julia and I met." The solicitude in his voice and hand sent a quiver through his

1

mother's stiff body from her black bonnet to the hem of her black silk dress.

Restive thoughts were rushing through Submit's mind like waters swirling down the Naugatuck River a few yards from the roadbed. Every atom of her being rebelled against the necessity of the journey and the ordeal towards which it was taking her—*the wedding*. She was trying to rise to this unhappy occasion for the sake of her favorite son who had been swept off his feet by the ensnaring tentacles of a scheming Irish colleen.

Submit's armigerous gentry friends, with not-so-subtle flickers of their eyelids, downcasting corners of their mouths, and quick lookings-away, had told her with unmistakable upper class mannerisms that such a marriage with a shamrock girl was quite unacceptable. Her mind tried to reject the racial implications. My God, an *Irish* girl forever soiling the purity of our English blood! The words "Papist!" "Paddy!" and "Biddy!" raced through a mind which was pervasively permeated with prejudice against such members of an immigrant lower class.

Submit Wooster's intrinsic disdain was enhanced by three hundred years of English misinformation, biased teaching in schools, rumors of sinister "Popish Plots" to take over England, massacres of Huguenots, and monastery scandals. Anti-Irish prejudice in New England had been enhanced by heresy statutes, the extreme narrow-mindedness of Puritan immigrants, recent anti-Irish riots in Philadelphia and Harrisburg, and frenetic "patriotic" activities of self-styled "native" Americans who felt that loyalty meant hating anyone different. Bigotry and intolerance were heavy in the air of New England in the mid-1800s.

Letsome had repeatedly tried to mollify Submit by emphasizing that the Sweeneys were gentry of Cork who

2

had come to the United States twenty years before the recent potato famine, and that William Sweeney was a well-educated man who wrote and spoke fluent Latin. His daughter, Julia, was born right here in Connecticut, had graduated with honors from High School in Waterbury and had spent two years studying with hired Trinity College tutors in Dublin.

Submit tried to bolster herself with the old self-strengthening New England axiom: "it's a hard row to hoe but I'll hoe it." The whole object of the effort, however, made her cringe. It was unutterably upsetting to her core beliefs.

The little train snorted to a standstill. Let lifted his mother's black ruffled parasol down from the rack as well as a suitcase carrying wedding clothes for relatives. Submit tightened her fingers over the polished parasol handle and followed her son down the train steps, feeling as if she were getting out of a tumbril to ascend the platform of a waiting guillotine.

Her son was already greeting, with astonishing cordiality, a very tall man with curly russet hair, sideburns, a small pointed red beard, a moustache that turned up over happy lips, and hazel-green eyes that looked as if they had just seen a whole street of people dancing an Irish jig. He wore a dark olive suit, pale green waistcoat and white cravat. As William Sweeney reached a welcoming hand towards her, Submit reluctantly conceded to him the tips of her cold, moist fingers which protruded from her black half-mitts.

"Mrs. Wooster!" he greeted her warmly, bending gallantly. She withdrew her hand to scrounge around in her black silk wrist-bag for an unnecessary handkerchief. "I hope the journey didn't tire you, ma'am."

"Not at all," she answered stiffly, trying to force a smile. Her draw-string lips and the draw-string of her wrist-bag closed simultaneously. In one flash of his quick green eyes

William had sized up his daughter's future mother-in-law and knew he must curtail his usual flow of Celtic affability. How could the cold, restrained lady in front of him be the mother of such a free-thinking, sensible and likeable young man as Letsome Wooster? She was clearly a prime example of a haughty, stern New Englander to which the Irish minority had become thoroughly accustomed.

You couldn't, he knew, change solid granite in a day but you could shine the sun of pleasantness upon it and allow ferns and wood-sorrel, plant-kin of the shamrock, to gentle it. He smiled and turned away to engage Letsome in conversation. He was thinking that if anyone could mollify a rigid, arrogant New Englander it would be his own outgoing and happy family—his wife, Mary, and his children Kevin, Julia and Maggie.

Submit had not yet met any Sweeney, not even Julia, for, although Let had many times suggested bringing Julia to Seymour for a visit, Submit had refused, hoping she would just disappear. According to her own creative interpretation of family history, no Swayne or Chatfield or Brockett or Terrell or Wooster had ever married a woman who wasn't from the proper social stratum.

Let had shocked her to the core in mid-August when he suddenly announced that he and Julia were getting married in two weeks. Submit had cried out, "Let! You cannot do this! You can't break my heart! You can't destroy your whole life, your career, your family and especially me!"

"Please control yourself, Mother," he answered with unusual firmness. "No tantrums, please! The decision is made. Julia is kind, beautiful, and intelligent, full of laughter and charm that passes description. I deeply love her. None of your upper class Connecticut girls can hold a candle to her."

The station rig drew up at a pretty white cottage at the north end of town. There was a small lawn in front with a border of rose bushes and marigolds. It was neat enough, Submit observed with some surprise, compared to her vision of mud, wattle, barking dogs and dirty children. As soon as the vehicle stopped, an aproned woman walked rapidly out of the front door with an auburn-haired girl coming after.

"Oh, my dear Mrs. Wooster!" exclaimed the plump, black-haired, red-cheeked, sapphire-eyed woman, extending her hand. "A hundred thousand welcomes!" Her rich brogue speech was as melodious as if she had been singing a song.

Submit extended her hand reluctantly and again tried to force a smile.

"Dear Mrs. Wooster, I'm Mary and this is our daughter, Maggie. Our Julia is superstitious about not being seen until the moment of the wedding."

A small shudder went over Submit which Mary Canty Sweeney detected. Mary threw her arms around Let, drawing him tightly to her, a touch of Celtic mischievousness, perhaps, for she knew that Submit's teeth must be clenching. The Irish imp on Mary's shoulder was chortling.

"Bless you, my son!" she exclaimed. "Welcome to the family Sweeney!"

Drawing away, Mary cast a glimpse at Submit. The poor woman's icy gray eyes, surrounded by pickle-colored shadows, seemed to have sunk into her head above her taut lips. Mary couldn't help adding to Let:

"It's a good family you're marrying into, Let. Stock of the O'Neills, High Kings of Ireland." Mary laughed and turned towards Submit. "Mrs. Wooster, you must meet our lad who is studying at Yale Law School. Or rather, I *should* be saying, he must meet *you!* Come out here, Kevin."

Kevin exited the house. He was of medium height, slim, brown-haired, with quizzical upturned eyebrows, bright blue eyes and amusement on his lips. There was something disturbing to Submit about his eyes which seemed to penetrate all her protective layers of dignity. She drew her shoulders together, as if to hitch the heavy cloak of pride over her exposed self.

Kevin gave a half-bow and lifted Submit's unextended right hand with dramatic overcourtesy. Her manner and appearance bore out every one of his assumptions except that she was handsomer than he expected. He noted her dignified carriage and well chiseled nose. With an inward twinkle, the thought occurred to him that if he could teach her how to smile and laugh in the Irish way, she might even be considered beautiful.

"A privilege to meet you at last, Mrs. Wooster," he said.

Submit shook his hand, then withdrew it quickly but had to admit to herself that these were remarkably friendly and good-looking people.

They all moved now towards the house. "I'll be wanting you to meet my sister, Gleona McGinnis, her husband, Darcy and the kids," said Mary. "You see," Mary went on, "Julia wanted only the two families at the wedding ceremony. She regards a wedding as something very sacred indeed."

"I should hope so," replied Submit.

"She's a most towardly, friendly girl and there'll be slews of people coming in afterwards for the wedding shindy. 'Twill be a great let-out entirely." Mary smiled, happy in the prospect of Irish hospitality.

It all seemed so inevitable, thought Submit. There was no way to stop the wedding at this late date. She urged herself to try to adapt to the situation but felt the walls inevitably rising within her. She noted to her surprise that the house was really quite lovely, with fine hand-crocheted lace curtains and beautiful carved walnut furniture from abroad. There were vases and pots of flowers everywhere. In the dining room a mass of ivy vines had been trained up along a trellis and half covered the dining room ceiling. In front of a bank of potted flowers on tiered shelves in the parlor was a statue of a monkish person on a pedestal with arms outstretched in a gesture of benison.

Let had told her many times that the Sweeneys weren't Catholic but she couldn't believe it. He had told her how William had known Mary Canty in his boyhood in Kilmurry near Macroom, Cork, how William's Catholic family had sent him to a seminary to study for the priesthood. William, after two years, had broken with the Church for reasons of stifling dogma, had returned to Kilmurry, married Mary and they had sailed to the United States to start a new life.

Let had told Submit about William's love of learning, his constant reading and study of history, his liberal ideas wrought from his England-oppressed background and his keen interest in science. His first job was as a textile dyer in Hudson, New York. Two years later he moved to Waterbury to work as a chemical engineer for Scovill Manufacturing Company, producer of brass buttons, rolled brass and cast copper. It was in Waterbury that Let had met him on one of his metallurgy business trips.

From the window Submit could see the long lawn going down to the Naugatuck River with a pleasant view of the hills beyond. Tables had been set up near a large arrangement of flowers and branches. Two red-headed boys were turning somersaults around the tables. To Submit, a typical shades down, curtains drawn New Englander, the idea of an outdoor wedding reception was indecent. How public! She turned and stood in front of the pagan statue.

Mary Sweeney now approached with a brown-haired woman and a freckled, red-haired man. "Mrs. Wooster, these are my sister and brother-in-law, the McGinnises from Hartford." Mrs. McGinnis wiped her hand on her apron, extended it and in a low, well-bred voice said, "It's a great pleasure, indeed, to meet the mother of so gr-r-r-rand a son. We're all much admiring of Let."

"How do you do," said Submit, forcing a weak smile.

"Yes," McGinnis echoed his wife. "A fellow rooster is Letsome Wooster." He laughed and let out a fine spray tinged with alcohol fumes.

Submit stepped back briskly from the fountain of Gaelic spray, toppling the terra cotta statue from its pedestal and smashing it to bits. Submit simply could not bring herself to say she was sorry. Who put the statue there in the first place? In her embarrassment, she felt like screaming. A wave of maroon went up over her cheeks but she remained silent.

"Oh, that's all right, Mrs. Wooster. Never you be minding," Mary said. "I'm sure we can find another St. Francis for Julia. He's kind of a patron saint for her because they both love all outdoor creatures." Mary saw the varied expressions racing over Submit's face and feared for her daughter's future with such an icy block of New England granite.

At this moment Chatfield, George and Sally Swayne arrived on horseback. Letsome had brought their wedding garb with him on the train. He now made the introductions. Slim, attractive and dynamic Sally brought electricity into the house with her fun-hunting eyes and sudden smiles. Mary had the impression of a beautiful swallow veering and diving in its search for prey.

Chatfield Swayne derived from the same tall, wide-shouldered mold as his sister, Submit, and his nephew, Let, but his appearance was less impressive, with rounded shoulders, a less characterful chin and a mouth masked by a blonde handle-bar moustache. He had a somewhat remote air, so different from Let, but he was capable of smiling which his sister found difficult to do.

George was almost too handsome, a dark-haired, stylish, haughty young man who had known Kevin slightly at Yale and had come to his cousin Let's wedding reluctantly, motivated only by family loyalty and curiosity. The three new arrivals retired to bedrooms to change clothes. Shortly Sally emerged wearing a ravishing gown of chameleon glacé silk in tones of green and bronze to match her eyes and hair, with a wide-brimmed silk bonnet to match.

The Congregational minister, Reverend S. W. Magill, now arrived and the wedding party was complete. Mary Sweeney came out of the kitchen and said to Submit, who was talking with Chatfield, "It's time now, Mrs. Wooster, for the wonderful ceremony to begin. Would you be following me to the garden?"

"The *garden?* Is my son to be married neither in a church nor under the roof of a house?"

"In a garden under the trees. God's first temple, you know," said Mary. "It was Julia's wish, most joyously agreed to by Let. Would you be saying now that God lives only in a structure put together by man?"

Her head and back rigid, Submit gripped her brother's arm and forced herself to follow the happily tripping figure of Mary Sweeney down the garden path to several rows of green benches arranged around an improvised altar banked with asters and chrysanthemums.

When the families had taken their places, Maggie Sweeney in a pretty pale green muslin dress came down the path carrying an Irish harp. She seated herself on a low bench near the altar and played three charming Irish tunes which Julia had selected, including Thomas Connellan's "Harp Tune" of the 17th Century and an Irish air, "The Young Man's Dream." Then Kevin sang in a good baritone voice a favorite song of Julia's to his sister's accompaniment, "The Fair Hills of Eire O" by James Mangan, giving the first verse in Gaelic, the second in English. Awaiting the bride, Maggie continued to play Irish tunes on her harp.

Something deep within Submit, in spite of herself, responded to the songs and lovely setting of oak and maple trees framing panels of the river and hills. It was indeed a beautiful backdrop.

Now Letsome and the minister appeared walking side by side. How superb Letsome was—tall, fair, elegant—aristocratic in every fiber of his being. He deserved the most stunning, best-born, best-bred girl in Connecticut or any place else in New England or New York! Good God, why was he . . . Submit tried to repress the tears that were springing to her eyes. She couldn't remember having felt the pressure of tears since her husband Albert had died six years before at the age of thirty-six when Letsome was only fourteen.

Now the white bridal figure appeared on her father's arm. A surprisingly handsome girl, tall, well-built, with black wavy hair, light olive complexion, bright rosy cheeks, a full-lipped smiling mouth and enormous eyes of startling peacock-breast blue. Submit thought she had never seen anyone look so happy. It was immodest to show such feelings but yes, she was attractive. It was easy to see how Let had become tentacled.

Never afterwards could Submit remember much of the ceremony. Lost in her own seethe of emotions, she recorded little of the ritual. She did recall when the two had been pronounced man and wife, Let had drawn the girl tightly to him and kissed her full on the lips in sight of everyone. How could he? What had happened to his restrained, undemonstrative upbringing?

Then the girl walked from the altar on Let's arm, stopped and threw her arms around Submit and said, "Dear Mother of Let, let me kiss you!" Submit accepted but could not return the kiss. Julia looked up at Let who commented, "I'm afraid it's been a tiring day for mother." He guided Julia away.

Submit felt again the full impact of Let marrying an Irish girl. How could he when he knew how she felt? She stood alone in frozen silence when the wedding reception guests poured into the garden. They were of all kinds, the people whom Julia knew and loved—the brass manufacturer Anson Phelps, the Scovills of Scovill Manufacturing Company, Selectmen and Sheriffs, school teachers, three Protestant ministers and Rev. Michael O'Neill, the Catholic priest. Also present were a Yankee book peddler, a turnip farmer, a number of Irish mill workers and children who ran freely all over the garden.

Despite the variety of ethnic groups, Submit could see only "Paddies"—a Gaelic invasion into the pristine sanctuary of New England. She found Letsome, told him she was feeling indisposed and would he ask Mrs. Sweeney if she could lie down? Mary guided her to an upstairs bedroom and closed the shutters.

For Submit, no shutters could block out the sounds of voices, loud laughter and twanging fiddles. Surely they couldn't be *dancing* out there! She got up and peeked out.

The garden was awhirl with revolving figures. Gyrations of the devil, as all good Methodists knew!

She pushed aside the shutter a little more. There was Let, a Trustee of the Methodist Episcopal Church, jigging with his Irish wife. There was dignified old Anson Phelps kicking up his heels. She shook her head, shut her eyes, closed the shutter with a bang and fell back on the bed.

What was the good old solid world of New England coming to? Perdition, that was it, brought by immigrants, especially the Irish. All of her life she had resisted all temptations and had instilled in her three sons and daughter the sacred teachings of her church. Now, perdition was being introduced into her very home, into her family forever. Oh, God, what have I done to deserve this?

Worn out by the turmoil of her feelings, she fell asleep. Three hours later, Let had to shake her awake in time for her to catch the train back to Seymour.

CHAPTER 2

THE HONEYMOON IS OVER

(September 12, 1850)

For the first time since her marriage two weeks previously, Julia felt the hawk-wing of fear moving across the field of her happiness but she was determined not to betray the slightest hint of it to her young husband. He was sitting beside her in the carriage which was taking them to her new home—which actually was his and Submit's home, in which she, Julia, was the interloper.

To the beat of horse hooves the happenings of the honeymoon week in New York ran through Julia's mind—that first luxurious dinner in New York at Julian's, the Jersey shorebirds and marrow on toast, the charlotte russe and champagne. She thought of their wedding night at Irving House with Let so gentle yet so ardent, an exciting match for her own fiery Celtic nature.

Next day the long exploratory walk down Broadway past Grace Church to Astor Place at Eighth Avenue, after which she had insisted upon seeing where, in front of the Opera House, the great actor Macready had been injured by a mob a few weeks before because he was Irish and a "foreign intruder."

Let had taken her into the splendid store of the Irish merchant prince, Alexander T. Stewart, where Let had bought her a green velvet cloak. The three-mile stroll had ended at lovely, tree-filled Battery Park where they had watched sailboats and steamboats. Let had other events planned for the first day in New York but Julia insisted on returning to their hotel for more exciting love-making.

On another day they heard a fine military band concert, had an elegant lunch, then had taken a walk along Fifth Avenue where they had stopped to see digging beginning for what the workmen said was to be "a great mansion." As they were watching, the future owners arrived. What a surprise to Let to recognize Anne Phelps, daughter of his old friend, Anson G. Phelps, who introduced her husband, James Stokes. It had been an amiable encounter until Julia opened her pretty mouth to speak, when, as the soft Irish r's rippled out, Mrs. Stokes jerked back her shoulders, her eyes became ice and, seizing her husband's arm, she exclaimed sharply, "James, we must be going."

Said Let, in instant reaction, "You know, Anne, it was good to have your father at our wedding a week ago. He danced the Irish jig faster and higher than anyone there, God bless him!" Anne Stokes grew sumac-red as they escaped.

"Well," Julia said, "I seem to have failed the test with friends of yours. You are beginning to see the penalties of marrying a colleen but somehow I can't bring myself to feel inferior. I'm very proud of who and what I am."

"And I'm proud of you to the roots of my being. People who act like Anne Phelps aren't worth knowing."

The honeymooners attended several theater productions, the most superb being the one they had planned their honeymoon around. It was the opening concert of Jenny Lind at Castle Garden. As long as she lived, Julia never forgot the astounding lark-loveliness of that young voice and the charm she exuded.

This day they had boarded the boat to Derby Landing where Let's phaeton had met them, driven by his odd-job man, Whiddy Hartigan, an amusing character who liked to converse with himself.

As they came closer to their new life in the same house with Let's so-cold mother, Julia recalled the words of her father. "People are ever and a day suspicious of folk from over the next hill, particularly New Englanders on their hard-won little granite mounds. They're especially disaffected these days towards our people because so many have fled here from the potato blight. Try not to blame the Yankees too much if they're not friendly at first, not towardly, like ourselves."

"We're almost to Seymour, Julia," said Let. "Only two more miles."

Julia thought she heard Whiddy mumbling, "Now, Hartigan, me boy, would you be thinking that our little town will be merciful or unmerciful to the sweet young Lady?" Answering himself, he said, "Well, I think I smell a bit of trouble ahead, me boy."

Let put his arm around Julia's shoulder. The blue-black iridescence of her hair was like the shining head of a grackle. Her remarkable blue eyes reminded him of azurite flames in a copper smelter. "Not sorry to be coming home with me are you, Julia darling?"

"Oh, Let, I suppose every bride says it, but I really am the happiest wife in the world." After a pause, she added, "Do you think your mother will like me?"

"So that's what's been troubling you. Of course she will. It may take a little time and you will have to be patient, but my mother's a wonderful person."

She surveyed Let's sun-blond hair, clear-cut features and honest greenish-brown eyes. She rejoiced in the strength, kindness and good cheer of his face.

Conversation was suddenly jolted into silence as Whiddy drew his horses aside to let a stagecoach pass. The way was narrowed because a group of Irish laborers was working on the road.

"Get out of the way, you damned Paddies!" shouted the stage driver. "Make room for the coach or I'll run you into the ditch!" There was a spiteful crack of the whip. One of the laborers lifted his hands to the back of his lashed neck while the others shook their fists at the driver.

Julia cried out, "Whiddy! Stop the coach, please, and let me out."

Before the horses had fully checked, she jumped out. Her voice was firm as she walked briskly to the coach and spoke to the driver. "Who gives you authority to lay a whip to a man? It's against the law, it's against human decency and it's against God's mandates. This man is every bit as good as you, if not far better! I'm reporting you to coach headquarters and to the Sheriff's office."

The stage driver roared, "You've got a broguey tongue yourself, you damned immigrant!" He whipped his horses harshly and drove off.

Julia turned to the lashed Irishman. "I'm dreadfully sorry. I'll be reporting that devil-driver, never you be doubting that. Let me have a look at your neck. The skin is red but not lacerated. The ignominy of it! Tell me your name."

"Timothy O'Toole, ma'am."

"Then take this, Timothy, and good luck to you. Buy a salve for the outside or inside of your neck and with anything left over, treat the boys!" She took from her purse a gold half-eagle and put it in his hands.

Timothy removed his cap and said, "Ten million thanks, Ma'am. You're surely the loveliest lady in all this love-forsaken country. The saints bless ye."

"Thank you, Timothy." Then she turned to the others. "You're all doing a grand job. I'm Irish myself. I've recently come back from two years in Ireland and I bring you its greeting: *Erin go Bragh!* Ireland forever! God bless you all."

As Julia went back to the carriage, the Irish workmen cheered. Then she could hear Whiddy murmuring to himself, "And it's Mrs. Wooster she is, Whiddy. Did you hear her, Whiddy Hartigan? Mrs. Wooster!"

"I'm sorry, Let. I should have restrained myself but I just couldn't stand the sight of such disgraceful abuse. I guess I have some work to do on self-control. Do you think I will be put to the test often?"

"I feel exactly as you do, Julia," replied Let, "but I don't think we can always handle such problems this way. Prejudice is very bad here at the moment. You may have to learn a greater degree of tolerance about a whole lot of things that lie ahead."

"I know, Let, but I have an Irish imp sitting on my shoulder and I simply can't stand injustice. Somebody has to defend these underdogs. It's our love which will carry us through hostility and hate, don't you think?"

He squeezed her hand. They both sat silently while the carriage drove into the outskirts of Seymour.

"Tell me about your Uncle Swayne and his family," said Julia, "especially about his wife who wasn't at the wedding."

"Well, Uncle Chatfield is a good man but a bit anti-Catholic. He tried but failed to block the building of the Catholic Church here in Seymour. He married Amy Goodwin of the Mayflower Goodwins. She was the so-called 'catch of New Haven,' but she knows it and is quite snooty. Their children, George and Sally, are full of life and fun. George is at Yale. Sally's out of school, marking time, I guess, until she finds the right beau. Attractive, don't you think?"

"I certainly do, and friendly. I like her immensely."

"She's always into mischief because of her adventurism and love of fun. Speaking of kinfolk, that's the old Henry Wooster place up there." He indicated a large white house with Colonial pillars. "The house was built in 1700 on property deeded to my Colonial ancestor, Edward Wooster, by Paugasuck Indian leaders in 1654."

Julia didn't comment for she was busy thinking . . . roots two hundred years deep on this side of the ocean . . . no wonder they don't like recent immigrants. I'm such a newcomer!

Let continued. "Edward Wooster and Francis French, two of my father's forebears, and Edward Riggs and Abel Gunn, two of my mother's, settled here in the woods, built log cabins, killed the wolves and panthers round about, and raised crops as well as dozens of children . . ." He realized he was talking too much and stopped.

"I'm listening, Let dear. I'm interested and very proud of your heritage."

"The next house, the fancy gray one with the two candle-snuffer towers, is where some cousins, the Gunn Dunlaps, live. Their property adjoins ours on the hill. We have a nice bit of meadowland up there and a fine view of the river."

"Oh, wonderful!" exclaimed Julia. "Why didn't you tell me you owned part of a hill? Hills are like people to me. They speak."

Let looked at her quizzically: "I think I know what you mean, my little Irish bride."

Julia heard Whiddy muttering, "You know what she means, don't you, Whiddy m'boy?"

Let resumed. "Now here is the famous Whittemore Tavern. I bought it recently and turned it over to my friends Awley and Maeva O'Neill to run. I'm going to let you out, then go up to the house to tell Mother we're coming." Julia thought it strange. So, Mother Wooster had to be forewarned . . .

"They're a good family," Let went on. "There was almost a riot in the neighborhood when I established them here—petitions, protest meetings and what not. Most of the Irish, you see, live in a community of their own near the foot of Knockmedown Hill near the river, about a mile from here."

"Knockmedown Hill," Julia said. "That must be the Yankee version of what the Irish settlers called the slope in honor of the lovely Tipperary hills, the Knockmealdowns."

Let knocked on the door of the Tavern. Both O'Neills appeared, Maeva and her red-haired husband, Awley, and, in a moment, Dennis and Moira. There were cordial greetings all around.

"Now, how about a spot of tea, Mr. Wooster?" asked Maeva.

"Or better still, Sir," suggested Awley, "how about a little poteen to celebrate the homecoming, a bit of heavenly dew, a little . . . er-r-r, Sarsaparilla?"

"Not now, Awley. Take care of Julia until I come back to get her in a few minutes."

"Yes, sir. Our pleasure!"

They exchanged pleasantries. After one sentence of Julia's, including several trilled r's, Julia said: "You may've noted that I've got a bit of an Irish accent even though I was born in Waterbury."

Maeva thought to herself, "So I see and so I'd heard! God bless you! Just think of it, Mrs. Submit Swayne Wooster's daughter-in-law!"

"Why do you think that? Is Mrs. Wooster getting something different than she thought?"

Maeva showed surprise in her eyes." I may've thought that but I didn't say it aloud, now did I?"

"I could *feel* what you were thinking, Mrs. O'Neill. It's a troublesome little way I have."

"Lord bless us!" cried Maeva. "A 'natural' you be, born with a special sense of reading minds."

"Yes, I sense more than I would like, sometimes. Please don't mention my little, shall we call it 'surmisin', to anyone. We Irish all have it, more or less, and I fear the Yankees don't."

"The gods let us have it," put in Dennis, "to give us one up on our enemies!"

Maeva continued. "Submit Wooster's set in her ways, against this and that and terrible patriotic. She sets great store by the Daughters of the Star Spangled Banner, for instance."

"What on earth is that?" asked Julia.

"Oh, they gather around an old pewter teapot and talk about their splendid forefathers."

"And how scum everyone else is," added Dennis.

"Yes, anti-Irish feelings are bad here," said Maeva. "It gets pretty unpleasant at the Inn sometimes. You can't imagine how many anti-Irish comments are made at the bar here."

"Right under your very own roof? Well, that bangs Banagher!" exclaimed Julia.

"And Banagher beats the devil!" Dennis finished the old Irish phrase.

"Well," continued Maeva, "You've got a great husband, the kind who likes everybody, even the Irish! Everybody likes him, but, for most of the other Yankees, Lord have mercy on us!"

"The God of Laughter is on our side," said Julia. She heard the Wooster carriage returning. "I'm very glad to have met you, Mr. and Mrs. O'Neill," said Julia, putting out her hand, "and let's use first names from now on."

"Do feel welcome to drop in whenever you go by. I mean that with a heart and a half. Now I'll be wrapping up a fresh-baked peach custard pie as a homecoming gift for you."

In a moment Let was there asking, "Ready to go home, Mrs. Wooster?"

"Ready!"

As they neared the carriage, Moira broke away from her conversation with Whiddy. "Goodbye, Whiddy," sang out Moira. "Be good to yourself . . . I mean yourselves!" and her laugh rang out.

Whiddy instantly replied, "I've greatly enjoyed our conversation and your lovely liltin' manner of speech, Moira. You wouldn't by any chance be Irish, would you?" He laughed heartily.

"Hand her up careful, Whiddy," he muttered to himself. Julia gestured to Let with a finger across her lips so that she might understand him. "Mrs. Wooster is lovely as a young green fern and her spirit's strong as oak, Whiddy. She'll need that oak strength. Watch over her Whiddy, me' boy. Keep from her all pixies and pucas, banshees and bugaboos."

Julia smiled with amusement but was beginning to feel the tension of her imminent get-together with Submit. Let took her hand in his. "Only a short distance now, darling," he said.

The carriage now turned past a towering elm tree and there came into view a three story red brick house with an ell at the left, two commodious chimneys and a spider web-paned front door. The crocheted curtains were drawn tight. There was a maple tree at the right, an orchard and a red barn behind, then the rise of the hill. Neat, dignified, everything in place. Their home.

Would Submit welcome the bride, the trespasser, thought Julia? Would there be a touch of welcoming sunlight in her eyes? The front door did not open. The sound of the carriage must have been quite audible. Let used the American eagle brass door-knocker. Finally the door opened slowly.

She found herself looking into the cold gray eyes of her tall, fair-haired mother-in-law, her lips held in uncompromising rectitude. There were crisscross lines at lip's edge, eyes' edge and all across the forehead. Submit had the same splendidly chiseled, slightly aquiline nose and high forehead that Let had and the same superb line of high-held neck out of wide shoulders. Vanity, remoteness, without a touch of tenderness. But I must start looking for the good in her, thought Julia. It is a handsome face, with strength and poise.

With visible effort, Submit slowly extended her hands. "I hope you had a comfortable trip."

She quickly let go of Julia's hands and put her arms around Let in maternal devotion. Then she gazed at Julia with a nothing-can-ever-separate-me-from-my-son look.

Julia found herself saying quietly, "No, nothing can divide you . . . one of my husband's dearest qualities is his love of home and family."

Mrs. Wooster broke away, startled at Julia's reading her thoughts.

"Now let's show the bride her new home!" said Let.

Julia flashed a warm smile at her mother-in-law and said, "Yes, please show me everything new and old in your lovely home, Mrs. Wooster."

"Come, darling," said Let, "we'll show you first the pretty music room I've built for you."

Julia took his hand happily and said: "Oh, aren't you coming with us, Mrs. Wooster?"

"No, I think not." Her sudden realization that Let's and Julia's heirs would be mongrels—half Irish—had struck Submit Swayne Wooster like a hammer. She went into the living room and sat very straight, eyes closed, in the spindle-backed chair under the gold braided, red coated portrait of General David Wooster which had been painted before the Revolution, in 1746, at the Court of King George the Third. She felt more comfortable with her own ilk.

CHAPTER 3

NEWCOMER VIGNETTES

(Autumn, 1850)

Lives, as Heraclitus knew so many hundreds of years ago, do not jerk and jounce in artificially sheared fragments gauged to the chapters and verses used to record them. They flow. In such a way the first few months of Julia's life in the new home turbled as over a rocky stream-bed, the confluence of many small episodes, thoughts, feelings, cross-currents and ripplings of circumstance.

On that first night in the new home, Julia lying in one of the deep, post-passion silences, heard a creak of the floor immediately outside the bedroom door. The genteel mother-in-law betrayed by old floorboards. No privacy even in one's own home! What impact would this have on her ability to relax totally and enjoy private times with someone to whom she felt so close?

Julia greeting her mother-in-law next day with a smile and "Good morning, Mother of Let," and being corrected, "I'll be Mrs. Wooster, if you please."

Julia slipped a daisy into her hair and was told, "Daisies smell bad or aren't you aware of that? It's irritating to a refined sense of smell."

Julia replied, "Ah, but for centuries they've been called by my people *noinean,* the flower of noon. They're beloved of the hills . . . and by me. I think I'll be keeping it in my hair." Then she was annoyed at herself. She must learn to respond with silence and be more accomodating to icy barbs.

Julia, moving lightly and happily over the house searching for quiet ways in which to brighten it, setting a vase of goldenrod on great grandfather Walter Wooster's circular Chippendale mahogany table. "You've spilled a drop of water on the table, Julia. Didn't your mother train you not to spill things? Nothing must happen to this old family table, owned by Captain Walter Wooster, the first soldier over the ramparts to raise the American flag at Fort of King's Fridge."

"If you will tell me where I may find some camphorated oil, the water-spot will be rubbed off in the time it takes to say *Erin go Bragh!*"

"What in heaven's name does that mean?"

"Forever be happy," replied Julia, smiling, thanking the elf on her shoulder for the suggested translation.

Julia pulling aside curtains from the west window of the living room beside the chair that had become hers.

"I wouldn't do that. It wrinkles the curtains," said Submit.

"Oh, it wrinkles my heart not to see those hills! Since this is my own special corner, I'll be tying the curtains back and enjoying the view, I think." Self respect did have to be maintained at times.

Sometimes Submit actually did make a complimentary remark. "What are you sewing, Julia?"

"A bit of lace for a fichu."

"You do very nice lace work, Julia, better than mine. I'm mainly a practical knitter, like the mittens I'm making now."

Julia and Let retreating after supper one evening into the little music room. Julia playing a few chords on the

Broadwood pianoforte that Let had bought for her, then opening the Irish songbook given to her by her father.

"Here, let's try this song by James Callinan, my father's friend," said Julia. "They went to school together in Dublin. It's lovely." Submit coming in to listen.

> On Cleada's hill the moon is bright,
> Dark Avondu still rolls in light . . .

Julia's soft contralto mingling with Let's strong tenor . . . "Now, let's try this one, darling," said Let. "I like the title, 'My Irish Wife'." Julia, knowing Thomas McGee's poem, dreading the implications of verse two but Let insisting:

> My Irish wife has clear blue eyes,
> My heaven by day, my stars by night,
> Apollo's self might pause to hear
> Her bird-like carol when she sings.
>
> I would not give my Irish wife
> For all the dames of Saxon land,
> I would not give my Irish wife
> For the Queen of France's hand . . .

Let ending with vehemence and stopping to kiss his accompanist. Submit rising to leave, with a rustle of silk.

"Oh, don't go, Mrs. Wooster!"

"Well, before I go, why don't you play me something I'm familiar with, one of the straight old English or American airs?"

"What, for instance, Mrs. Wooster?"

"Well, 'Robin Adair', for instance."

"Oh, lovely! I adore it, but actually it's an old Irish song, *'Eibhlin a Rinn'*."

"Well, not that, then. Let's sing 'My Country 'Tis of Thee'."

"I love that, too. It's adapted from an old Irish folksong."

"I don't believe it, Julia."

"It's just the beautiful truth!"

"Good night. It's past my bedtime!" said Submit, leaving abruptly.

"I'm sorry, Let. It just slipped out. Am I never to say anything *for* the Irish? Must I take all the 'againsts' without any rebuttal?"

"I love you, Julia. Be patient with Mother. She has her attitudes . . . but she'll be changing, I think, as she comes to know you."

"The frosty granite of New England never changes, Let."

"But it does, Julia. Even a fern may change a rock, insinuating itself every so gently into little interstices."

The first day at church, glances and whispers . . . men craning to look . . . Some women hurrying away after the sermon to avoid introduction. Caresse Smith, the reverend's pretty French wife, waiting at the church door to offer a warm handclasp.

The Chatfield Swaynes duly coming forward, mitt-ends extended to Julia by Amy, a warmer hand by Chatfield and a very warm one by Sally with a kiss on the cheek. Later that day a home visit by Mr. and Mrs. Chatfield Swayne, very brief, very perfunctory. Submit and Amy pairing off to talk together. Let and Chatfield talking brass mill business. Julia sitting patiently with folded hands trying graciously to tolerate the complete ignoring. Was this not a call on Let's bride? "I must be patient, I must be patient," Julia repeating to herself.

That other call, the following Saturday, from Almira Aurelia Humphreys. Let, home early from the factory, catching sight of her from the front window, and exclaiming, "Here comes Almira Humphreys. I'm not here, positively not! I'm taking a walk in the garden." Submit turning apologetically to Julia:

"That's one of the few wrong-headed notions he has. She's a wonderful woman, one of the really impawtunt people. She's the granddaughter of General David Humphreys. I'm distantly related to him, too, on the Chatfield side. I guess Let's told you that he was the one who, at Mount Vernon, actually persuaded George Washington to become our first Presidential candidate."

Almira Humphreys arriving to pay her bride-call, firm-mouthed, swan-proud, sweeping into the house, greeting Julia with a brief extension of her hand . . . Then conversing with Submit exclusively, as Amy Swayne had done. Julia smiling but inwardly astounded by the bad manners.

On another occasion, Julia pausing at the door to talk with the Genoese statuary man and Submit reproving her. "It's much beneath one's dignity to talk with any of these itinerants if one doesn't intend to patronize them."

"But they're all such delightful people—the tinker and the notions peddler, the Indian herb-woman and especially the French vendor."

"One must choose one's acquaintances with discretion and care, Julia."

Julia loving the common townspeople she met during her long walks. For instance, Page Sanford at the blacksmith shop, son of "Pitchfork" Sanford who had killed a man with a pitchfork, been convicted and condemned for life to wear a hangman's rope around his neck. Julia found his talk pithy and wise.

Julia enjoying Father O'Laverty over on Washington Avenue, who could often be found watching the finishing touches being put on his new church or working in the churchyard planting flowers. Father was in his late thirties, a poetic-looking man, thought Julia, very kind, very different from straw-skinned, weasel-eyed Reverend Epaphroditus Smith of the Methodist Episcopal Church whose young French wife, Caresse, is a darling. How could she have married that sour prune?

Julia exploring along Bladen's Brook, Little River and the Naugatuck where wildness of beauty alternated with the busy mills of Seymour. All the mills being of interest to Julia through her husband's enthusiastic descriptions, especially the woolen mill built by General David Humphreys which used fleece from merino sheep he imported from Spain "against the rules", and the brass and copper mill where Let was now Superintendent despite his young age.

Walking was in Julia's ardent blood, as her long-legged Celtic tribal ancestors had walked the green hills and glens of Ireland. Often she returned home by the river road and stopped at the miserable shacks of blacks on the floodable flatlands to talk with old Tribulation Cumming or his daughter Fallopia who had eight children, each sired by a different father. Tribulation, who helped to support them all, declaring it was "God's will".

Julia moving up the slopes of Knockmedown Hill to where the Irish lived on plateaus above the blacks, and talking merrily with Hartigans, Whooleys, Mulligans, Brodigans and O'Kanes. It was Whiddy Hartigan's family that Julia had come to love best, with the bright-eyed children and quick-witted parents.

Often Julia escaping from the confining 28 Pearl Street house to the beautiful hill that rose gently behind it, the highest slope named "Deer's Delight Hill" with that sudden flash of poetic feeling that sometimes leaped out of stern Puritan mindsets like a lark singing from a rocky perch.

"Where are you going, Julia?" asked Submit.

"Just for a wee walk on the hill. I'll be back quicker than the clout of a leprechaun's hammer."

"I have no idea what you mean but I do know it's not safe. There are all sorts of queer folk wandering around, tinkers and peddlers and gypsies, runaway niggers and rabble-foreigners. It's not like the old days when it was all hemmed in by good old New Englanders and there was nothing but deer and woodchuck running across the meadows. I advise you to stay home, Julia."

"I think I'll chance it. Let understands my love of hills. Likely there's nothing up there but the little folk and a few lovely deer."

Like a typical Celt filled with the joy of Nature, she loved her thoughts when alone with the beauty of hills, trees, meadows, flowers, streams, ponds, clouds, sun, wind, animals and birds. She walked on many an afternoon up to the very top of the hill. She had given names to their six cows—Silk of the Kine, Brown Drimin, Maol the blunt-horned, Bofind the white cow, Boann and Queen Maeva. She talked with them and petted them while they happily munched. Crows never cawed warningly when she drew near.

It was a beautiful hill with a soul-lifting view, as lovely as the Hill of the Angels at Hy or Grennan Mountain above Londenderry and the North Atlantic, where Julia had stood, three years before, proudly remembering that her forebears, the O'Neills and Suibhnes, the Sweeneys, had ruled from there as High Kings of Ulster. The view was as impressive as from Cashel above the Golden Vale of Tipperary or Tara, above the plains of Meath, seat of Irish kings and full of ancient monuments dating back to 5000 BC. Julia loved the silence and peace. This was her place of escape, her joyous free-spirited fantasy world and she began to call it *Mullach na Sidhe*, Hill of the Fairy Folk, the Enchanted Hill.

From the summit all undulations of the Naugatuck Hills, spurs of the main Catskills further to the west, crowded into the sky, north towards Oxford, Waterbury and Hartford, south toward Derby and Long Island Sound. Tall, two-shouldered Castle Rock stood directly across the river, a tower against the sunset and the ever-mysterious west. To the north, Rock Rimmon cut a sharp profile, sheer against the otherwise gently-rounded hills.

Sometimes Julia walked down the hill's south side to the pool and stream, near the wall that separated Let's property from that of the Gunn Dunlaps. She walked over the east slope, full of strong-scented flowers and with great granite boulders bright with mica and garnet. She often waited until sunset's cascade of colors rendered the final bolstering of her soul for the return home. According to an old Irish proverb, the rapid dwindling of an autumn evening is as fast as a hound running on the moor, so she hurried home to help set the table for supper prepared by Eliza Hull, wife of their hired man.

Julia always came home wind-blown, rosy-cheeked, heart-refreshed and with a spray of wild flowers or a leaf cluster in her dark hair. Submit made sure she herself was busy polishing furniture or silver, crocheting or mending. After all, New Englanders didn't waste their time with trivial pursuits. Time was precious and should be used for tangible accomplishments, not meandering and day-dreaming.

Julia timed her return with the arrival home of Let from the factory. He was always full of hearty demonstrable affection, drawing her to him so enthusiastically that often the flowers fell out of her hair. As Julia moved happily into the company of Let, Submit cooperated by retreating to her chair in front of the fire with a good book. She did seem to enjoy the happy interactions of Let and Julia although sometimes she subtly shook her head at their overt affection.

CHAPTER 4

HOLIDAY CHEER

(November, 1850)

Submit Wooster had never dreaded the prospect of a Thanksgiving dinner more thoroughly than this one. The preparation work was considerable in spite of the help of Eliza and her married daughter, Luma. Maeva O'Neill made peach and pumpkin pies and Julia was helpful but the human factors were oppressive to Submit. *My God, how does one comfortably blend English and Irish and why should one be put in such a socially embarrassing situation?*

Let had insisted upon inviting the whole Sweeney family. Luckily all but Kevin were dining with Mrs. Sweeney's family, the McGinnises, in Hartford. Let had sent Whiddy to New Haven to bring Kevin back from law school. It was bad enough to have one Irish person, Julia, at the table. But two! That was asking too much of long-established New England gentry, especially with Cousin Almira Aurelia Humphreys and her daughter, Helena, coming plus Cousin Elvira Dunlap and her family, and the Chatfield Swaynes. Julia was shelling walnuts in silence as Submit displayed her nervousness. Submit squared her proud chin and scurried around, taking out her feelings on Eliza. The two o'clock dinner was only three hours away.

At half past one Chatfield Swayne's carriage drove smartly into the yard. Amy came early on the pretext of being eager to help but actually to see how Submit was faring. Submit sat down with her in the music room for a few minutes of relaxation. Sally came flouncing merrily into the kitchen. "Hello, Julia, how are you? Hasn't that brother of yours arrived yet?"

"No. You're to sit next to him, Sally. I switched the place cards."

"Good. Didn't see too much of him at the wedding. I liked him though he seemed kind of serious."

"Oh, no. He's lots of fun and full of charming guile."

Submit returned to the kitchen and said, "Julia, will you please go into the dining room and fill the mugs from the eggnog bowl?"

Julia suspected that Submit's tactic was to minimize contact between Irish and elite. She smiled. She was determined to be amused today, not disturbed. Kevin arrived next. Julia took him to the dining room while she filled the mugs. Kevin read the place cards which Julia had hand-painted and inscribed.

"Any juice of joy in this eggnog, Julia?"

"No. My mother-in-law's against it."

"Ye gads and merry Bacchus! Have you got any rum or whiskey in the house for puddings and colds and such?"

"Yes, that we have."

"Good. I feel a cold coming on . . . bring it to me and never say a word. This party needs livening up a bit and I know the perfect person to do it!"

Julia came back from the pantry with a nearly full bottle of rum. Kevin laughed quietly as he went around the table adding it to mugs according to the place cards and his own Yale intuition. The Reverend Epaphroditus Smith received the largest infusion. The next biggest portions were bestowed upon the eggnogs of Submit Wooster, Almira Aurelia Humphreys, and Amy and Chatfield Swayne, with generous allotments also to Gunn Dunlap and George and Sally Swayne. When Kevin finished, he sang lines from the Irish drinking song:

> Oh, to drink with the Devil,
> Though it may be hilarious,
> Must be regarded
> As somewhat precarious!

Everyone gathered now in the living room, Submit performing the role of greeter, Let remaining close to Julia and making her a part of his own welcomes.

Let also put his arm around Kevin's shoulders and drew him into the circle.

Sally found Kevin even more attractive than at Let's and Julia's wedding, better looking, more exciting and sharp-witted. Every line in his face was mobile, his quirky eyebrows particularly expressive and his hands overflowing with gesture. Sally's own restlessness responded and Kevin played the game, matching her flirtatious come-ons with his own quick responses.

After they were seated Kevin could not help observing the totally different girl opposite him, Helena Humphreys, with her quiet low-pitched voice and her few but well considered comments. Submit immediately noted that Kevin had a well-toned speaking voice but his laugh was too loud. Why couldn't the Irish restrain their emotions with a modicum of quiet dignity?

The Reverend Epaphroditus Smith made a long, tedious benediction, thanking the Father in Heaven for abundant crops, overflowing corn bins and heaping platters—a long alimentary blessing sanctified with long-winded verbiage. Into the silence which followed, Kevin set forth where the gathered angels feared to tread:

"I'm reminded by your comprehensive harvest benediction, Reverend, of the story of the farmer, let's call him Corny Corntassel, who decided to do a futuristic benediction on Thanksgiving. He took his family down to the cellar, faced the well-stocked shelves and blessed everything in view. Didn't have to say grace again for an entire year!"

This appealed to George Swayne and he vented a loud guffaw. Let laughed. To everyone's surprise, the minister's wife, Caresse, laughed loudest. Helena put a lace handkerchief to her mouth to keep back a wide smile, bringing the look of a grieved beagle to her mother's face. All the others were aghast at the implied teasing of their devout minister but remained silent. The company broke up into small chattering groups.

A few minutes later, Chatfield Swayne began holding forth on the Fugitive Slave Law. He and his nephew, Let, rarely agreed on anything outside the field of brass manufacturing, on which subject their two minds blended smoothly. Let was determined not to argue with anyone during this family celebration. Chat continued to gesticulate with his fork and pontificate on the question of its being the constitutional duty of every law-abiding citizen to turn over escaped slaves to the United States Marshall. Chatfield's loud and compelling voice caused other conversation to stop.

"Yes, it's one or two women who are a menace to this town!" Everyone knew he was referring to Lydia, someone who was loved and respected. Epaphroditus Smith, beginning to feel his eggnog, exclaimed stridently, "Hear! Hear!"

Kevin hesitated. He did not wish to introduce discord into the family scene but he had been honing his debating skills at law school and the challenge was too much for him.

"I'm sorry, Sir, to disagree with you, but, as has been pointed out by William Lloyd Garrison in *The Journal of Freedom*, there are higher laws than those made by courts and judiciaries, namely God's Law and the Law of Humanity."

"Did you not tell me, Mrs. Wooster," put in Julia, "that your ancestors, the Riggses, sheltered the regicides in their fortified house in Derby?"

Submit, who did not wish to contribute any weight to Kevin's statements, merely stiffened her face as did Amy Swayne, who also had Riggs ancestors.

"In my opinion," Kevin went on, "there should be punishment not for fugitive slaves but for all those who connive with slavery against everything that America stands for."

"Are you an American citizen?" asked Chatfield.

"Absolutely. I was born in Hudson, New York, and my father, who came to this country twenty-five years ago, is also a citizen. None of us here at this dinner table is of original native American descent, I believe—Indian, that is. We're all immigrants, descendants of simple farmers, beehive keepers, carpenters, shoemakers, clerks and bonded servants out of the British Isles."

A palpable shudder of horror went round the table. "Yes, immigrants," Kevin continued. "The word in recent days has had a main connotation of the Irish—the starved potato famine Irish who are now swarming over the shores of America and crowding against the so-called 'native stock,' which, by comparison, has taken on the often false gloss and armorial burnish of a contrasting aristocracy."

Let stepped into the breach. "I must confess I agree with you on the slave question, Kevin, although one can understand both sides. I could never turn back a desperate, freedom-loving soul to the degradation of servitude."

"I'm sorry to hear you say that, Let," said his uncle Chatfield. "The law is the law. That is the foundation of any sane society. You're studying the law, I believe, Kevin."

"Yes, sir, but the law always has many interpretations, keyed, as it should be, to the highest aspirations of society and the overall laws of humanity."

"I'd hesitate to choose you as my attorney," exclaimed Chatfield gruffly.

Instantly Kevin replied, "An attorney may also exercise discretion of choice in clients, Mr. Swayne."

Let decided it was time to shift the subject entirely. "I see by the paper that gold is getting harder to find in California."

No one replied, so Kevin said, "Yes, it's not so easy to make a fortune out there. The nuggets aren't lying around loose anymore."

Helena, surprisingly, entered the general conversation. "Oh, how I wish I were a man! I wouldn't mind the dangers of the goldfields just to have the adventure. Don't you think so, Mr. Sweeney?"

"Why yes, Miss Humphreys. Adventure is, after all, where the excited mind creates its own circumstance. The gold mine of adventure is almost anywhere."

"Perhaps, but the excited mind has to have the spark of circumstance to blow upon or else there will be no great fire."

Kevin began to realize the girl's situation—the overpowering mother, endless unnecessary restrictions and her longing for release from maternal bondage. She was more intriguing to him than always sparkling but always flirting Sally.

Let returned to Kevin's comment about mining gold. "There was a returned traveler from California down at the Tavern the other day who seemed to bear out your comments,

Kevin. He said there was still plenty of gold to be had in California but there were better ways of making money, particularly business opportunities in San Francisco."

"Couldn't you induce the O'Neills to try tavern-keeping out there in California?" suggested Gideon Dunlap.

"Yes!" said Epaphroditus Smith in a loud voice. "Then we could get the old tavern back in good Christian hands again!"

"And have decent neighbors again!" said Almira Humphreys.

"Christian! Why, Dr. Smith," protested Julia. "The O'Neills are just about the most Christian people I know!"

"Jesuits and Papists!" shouted Epaphroditus, feeling less and less restrained.

Caresse put her hand gently on her husband's arm but he threw it off brusquely.

"Those are irrelevant and irreverent words, Sir," said Kevin, whose face had flushed. "My family and I happen not to be Catholic but I know very well that a good Catholic is a good Christian."

"Papists!" said Epaphroditus Smith through his mutton-chop whiskers.

"Won't you pass your plate," suggested Let, "for more turkey, Parson?"

"Yes, I will, Sir, thank you, and, Mrs. Wooster, I would like another mug of that superfine eggnog. Excellent flavor. Yes, *excellent!*"

Kevin quickly looked at Julia and they winked at each other. Then Kevin said, "I'll fill the glasses around the table, Mrs. Wooster."

At this point, Almira Humphreys said, "Well, anyone who's read *The Awful Disclosures of Maria Monk* can have little sympathy with any Catholics."

"I should say as much," said Submit. "That book tells the whole horrible story."

"But, my dear ladies!" exclaimed Kevin, trying to control himself. "Didn't you know that Maria Monk's book has been shown to be a complete hoax? There isn't a word of truth in it. She was a woman of the streets in Montreal. The book's contents were from Maria's experiences in a reformatory, not a convent!"

"Well, I declare!" said Almira astutely.

"It all goes to show, Mrs. Humphreys, that it's best not to believe newspaper stories immediately just because they're in print. Hate and prejudice are like venomous spiders spinning webs for the unwary. If you went into the Catholic church . . . what's the name of the Catholic priest in this town, Julia?"

"Father O'Laverty. Take care, Kevin dear."

"I have no doubt that if every one of you went with an open mind into Father O'Laverty's church on any Sunday morning, you'd find the same holy reverence and beauty of service that you no doubt find in Reverend Smith's church."

The word "Sacrilege!" went skirring through the whiskers of Epaphroditus Smith.

"Those can be fighting words in this town, Kevin," said Gunn Dunlap.

"One should not fight about religions. Discuss, yes, do battle, no," said Kevin.

"Huh! The great lawyer speaks," said Gunn as he took another swig of eggnog.

Once more the host came forward with a verbal olive branch. "I'm sure there's a great deal of truth in what you say, Kevin. All church spires point to God."

"Yes, but by the Almighty," exclaimed Reverend Smith, "some men are right and some are wrong!" He pounded the table so hard that the carving knife fell off the nearby platter.

He tried to get up but stumbled and fell back awkwardly into his chair. Straightening himself, he continued talking loudly. "How can you sit there and say that one church is as good as another, one doctrine as good as another?"

"I don't in the least mean to be sacrilegious, Reverend Smith," said Let, "but I think we should try to understand other points of view. We need to see beyond our own pews, our own church beliefs, our own steeples."

Through plum pudding and squash and pumpkin pies, Let and Julia now guided the conversation along undangerous paths. Realizing the potential hazards of the rum infusions, Julia suggested that they all remain seated in the dining room rather than transferring to the living room but Sally now said:

"Let's all of us young folk go for a drive. We can head for the Woodbridge place. The writer Donald Mitchell, better know as Ik Marvel, is up from New York visiting his cousins and there should be plenty of young people around."

"Too many," said Let. "He's probably pestered to death since his *Reveries of a Bachelor* has been announced for publication."

"Mrs. Smith cannot go!" proclaimed Epaphroditus, perhaps realizing that he needed help in walking. "She's going home with me."

"Helena can't go either, of course," announced Mrs. Humphreys. "She'd catch her death of cold. It looks as if it's going to snow any minute."

"Mother, I really want to go," said Helena. I've never met Ik Marvel and I adored his *Lorgnette* and his *Battle Summer*."

"Oh, Mrs. Humphreys," said Caresse. "It's a beautiful day. It won't hurt her."

"Under *no* circumstances. Helena, you must be going home right now to get your rest." Helena said goodbye to everyone and left on foot for the walk home.

Kevin was furious. As soon as the young people, muffled up and laughing, were outside the door, he said, "Let's get Helena anyway and carry her off! We'll bring her back before her mother gets home and no one will be the wiser."

"I think," added Sally, "that Aunt Aurelia's afraid of Helena's marrying and leaving her all alone. If Helena weren't such a saint, she'd have rebelled long ago!"

Helena was climbing the stairs to her bedroom when Kevin's and Sally's fast walking brought them to her door. Sally put in her words of argument but Helena shook her head. "No, Sally. I'm supposed not to be well enough to do such things."

Kevin responded, "Miss Helena, I think you're much healthier than you realize. It's time for you to *live!* Didn't you say something about adventure? Here it is!"

Something defiant leaped into flame in Helena's deprived spirit. "I'll go! Mother won't know I'm gone. I'll bring the *real me* along! Thank you, Sally and Mr. Sweeney."

"There is just one condition, Miss Helena . . . that you call me Kevin."

"Hurry, Helena," said Sally. "Your mother might come home early to see whether her favorite invalid collapsed on the way . . . hurry!"

"I'll get my coat. I'm coming, Sally and Kevin. I'm definitely ready to experience a few escapades in my life. I've waited a long time."

CHAPTER 5

THE HILL

(December 2, 1850)

A fire was burning in the hearth between them but discomfort was smoldering in Submit's heart. She was thinking how pleasant this should be with mother-in-law and new daughter-in-law knitting in front of a cozy fire on a cold December day. So often, however, stony silence was the only response which seemed appropriate between them. She often tried introducing bits of conversation but only got a few words from Julia in return. Was Julia afraid of her? *I always try to be courteous. Could she be fearful of the obvious social gulf between us? I must try to make her feel more comfortable.*

"What were you smiling at, Julia."

"I was remembering Jenny Lind's marvelous concert. Surely I shall never hear anything so beautiful again in all my life."

"I don't understand why she had to sing so many foreign songs. We're getting too foreign in this country to suit me. What's wrong with American music? It must be time for the paper, Julia. See if it's come, will you?"

Julia put down her sewing and started to rise from the chair but felt a slight dizziness, as she had been experiencing for three weeks. She suspected happily what it meant and

43

had confided to Let but begged him not to tell his mother yet. She didn't want to bear the sharp bluntness of Submit's comments until contour betrayed the secret. She found the *New Haven Journal and Courier* on the doormat and placed the paper in her mother-in-law's hands.

As Julia seated herself again she could feel the cold gray eyes penetrating her, womb to spine, like lensed gimlets.

"Powdered peony root," said Submit.

"What?" asked Julia.

"Peony root is an excellent remedy for the nausea of pregnancy."

Without looking up from the rose and shamrock traceries of her lacework, Julia responded, "I'll mention that to the next pregnant lady I encounter."

With an annoyed little crackle of paper, Submit spread out the first page of the *Journal* on her lap. Why had this daughter-in-law not confided her secret? Had she not every right to be told, she the grandmother of the future child?

"Julia, do you think mothers-in-law are stupid? I've been noticing your new finicky ways at table and twice I've heard your retching in the early morning. I'm a little embarrassed that the child is coming so soon after the wedding."

Julia winced at such negativity about such a happy situation but remained silent, which she had to do several times a day. Sometimes it was quite difficult.

Submit had fallen into the habit of reading a few quotations from newspaper articles aloud to Julia before settling down to a more intensive reading by herself. Often she found disparaging journalistic comments about the Irish, made to order for quotation. She began with a few harmless items.

"'A placard has been posted on Parisian boulevards announcing that ladies are in request for California.' Ladies or trollops, I wonder," commented Submit.

"'First fugitive slave cases in Boston. Warrants issued for the arrest of William and Ellen Crafts who escaped two years ago from Macon, Georgia.'

"Right here in Seymour," Submit continued on her own, "we had a slave owner from Alabama who last week caught two of the three slaves he was hunting for, right in back of Lydia's house. She'd been sheltering them. One escaped. We have no business interfering. It's against the law."

"But one can't codify God's law and make it apply to all kinds of differing social situations," said Julia. "Is the condition of slavery covered in the Bible?"

"It isn't against God's law to own slaves or any other kind of property."

Julia again decided to keep silent. She felt very strongly on the subject but not enough to trigger more controversy with an ossified set of beliefs.

Submit kept reading. "'Two watchmen were badly injured in Boston on Sunday evening in a riot among the Irish population near the Worcester Railroad.'" She looked up at Julia over the rim of her glasses. A flush swept over Julia's cheeks but she kept on knitting. She knew this was the kind of anti-Irish item Submit loved most to find and read to her.

"Well, I declare, the Irish again," Submit continued. "'Edward Robinson, first engineer on the Steamer, *Globe*, was stabbed and killed at Mackinac by an Irishman.' The Irish, always the Irish, making trouble! Where are you going, Julia?"

Tears were in Julia's eyes. She had risen abruptly. "I think I shall be going back to Waterbury to live in the gentle, truly

Christian, civilized family from which I come—where the qualities of kindness and tact are always present."

Submit knew she had gone too far. Why did she read those anti-Irish news items? A brief feeling of admiration arose in her mind as she became aware of the dignity and righteous indignation in the young figure before her but it was overcome by sudden panic about Let's possible reaction.

"No, Julia. Don't go! Those articles were in the paper, you know. I didn't invent them. You would have seen them anyway." She considered apologizing but couldn't bring herself to do it. Good God, why did Let have to bring Julia into their household? She and Let were so happy together before Julia arrived.

Julia felt she had to take a stand, firm but polite, once in a while to maintain her self-respect. "They didn't need to be read with the intention of stabbing me in the heart. How would you like it if I talked to you, day in and day out, about the scuminess of the Brockets, Swaynes and Chatfields? I'm proud of all your people and I say so, but I'm proud of *my* people, too. When all of England and Europe were dark and ignorant in the Middle Ages after the Roman Empire disintegrated, the learning and beauty of Ireland spread out like rays of the sun. There were princes and poets in Ireland long before there were any among the naked, blue-tattooed, pagan, idol-worshipping tribes of Britain and long before the English language was even in existence.

"The Mac Sweeneys go back to those princes, kings and poets, back to King Niall of the Nine Hostages, one of the oldest traceable lineages in the world. Celtic castles tower over the green hills of Ireland from Tory Island and Sheep's Haven Bay in Donegal down to the hills of Cork and Kerry.

"It appears, Mrs. Wooster, that I am not welcome here so I think it best that I take a little holiday and spend it with my family. Irish homes are full of happiness and laughter, which I thrive upon."

Julia wondered why such a strong stand had emerged from two minor anti-Irish news items. But it was the daily assaults by Submit against the Irish which little by little overwhelmed her restraints. Perhaps Submit was so accustomed to bashing all immigrants, that she didn't realize her impact on others. Well, it was time she did!

Submit sat down abruptly, dumbfounded that anyone could be *proud and happy* to be Irish. It was an entirely new concept to her. She had been taught that the Irish were barely out of the stone age while England had had noble aristocrats for centuries. "I've heard all my life," said Submit, "that every potato farmer and animal herder in Ireland call themselves kings, especially after beer-guzzling in taverns. But you're not going away, Julia, are you?"

"Even St. Patrick had limits of tolerance, Mrs. Wooster. I have tried very hard to be a good and kind daughter-in-law but I don't seem to be making any progress. You apparently think I am barely human."

"My goodness, Julia, you startle me with your frankness. You wouldn't want me to suppress the truth, would you? Please don't confide our little chat to Let. He might take it out of context. Are you really considering leaving?"

"I'm going for a long walk on the hill in blessed solitude. I'll let you know my intention when I return. How true is the old Irish proverb: If you wish blame, marry. If you wish praise, die." She walked away rapidly, tears blurring her eyes.

The light of late afternoon was adding yellow hues to the blue malachite hills. Today the tree branches were witches' arms. Reaching the top, Julia paused to look over the wide sweep of land, her gaze lingering on Castle Rock and the silver glints of the Naugatuck flowing towards Long Island Sound.

Directly to the right below, set among maples and pines, was Wooster house, a thread of smoke issuing from the chimney. She thought what a perfect home it would be with just her and Let and their uniquely beautiful love, without the constant antagonism and conflict caused by Submit. Couldn't Let arrange a viable alternative somewhere, somehow? Being kind and generous to elderly relatives is certainly a commendable cultural trait and one which the Celts have been successfully doing for millennia. But some of the elderly don't deserve it.

It was a heavy cross to bear for an otherwise happy newlywed, to enter a home full of uni-directional, unstoppable, daily malice. Whether or not Submit realized how negative she was, Julia thought, no amount of kindness, smiling, graciousness, or silence has any effect. From time to time, I must assert myself as I chose to do today. I would love to discuss it in detail with Let but so far he seems to have little insight into the situation. I must wait until he does.

Would the grandmother hate the child because of its half-Irishness? Should I take myself and my child away to my own beloved people in Waterbury? No, it's Let's child. I love him as a soul-mate. I must endure. Courage, Julia . . . It may be that you put fear into that bitter woman today. There comes a time for a sword in the glove of patience. I am not a saint like Saint Patrick. If only I could see more evidence of kindness and love within that cold, embittered, venomous woman it would be easier to tolerate her endless barbed assaults.

Julia began to walk east over the summit of the hill towards the rocky pasture. A young stag took flight, racing as lightly as thought across the tawny grass. All the old Irish associations leaped into Julia's mind: Amergin's stag of the seven tines, the royal beast of the Irish Tuatha de Danaans, the white hart of the Druids. At the red fence the deer came to a halt and gave Julia a long look. In that moment of communication, Julia's heart leaped anew with the ancient mystery of man-and-beast-as-one. Then the agile deer bounded over the fence, across the pasture and stone wall into the Dunlap meadow.

Julia stayed where she was, savoring this magical little glimpse of nature's endless wonderment. She walked quietly to the cart gate, opened it and went into the rocky area until she came to the twenty-foot heap of granite boulders in the center. She looked over the eastward hills towards Amity, Mount Carmel, Harmony and Bethany, those lovely Biblical names set like benedictions on the obdurate, granite Yankee hills. Benevolent ideals must lurk somewhere in the depths of those icy, stern New England souls . . . why so deeply hidden?

She stopped and looked at the sky turning topaz. She moved lightly across the bouldered meadow until she came to a large granite boulder almost ten feet in diameter, attracted by its sparkling mica and red-glinting garnet catching its flame from the sky. She looked down at the shining igneous inclusions and noted one small fissure filled with dust and a few disintegrating leaves. An idea occurred to her.

Here was a strong solid block of granite which had successfully resisted the powerful forces of nature for millions of years, including storms, earth movements and the grinding force of glacial ice. It reminded her of the tenacity of misbeliefs so solidly held by Anglo-Saxon New Englanders for so many decades, now unleashed with full force against Irish immigrants and all foreigners. Could such engrained prejudices be breached by gentle, prolonged persuasion?

Could the heart of a hard immoveable rock be tenderly opened by kindly patience? Could a plant survive in such a stony surround with so little nourishment for its own soul?

She walked towards the pond and closely examined the plants along its edge. She picked up a sharp rock and softly scraped around the base of a small cinnamon fern, gently teasing it out of the moist earth with its roots intact. She filled her pocket with soft earth. Then she took out her handkerchief and doused it in the pond. Returning to the large granite boulder, she carefully placed the fern in the little crevice which was dammed at both ends by granite. She filled the foot-long fissure with earth, surrounding the fern gently. She squeezed water over it from her handkerchief, tenderly patting down the soil while offering an Irish prayer for its continued life:

> May the sun shine warm upon your face
> And rains fall soft upon your destiny.

She would have preferred to plant an Irish fern but knew that such ferns had so far resisted attempts at transplantation from Ireland to the United States, requiring persistent rain throughout the year.

She walked happily to the hilltop and looked down. To her surprise she saw that someone else was enjoying the lovely view only thirty feet away. Standing in front of a small cave-like opening was a hatless, dark-haired man, one olive hand resting on the side of the rock. She saw that he was a good-looking mulatto. She quickly guessed that he must be the third slave whom Lydia Kinney had hidden and who recently escaped his Alabama owner's search. He looked up, his eyes bulging in fright and he immediately turned and began running.

"No, wait!" she called. "Don't run away! Let me help you!" Something in the honest insistence of her tone caused him to stop. He turned and cautiously approached as she hurried down the rocky area. "Don't run away! Everything is all right. The Alabama man left town early this morning. Come here, please."

The young man walked slowly towards her, his eyes fastened upon her as if to weight her trustworthiness. She was struck with the chin-up dignity of his bearing, no shambling chain-encumbered walk, no subservient stooped shoulders. An "up-standing fellow", the New Englanders would have called him if his skin had been white. There was no African flare of the nostrils, no tight curling of the hair. He could easily pass for a handsome Spaniard.

"You're sure of that, lady? That the man from Alabama has left town?"

"Quite sure. Now you can return to Mrs. Kinney's house safely and be taken on to the next station."

"I don't want to do that. We very nearly got her into a mess of trouble. Such a fine lady. I'd prefer to stay here. Isn't there a job in this town for me?"

Julia remembered that the Dunlaps were looking for a coachman. If she could conduct this man down to Tribulation Cumming and have him stay there for a few days, it might be worked out. She explained the plan.

"Yes, I'll chance it. Thank you lady, mighty kind of you."

"My name is Mrs. Letsome Wooster. And yours?"

"Well, you can call me Lazarus, ma'am, seeing as you've sort of raised me up from the dead from my tomb in that rock. Lazarus Jones."

"All right, Lazerus. Walk with me down the hill to Mr. Cumming's place."

"I don't see why you're taking so much trouble for me."

"Well, I'm a different color, too, Lazerus. I'm an Irish shamrock. I'm green. Black and green don't seem to be the best colors these days, do they?" They both laughed.

CHAPTER 6

HELPING THE NEEDY

(December, 1850)

November haze hovered over the blue-brown hills of Seymour until December crept windily and coldly in with white snows on black branches and sounds of sleigh bells like icicles falling on spinet keys.

Dozens of Christmas baskets were being filled at 28 Pearl Street, an annual ritual. Submit and cousin Almira Humphreys always drove out with a carriage full of baskets which they delivered just before Christmas in Darkey Hollow to the Cumming tribe and to any mill workers who were strapped financially. The Irish on the terrace above were not included no matter how poor. Such lower class immigrants should fend for themselves or go back where they came from.

This year, 1850, Julia offered to take over the distribution. "I'd like Helena to go with me," she suggested to her mother-in-law.

"You're arousing comment, Julia, often taking walks past Knockmedown Hill and passing time with all those common vulgar darkeys and Irish."

"Vulgar? Forgive me, Mrs. Wooster. Poor, yes; vulgar, no. They're full of gentleness and kindliness of a rare sort, a kind of poetry."

"Poetry? Absurd! They don't even know how to read and write."

"I mean poetry of feeling and attitude towards life."

"Helena's not well enough to do much walking."

"Not well enough? Two days ago we walked to the Brass Mill and back."

"Merciful heavens. Ladies *never* go there!"

"Let showed us through the rolling mill, boiler rooms, stamping mill and copper works. We found it extremely interesting. I understand his business far better now. What fascinating work! The workers loved meeting us."

"Shocking. Did Helena spend the next day in bed?"

"All she needs is exercise and love. She's more restricted than a slave!"

"She gets all the love any girl could possibly need. Cousin Almira is a *wonderful* mother."

Julia kept silent. Helena was acquiring vigor of body and spirit with which to face up to her mother's smothering mandates. After further admonitions, Submit gave her approval.

The two girls started off in the Wooster sleigh, the bells on Banba's harness ringing merrily. Julia particularly loved this horse whose name she had persuaded Let to change from Betty to a lovely old name of Ireland.

In ten minutes they were among the dingy houses of Knockmedown Hill where dogs, cats and raggedy children, even on a cold day, were playing happily. Julia suggested the Hartigan family first because this was Whiddy's family and there were five younger children. She tied Banba to the tumbledown fence and the two girls were soon in the midst of laughing, shouting Hartigans. Most of the children were of the dark Gael type but the youngest, Heafy, aged four, was fair-haired and looked like a cherub.

Now Mary Hartigan warmly exclaimed, "And to think all we could afford this year for Christmas dinner was just a bit of salt pork and bread, and you've brought us a fat goose! May joy stay with you both all the rest of your days!"

Julia asked Mary for advice on distributing the other baskets.

"Well, I think to the Mulligans since Criddy Mulligan's hand was caught in the wire-gauging machine at the mill the other day and he'll be out of work for a long time. I'd say to the old Brodigans, for they can't help themselves much, and I'd say the Gangooleys because all he makes goes down the drainpipe of his throat and there's nothin' left for his wife but cold tea and dry bread."

"These it shall be," said Julia.

Helena, who had never been among these people, delighted Julia with her kindliness and understanding, her humor and her tact. How could she be the daughter of Almira Humphreys and yet adapt herself so quicksilver-rapidly and so charmingly to these poor Irish people, catch their natural rhythms, answer their wit with her own flashes of humor and seem to revel in the experience? Julia came away from Knockmedown with a new affection for Helena and a question:

"Forgive me for asking, Helena, but what was your father like?"

"He loved the whole wide world and the whole wide world loved him."

"Then you're like him, Helena. After we take baskets to Darkey Hollow, let's ride across the covered bridge and explore the other side of the river."

"Wonderful idea. The other side has a touch of history in it."

Julia drove the sleigh down the hill towards the Irish section and the beginnings of Darkey Hollow. "Heavens! What's all that singing?" The shrill sound of female voices had broken out. A short moment brought them to Crotty Hartigan's Tavern. The local Women's Temperance Society was gathered before the swinging doors to Hell. They didn't dare enter and chant the devil to shame in his own bailiwick. They stood outside, fur-tippeted, wool-scarved, dark-skirted and sang with all the force which self-righteousness and fanatic zeal permitted.

The raucously-croaking temperance ladies were in the midst of the song, "Hurrah for Bright Water!" when Crotty Hartigan opened one of the swinging doors to let out two of his happy off-balance patrons, Tim Gangooley and old Patrick O'Neill. There was an audible shudder in their singing voices as they watched these tottering-on-the brink-of-hell creatures. Hartigan stood with a big smile on his face, then reached into the pocket of his apron, took out a silver dollar and flipped it to the singers, calling out:

"Here's a gratuity for ye, dear ladies! Thank ye for the lovely serenade. My patrons and I greatly enjoyed it. They all had an extra round on the strength and power of your singing. Please come again! You're good for business!"

Phoebe Perry called out shrilly, "The devil is in you, Hartigan." Crotty threw her a kiss and retired behind the doors.

Stifling giggles in their muffs, Julia and Helena hurried down the hill. In Darkey Hollow half a dozen kids were shrieking jubilantly as they played in the light snow outside the shanties. Old Tribulation was standing beside his doorway leaning on a cane, smiling. To the girls' friendly greetings, he answered:

"How de do, Missies. How de do. Welcome to de Land o' Goshen!"

As they handed him their baskets for his own household and other colored folk in the Hollow, he exclaimed again, "'Tis indeed now the Land of Goshen! Overflowin' with milk and honey, cranberries and turkeys! The Lord bless ye!"

"How's your youngest daughter doing?" asked Julia.

"Fallopia, you means? Nothin' the matter with her 'cept she's doin' as the Lord intended. Expectin' another little pickaninny about any time."

When they were out of hearing, Julia said: "Isn't that a priceless name? I expect old Tribulation or his wife must've heard it from a midwife."

"And found a kind of African melody in it," said Helena, laughing.

What a joy, thought Julia, that Helena's sense of humor rose, as always, above the false sense of prudery of her Yankee mother.

They finished distributing their baskets, then drove down to Bank Street and across the old covered bridge to the other side of the river, where they halted Banba. The river was full of ice chunks and the current was strong. The water churned and bubbled lustily around the bridge piers.

"It's wonderful," said Julia, "the way water sings against an obstacle." The time had come, she thought, to share her secret with Helena. "I hope I can teach my child this lesson above all other things, to turn the other cheek."

Helena's eyes widened. "Julia, are you trying to tell me something?"

"Yes, I am. I want you to be the very first outside the family to know."

"Oh, Julia!" Tears sprang into Helena's eyes and she drew Julia towards her and kissed her. "I'm so happy for you and

Let. I would love to have children but I can't ever have a baby."

"Good Lord, who ever told you that?"

"Mother's been telling me that for years. That's why I can't ever marry."

"Can't marry? Has any doctor ever documented such a verdict?"

"I trust my mother, Julia. Who could know better than a mother?"

Julia bit her lip. "Giddyap, Banba!"

There were few houses along this stretch. Tree branches leaned far over the road and little frozen ponds glinted in the afternoon sun in bouldered, brambly fields. Now and then a squirrel frisked across the road or a crow cawed warnings from a pine-top. They encountered neither sleigh nor person.

"Along here, Julia, is a very old cemetery used by residents in the mid-1700s when the settlement was called Chusetown after Indian Chief Chuse.

"Old for America, that is," replied Julia. "How I'd love to show you the fair green hill in Roscommon, Ireland, the burial place of kings three thousand years ago or the stone dolmen at Howth, near Dublin, over the body of Aldeen who died of grief for her husband killed in battle in 270 A.D."

"How beautiful your Ireland must be, Julia!"

"It's lovely as the day, as they say over there. To hear my mother-in-law talk about Ireland, it's just one long pig-pen with a few scattered shanties. Sometimes I dread bringing my baby into such a Yankee world, Helena. Do you suppose my baby will be hated as much as I am because it will be *half* Irish?

"You're not hated, Julia."

"Oh yes I am. You should spend a day living in the Wooster house." Tears sprang into Julia's eyes. They had reached the road and Julia went towards Banba to untie her. Then suddenly she cried out, "Wait, wait. What's that noise? Step back, Helena. Step back! Runaway horses!"

A sound of wildly galloping hooves came down the river road but it wasn't a runaway horse but two young men in a carriage. The driver was whipping the horse along and singing at the top of his voice an Irish song, "The Rakes of Mallow." The other was clinging to the singer and laughing loudly.

"Did you see what I saw?" asked Julia.

"I saw Dennis O'Neill and another young man driving like mad!"

"It wasn't a man, Helena. It was Sally Swayne!"

"Sally? Oh, my goodness. Sally in a man's clothes?"

"How else could she have a good time with Dennis without raising talk? Sally's a girl who strikes sparks from the flint of life. I must say I admire her!"

"Yes, but could she burn herself out some day?" asked Helena.

"Yes, but in the meantime, it's a drama-filled life full of fun!"

"She seemed quite interested in your brother at the Thanksgiving dinner."

"She's interested in every male who walks vertically but my brother isn't impressed. I think it was *you* who intrigued Kevin most at that dinner."

"He's invited me twice to New haven since then, Julia, but Mother absolutely forbade such a long expedition. Please explain this when you next see him. I'm not sure he understands the tight bondage of my maternal shackles."

Julia felt her cheeks burning. "Of course I'll explain but you should be entirely forthright with him. Don't invent any excuses for your mother."

"We mustn't ever tell anyone what we saw on the road."

"No, that's Sally's secret . . . and ours," replied Julia, "but I have an Irish premonition that life may become somewhat more complex for her soon."

CHAPTER 7

CLOSE CALL

(January, 1851)

Almira Humphreys' solicitudes for her daughter's health were inconsistent. On occasions when her own social life might suffer from Helena's absence, maternal concern diminished or disappeared. In spite of Helena having a worsening cough and sore throat for two days, her mother insisted that she accompany her on a carriage trip into New Haven in early January of 1851 to hear Henry Ward Beecher preach at the Congregational Church.

The result was that Helena came back with intensified symptoms which steadily worsened. Almira delayed calling Dr. Benedict for two days, hoping the symptoms would go away but they didn't. The doctor appraised her severe pneumonia, shook his head, explained the grim prognosis and did what he could with his pink pills and a molasses cough mixture.

Helena got worse, with higher fever, more severe coughing and finally delirium on the fifth night. Almira had dismissed her childhood friend, Dr. Abiram Stoddard, three years before for giving Almira a piece of his mind about the way she kept her daughter a virtual captive. Now, however, with Helena going down the dark slope before her very eyes, the hatchet of pride must be buried before it was too late. In the early morning she marched down the street, banged his door knocker, stood firmly with straight lips and asked if he would visit her daughter.

"Well, Almira, I thought you had given up on my old fashioned ways."

Almira stammered. "Well, I . . . Abiram . . . I . . ."

"I see, circumstances alter cases. I'll be right over, Almira. I'll do anything I can to help that lovely girl of yours." He wanted to say: "How such a jewel ever sprang from your loins is one of God's Great Mysteries."

"Don't consider me a magician, Almira. We've lost important time here and sometimes we don't do well with serious infections."

Dr. Stoddard already knew about the case since he and Dr. Benedict always cross-consulted on the severely ill and on difficult diagnoses. After carefully examining Helena, a clouded look came over his face.

"Serious?" whispered Almira across the bed.

"Very," Dr. Stoddard's lips soundlessly shaped the words. When they were outside the room, he said, "There's little we can do at this stage except wait for the crisis and hope she comes through. Almira, you look sick yourself. Eyes watering, red face. Let me take your temperature."

"No, no!"

"Do you want to be incapacitated also?"

"Merciful heavens, no. Who would take care of Helena if I became ill?"

"My dear Almira. That's the trouble with you. You think that no one in the world except yourself can take care of Helena. I'll get a nurse for you."

"You know I don't like nurses, Abiram. They get too personal."

Dr. Stoddard put a hand on her cheek. "You're burning up with fever, Almira. Let's ask Submit to help out for a few days. She loves medical fussing and we'll ask that lovely daughter-in-law of hers to help with Helena's care."

"Lovely? Humph," said Almira with an equine snort.

"Yes, very lovely, and smart as all get-out, too. Unfortunate for her that she's not a Yankee. Has to buck bigotry, arrogance, hostility, envy and a lot of other unpleasant attitudes in this town."

"I simply don't understand you, Abiram!"

"Most of the ladies of this town don't want to understand." I've heard 'em talking in my parlor and I know exactly how much Christian goodwill there is towards Julia Wooster, Caresse Smith, Maeva O'Neill and anyone who happens to be a little bit different! Love me, love my pedigreed dog, my blue-blooded cat and my patrician parrot! Ye gads!" He stormed out of the house and rode in his buggy to Wooster house. There he laid the situation before the two women.

Julia immediately said "Oh, yes, I would love to help." Submit also agreed to help.

"There's some danger but I'll show you how to protect yourself."

"I'm very strong and younger than Mrs. Wooster. Let me do it all."

"No, I think you should take turns taking care of both of them. It means night and day, you know, for a few days. I'll give you explicit instructions. If you find you can't handle it, we'll get a nurse in from New Haven."

At nine o'clock that evening Dr. Stoddard came for his fourth visit of the day. Julia was on duty after Submit's stint. Helena was sinking rapidly and he had told Julia there was little chance of saving her. Helena's breathing was irregular and rasping. Almira had risen from her bed, wrapped a blanket around herself and insisted on sitting in a chair across Helena's bed from Julia.

As Julia watched the young flushed face and the flittering-eyed, square-jawed, wrinkled one, she had a curious feeling that, mingled with the maternal solicitude of Mrs. Humphreys was a strange emotion, drifting like a noxious vapor from Almira, of let-me-watch-her-die-so-I-don't-have-to-share-her-with-anyone-anymore. "It's as if," thought Julia, "she were saying, 'Now Helena will be mine, all mine! She will lie beside me—my child forever!'"

"I can't let this premature death happen," thought Julia. "I've seemed to have, now and then, some healing powers with humans and animals. God never punished anyone for asking His help." She put her hands together in front of her, closed her eyes and began to pray out loud, but softly.

"Oh, God of All the Good and Beautiful. Oh God, called by the Druids, my ancestors, The Mighty Essence . . . Oh God, from whom comes all suffering and all healing, help this lovely young spirit who has scarcely begun to live. Oh, you Everywhere-Dwelling Great Force . . ." Julia rose and placed both hands on Helena's forehead, her palms resting lightly on the temples, the fingertips meeting in the center, and continued to pray quietly but audibly.

"What are you doing, Julia?" said Almira Aurelia sharply. "What queer pagan thing is it you're saying? Sounds like witchery to me . . ."

"Sh-h-h, just praying." Julia prayed soundlessly now, with more urgency than she had ever prayed before. She summoned into her mind every strong and radiant thought she could evoke, thoughts of God far beyond the stunted image of a Deity mounted on his parochial cloud. She appealed to Him in terms of what He had created—vast beauty, vast power, vast joy, chords of inconceivable music, spectra of unimaginable color and pervasive light.

Could not one small spark of this benevolent light be spared for the beautiful heart and soul of Helena, so young, so pure. Oh, Everlasting God, one tiny spark, I pray you . . . There was a long silence, broken only by Helen's struggling, irregular breathing.

After fifteen minutes, the silence was broken by Almira. "Look! Listen! Her breathing's becoming less rasping, less desperate. I think she's better!"

Julia saw Almira's eyes dilate with a strange mixture of terror and joy. She saw Helena's face beginning to become less flushed, more peaceful. "I think she *is* improving," said Julia. "Perhaps her crisis is over."

"I watched her face . . . I think you did something powerful for her, Julia." The words seemed to be wrenched reluctantly out of her by the intensity of the moment but she was clearly impressed and mystified.

"I only happened to be here at the apex of the crisis, Mrs. Humphreys. Our prayers, yours and mine, may have helped a little. Love always helps."

"I watched her face while you knelt beside her. It was very unusual. Something definitely was happening." She looked intently at Julia.

When Helena clearly began to improve and was back to full alertness in two days, Julia began to stimulate her by talking about the future. "We'll go to New Haven, Helena, and have some fun, go to the shops and have Kevin show us around town, including the old Yale campus. Would you like that?"

"I'd *love* it!" Then, always the afterthought. "But will Mother allow it?"

"I'll see that she does. We're going to become more adamant!"

One afternoon when Mrs. Humphreys had entirely recovered and Helena was much better, Dr. Stoddard came in. After examining her, he said, "Well, young lady, you're almost well. Time to get up and move around. In a few days I'll let you out to taste this mild mid-winter spell of nice weather we're having."

"Oh no, Abiram!" said Almira. She's too delicate."

"Delicate? Who says so? She survived against considerable odds. She's full of strength and stamina, Almira. Full of vigor and vitality!"

"She is still very weak, you old fool, you know . . ."

"I know nothing of the sort! I brought this girl into the world and I know her from toe to topknot! We parted company on this topic before, Almira, but I'll stick to my guns. All she needs is exercise, plenty of activity and a normal life!"

"Thank you, Doctor, thank you for treating the case." Almira moved with the decisive step of dismissal towards the door.

Dr. Stoddard paid no attention. "You have your friend, Julia, to thank for an important part of your recovery, Helena. She did a superb job of nursing."

"Yes, she did and I love her dearly," responded Helena.

"Julia has a very special talent for healing," said Dr. Stoddard.

Julia's heart began to pound for she'd been shaping a bold question. Now or never, she told herself. *Carpe diem*. "You're very kind to say what you did, Dr. Stoddard, but it's your fine doctoring and Helena's own basic good health and youth that cured her. Now I have a further question to ask. Helena has been told many times that she is incapable of having babies and therefore shouldn't marry. Is there any reason why Helena can't have babies?"

"Lord Almighty! Where did she get that ridiculous notion? Of course she's fit to bear children!" He picked up his bearskin cap firmly and, jamming it on his white head, strode to the door. There he paused and roared with leonine fervor, "She's perfectly capable of having a dozen babies, including twins!"

Almira Aurelia Humphreys quickly disappeared into her own room, slamming the door.

CHAPTER 8

SHAMROCK LAUGHTER

(February, 1851)

Julia was so tired from nursing Helena through her almost-fatal pneumonia that Let suggested she spend a week recuperating with her family. She could hardly wait to refresh her soul at her family's Gaelic Fountain of Laughter.

Before Julia could pack her Brussels carpetbag and be driven by Whiddy to the train station, Submit had made it plain what she thought of the whole idea.

"Never in all the time I was married to my dear husband, Albert, did I think it necessary to spend a single night away from him in the home of my parents."

"You must have been a good wife, dear Mrs. Mother-of-Let," said Julia with a pixie dancing on her shoulder. "But I thought you told me that, after you were married, your widowed mother divided her time between you and Uncle Chatfield, so there was really no parental home to visit."

Submit flushed and struck sidewise. "I will have you speak of my brother as Mr. Swayne and me as Mrs. Wooster until I give you permission otherwise."

"I will do that, if you wish, Mrs. Wooster, but Let doesn't approve of such formality in the heart of a family, you know."

"Formality and dignity are, and have always been, signs of the true aristocrat. We gentry never lower our standards. Others don't seem to care."

Julia tightened her jaw but let it pass. She was so happy at the thought of going home to a family where all was warmth and approbation and love that she could afford to let her mother-in-law have, as always, the last loveless word.

When Julia walked down the stairs from her room a few minutes later, she smiled and said, "Goodbye, Mrs. Wooster. Be happy while I'm gone."

"Happiness is for fools!" said Submit. "It's hard work that counts."

As Julia stepped into the front yard, her heart rippled with merriment for there was Whiddy Hartigan walking around and around the hitching post, dragging the whip behind him and talking to himself. She could feel her own elf walking in circles on her shoulder in time with Whiddy.

"Good day to you, Whiddy. Why are you revolving 'round the post?"

He gave a singular smile along the curves of his scalloped mouth. "Three times 'round is luck, Miss Julia, as you colleens very well know."

Julia thought of the Irish legendary hero, Cuchulainn, always driving his chariot three times around the fortress mound at Emania before a battle. As old in Hibernia as sun and moon worship, this revolving good luck charm of three was the same number as petals in the shamrock, the symbol of Ireland used by Saint Patrick to illustrate the Catholic Trinity doctrine in the Fifth Century.

Whiddy took her bag and helped her into the buggy. "Would you like to drive, Miss Julia? A little touch of freedom such as I'd be guessing you'd not be having much of under her ladyship?"

"Yes, Whiddy, what a nice idea. I'm glad you hitched up Banba."

"You and Mr. Wooster are the only people outside my family to say nice things to me. Other people take me for a damn fool Irishman."

"You're very witty and intelligent, Whiddy. You're smarter than all those who run you down, but you do give people ammunition when you walk around posts and talk to yourself and do other odd things. Why do you do them?"

"Well, it amuses folks and I enjoy using my acting propensities. At one time I thought of becoming an actor."

What a fun person to be with, thought Julia. As the two drove down the hill, Julia holding the reins, people stared at them. It was unheard of that anyone should sit beside Whiddy and find anything to say to him. Yet there they were, talking and laughing as merry as you please. That girl made friends with everybody. She had even been seen chatting away with Page Sanford in front of his blacksmith shop, with old Morris the harness maker, with Collis Huntington the tin peddler, and old Eunice Mauwehu, the Indian woman. Some Seymour citizens were heard to say, "She's like a fresh breeze wafting through the town, bringing much-needed friendliness and laughter to these parts."

Now the horse and buggy had reached the station. In the sight and hearing of the half dozen on the platform, Julia put out her hand to Whiddy as the train arrived and said: "Goodbye, Whiddy. May God go over the hills with you."

"Thank you for keeping me in discourse, Miss Julia. You'll make a rational creature of me yet." Smiling, he turned away, mumbling to himself, "Whiddy, me boy, it's time to pick up your role again as the village idiot."

From the train window Julia saw Whiddy marching three times around one of the iron rods that held the platform canopy. She laughed out loud.

Julia ran up the steps of the little white frame house in Waterbury and burst in upon her surprised family, causing hugging and kissing. Kevin was there, too, in the break after midyear exams.

Tea, beer, apples and nuts were brought out and convivial conversation flowed. Julia elicited lots of laughter with her latest mother-in-law quotes.

"I'm so happy to be out of that venomous atmosphere," said Julia.

"As for myself," said Kevin, "I'm sure I couldn't spend two days with the old bitch without bringin' me two hands around her throat a bit too tight."

"Come, come, son," said Kevin's father, "those be unwisdom words for one planning to administer the equitable laws of the land."

"How dreadful that another solution can't be found to house your mother-in-law," said Mary. "I'm reminded of that old Irish rhyme:

> Two women in one house.
> Two cats and one mouse,
> Two dogs and one bone,
> May never accord in one."

"You and I accord pretty well, Mother!" said Maggie. "Don't be throwing me out the door quite yet!"

"Ah, Cushie, you're me own blood daughter and you're really not a woman grown yet. You'll be finding some young lad soon and flying out the door, perhaps even in secret, to harmonize with him."

"I may not be fully grown yet," replied Maggie, "but the idea of harmonizin' sounds pretty good to me!" They all laughed.

"I'm still of a mind," said William, between puffs on his short-stemmed Gaelic pipe, "that Julia can learn to live with the old lady. Malignant repartee eats at the liver. I think accord can be built with saintly patience and silence."

"I agree, Father, and I often use silence but it's not easy for anyone with Irish blood to keep silent all the time in the face of constant insults. The hostile assaults never end. You'd think she'd get fatigued with being acid and bitter all the time, like an unripe quince, but she never seems to tire. The only way to end it is to leave the house and go walking on the hill."

"Yes, Father," said Kevin. "It's very difficult for us always to heed the words of the Lord, 'And unto him that smiteth thee on one cheek, offer him the other.' Nice thought on paper but somewhat more difficult in the actuality."

"I understand you both better than you may think," said their father. "My red-headed anger used to explode fairly often in my youth but you can all testify that I haven't let the flames burst out very often for many a year. To return to your case, Julia, absence of the retort expected can be a retort resounding. Words held back are rarely regretted and silence can be a thunderous rebuke!"

"Yes, I almost always hold my temper with Mrs. Wooster but it sometimes takes monumental will-power. Let has no idea how Submit constantly pleasures herself by tormenting me. She hangs an entirely different tongue in her mouth when he comes home. She is suddenly all sweetness and courteous charm."

"As for anti-Irish feelings," said William, "there are a keg full of reasons. Competition for jobs, religious distrust and the lesser quality of some recent potato famine immigrants. Chiefly it's just the Irish being different. The ancient Greeks and Romans looked down on anyone different from themselves, unable to speak their language properly, and regarded them as stupid, crude and inferior. I, too, have been deeply hurt but I've tried to trust the goodness in people."

"You're a fine man, Father," said Maggie, "especially if you let me do some harmonizin' one of these days!" They all laughed again.

"Julia has innate patience and serenity," said Mary, "but if she can't come here to have her baby, I'm going to Seymour to take care of her there! If that woman, Submit, isn't on her best behavior . . . I plan to drown her in laughter!"

"You're coming, then, Mother? How wonderful!"

"You know, Julia," said Kevin. "I'm gathering strong ammunition for you."

"What do you mean?"

"Well, after that contentious Thanksgiving dinner, I got to thinking again about the whole damned business of why we Irish are so hated and why the old-time New Englanders are so damned peacocky and proud. The societies they form are harbingers of hate. I wrote a number of themes on Irish and Yankee conflicts when I was a Yale undergraduate and I've kept it as a hobby. Recently I have done more work on the project for a case I had to present at Law School and I may turn it into my Senior Thesis. The historical facts are mind-boggling."

"Good idea, son," said his father, "but stir the pot gently."

"It's given me perspective, Dad. Not only have I discovered some of the outstanding contributions of the Irish to this country but I've also been learning a lot more about these holier-than-thou, so-called descendents of the finest noble families of England. Yes sir, I've got some astonishing ammunition for you, Julia, about Seymour's so-called gentry. It's not all negative stuff. I was thrilled to learn that four out of our thirteen Presidents had some Irish blood in them—Madison, Monroe, Jackson and Polk."

"*Some* Irish blood?" put in William. "Why, Andy Jackson was *all* Irish. I've wet my own lips with liquor at his father's tavern at St. Nicholas's Gate, Carrickfergus, in County Antrim. *All* Irish, me boy, all Irish!"

"Did you know," went on Kevin, "that there were hundreds of Irish soldiers in the American Revolution? One quarter of those from Connecticut had Irish names. It was the Irish who saved the day at Valley Forge. When General Washington asked his army if they wanted to carry on, it was the Irish who shouted back, 'Aye! Aye!'"

"Submit's proud society, the Daughters of the Star Spangled Banner, feeds mainly on self-perpetuating delusions," said William.

"Well, bad scran to her!" answered Kevin. "She belongs to that body of witches and banshees, does she? How can Let tolerate it?"

"I've heard him speaking with her rather strongly about it," replied Julia, "but her hardness is like that of Osgur of the Fianna, a twisted thorn with a sheath of steel upon it. When the Daughters meet at our house, Submit hasn't yet seen fit to invite me but I sit on the stairs and listen to their haughty yappings—Mrs. Charles Goodyear or Mrs. Henry Beecher or Mrs. Benajah Johnson, directly descended from Elder Brewster. Or Amy Goodwin Swayne, whose ancestors came over in the Mayflower. Must've been a mighty big ship, I'd say! Then there's Mrs. Elvira Gunn Dunlap who's so proud of her hubby's great-grandfather Dunlap who did the printing of the Declaration of Independence."

"That name interests me," said William. "The John Dunlap who printed the Declaration of Independence was as Irish as Mulligan's pig and Hooligan's cow! He was from Strabane in Ireland."

"I can't believe it!" Julia said, laughing. "There's no prouder dame in Naugatuck Valley than Elvira. You should see her swanning around in her phaeton with her colored coachman, Lazarus Jones, and two proud-stepping bay horses."

"I'm telling you, Julia, my father had friends in Strabane and a very pretty town it is, with its sloping green lawns along the River Mourne. I've often heard tell there of the John Dunlap who went over to the Colonies and set up his print-shop in Philadelphia and rolled out the famous Declaration."

"Save that little jewel, Julia, for the appropriate time," said Kevin.

"That I will, with a heart and a half," said Julia laughing.

"Don't haul the moment to you, my girl," said her father. "Allow the moment to come of its own free spirit, for edification rather than revenge."

"Don't worry, I'll gentle it. Submit is always rubbing my face in pigpen mud. She loves mentioning her Brocketts who were high lords in Yorkshire, and her Chatfields who were 'armigerous gentry,' whatever that may mean."

"It means the noble class who are entitled to show off an impressive coat of arms on their family shield," explained William, puffing away at his dudeen.

"And me with my O'Neills who were armigerous gentry for thousands of years before the English even existed!" exclaimed Mary. "It's really laughable."

"What were some other family names Submit mentioned?" asked William.

"Swaynes and Gunns and Riggses and Upsons and Tomlinsons . . ."

"I'll be taking some of those names down, Dad. I'll bet I can find some real blots on their armigerous escutcheons in the New Haven records."

"You may discover that I am also second-son English nobility and then I may join one of the exclusive societies myself," said William. Everyone laughed. "It is possible that some of those names may be Irish or Anglo-Irish."

"Oh, no, which ones?" asked Julia. "That would be too good to be true!"

"Well, Riggs and Gunn. Even Swayne might've been Irish many moons ago. The Gunns go back to the Norse Vikings who peopled the Isle of Man. Some went into Scotland and became two clans of Gunn. In the twelfth century the Countess of Atholl fled from some conspiracy with her two sons, David and Sweyn—mind that name. Sweyn became the great Gunn of Ulster in Ireland."

"It's unbelievable!" cried Julia, rocking back and forth with glee.

"Wouldn't it kill the old lady," said Mary, "to think she might have a pint or two of Irish blood in her? Might you ever have been mentioning that Sweeneys are kin to O'Neills, High Kings of Ireland? I tipped her off to it at the wedding but she has very selective ears."

"I did mention our ancestors to Submit, and what do you think she said? That every swineherd and goatherd was probably called a King in Irish taverns."

"She didn't!" shouted Kevin. "I'll wring her old scraggly neck!"

"I do have a favor to ask of you, Kevin," said Julia. "Her husband, Albert Wooster, died in 1844 at the age of thirty-six. They were known as 'the handsome couple.' Would you see what you can find on him? I'd also love to learn more about her father, Joseph Chatfield. She never mentions either one."

"With pleasure, Julia. My research may stun them, those proud-stomached, pompous-prancing, high-nosed, high-falutin' bitchy Yankee dames!"

"Let's all go for a walk down to the river," suggested Julia, "and be forgetting about all such adversarial topics. Flowing water often calms turbled thoughts just as flowing beer often exacerbates them. Let's see if there be any signs of blue or violet hepatica peerin' through the snow."

"Good idea," said Mary. "And to think that by the spring I'll have a darlin' grandchild to take awalkin' through the world with me. Ah, may the little one not resemble, in any way, the vitriolic, unsmilin' old Yankee cobra, but may he or she be all lovely Irish, enjoyin' and laughin' her way through life!"

"Yes," said William, "that's our question for the day: why is laughin' better for the human soul than spitting venom at people? Let's see if we can find the answer in the happy gurgling waters of the Naugatuck."

Chuckling, he plucked from the hall rack a bright green hat to put on his red head, offered his arm to Mary and out they went with a jaunty Celtic stride.

CHAPTER 9

Hilltop Escapade

(April, 1851)

One warm morning in early April, Let remarked at the breakfast table that he would have Tom Tibbals come over with his divining rod to locate water for the new vegetable garden he was planning for the slope above the house.

"You don't need to do that, Let," remarked Julia quietly. "I'm pretty sure I can find water for you."

"What's your trick, darling?"

"The Irish have known how to find water since the Druids and long before. My father has a knack and I believe I have it, too. I'd like to give it a try."

Submit gave her a look as if she were a witch and tightened the purse strings of her lips. "I'll send Hull to get Tibbals," said Submit.

"No, Mother, I have faith Julia can do it."

"It's not a thing for a woman to be doing. I've always thought the devil had his tail in that water-finding business!"

"The devil is afraid of water because it makes him sizzle," said Julia with a laugh. Let joined in the laugh. A purple shadow passed over Submit's face.

"I'll try late this afternoon at magic-time just before sunset," said Julia with a wink at Let. "I'll be needing a

Leprechaun Consultant and they come cheaper after hours." She and Let laughed.

"The best hazel bushes," Let suggested, "grow at the hilltop pond."

"The Druids used coniferous yew rods as water wands, sometimes with bells attached. I prefer to use the wand of my mind."

"I'm very fond of the wand of your mind," said Let, smiling.

In the late afternoon Julia left the house. The peaceful air smelled sweet and Aprily. The great maple at the foot of the hill was covered with a flush of small red leaves. The rambler roses on the trellis were in bud. Clear calls of robins came from the orchard. Swallows added their metallic chirping as they darted acrobatically for their last insect meal of the day. Julia loved being alone with the myriad beauties of Nature and she needed to be alone to locate water.

She looked at the topaz loops of the Naugatuck River and the rounded granite hills rolling away into the distance, becoming lavender-gray against the crocus sky. What a beautiful world, she thought. How can anyone invent unpleasantness in such a world as this? She walked over the slope, thinking of secret underground trickles. Where were the hidden springs? As she criss-crossed back and forth, she could not feel the pull of any hidden water.

At the slope's south end there was a thicket of bushes among which was a hazel bush. "I'll sit me down beside the hazel," she said quietly. "Hazel is one of the seven sacred trees of Ireland. It is the tree of poetry, beauty and wisdom that grew by Connia's Well. Lend me your wisdom, little hazel bush."

She stroked a cool branch on which the buds protruded like small dark beads and there was love in her heart. Her father had taught her the ancient Irish lore that there is an in-dwelling Spirit in all things, even trees and stones. "God," sang the bards, "is the Mighty Essence—everywhere, in all things, both animate and inanimate." A tiny particle of crystal in a rock may send out a little energy packet as a reflection of energy from the sun. One has to be ready to sense it.

"Lend me your wisdom, spirit of the hazel. Let me see or feel the water under the ground, the pool of beauty and life."

Sitting next to the hazel bush, she half-closed her eyes, shutting out all troubles and antipathies, thinking and loving intently. Through the veil of her eyelashes the whole hill-slope began to take on an iridescent shimmer. Then, not two yards from her feet, a pool, blue as gentian, appeared for half a second, then vanished. She opened her eyes wide. There was still a flutter in the air as if some essence had vibrated there. She was alive with the wonder of it.

"Oh, spirit of earth, of water, Whoever, Whatever . . . My thanks to You. I know now where the cool water lies." She quietly bathed her spirit in the faded image of the pool. Then she thought, I must go up to the hilltop meadow to see whether there are any new flowers. Gently she broke off a twig of hazel and placed it in the ground where she had seen the blue mist.

She walked towards the board fence which separated the meadow from the stream-fed artificial pool where the cows drank. She was about to climb over the fence when she heard voices behind a boulder on the other side.

"C'mon, Sally, let's both take off all our clothes right now and not go at it piece-meal as we usually do. I'm eager to love you," said a male voice which Julia immediately recognized as that of Dennis O'Neill.

"I agree! I can't wait," said a voice clearly Sally Swayne's.

Julia looked around. There was no cover except the fence, surrounded by open meadow. She knew she should run away but fear of discovery and undeniable curiosity urged her to stay. She huddled quietly behind the fence.

After several minutes of silence, Sally said, "You touch and kiss so wonderfully, Dennis, but now I want to be kissed and kissed . . . you know, everywhere, the Dennis way, which you do so fantastically."

After another few moments of silence, there were groans and "Oh, God, Dennis. Jesus, you're good. Let me rest a few seconds then I want more, more. It's so exciting."

After less than a minute, "Yes, Dennis, yes. Gently now . . . yes, more, more . . . Oh . . . yes! . . . It's so intense . . . Yes, yes! Oh-h-h-h. Let me wait a minute, then one more time!"

Julia wondered exactly what they were doing. It sounded very exciting but she couldn't visualize it. After another bout of "Oh, Gods," this time with actual screams, Sally said:

"Now it's your turn, lover boy, turn over on your back." Silence, mixed with groans, went on for several minutes until Dennis said, "That's it, Darlin', I can't stand any more. It's time to do a little mergin'."

More minutes of silence with increasing sighs. "Yes, Dennis, yes! God you feel good! Go on and on, slowly now, not too fast." Several more minutes of silence, then increasing groans from both, then loud screams from Sally and heavy grunts from Dennis, then silence."

Several minutes later, Dennis said "Give me a few more minutes, my Darlin'. I'm not finished with you yet! I'd be loving you again if you're up to it but I need a little time to recharge my Celtic batteries . . ."

Julia realized she was breathing heavily. My God, she thought, that was so exciting! What were all the preliminaries about, leading up to the Grand Finale? I think I've been missing something . . . maybe I should be finding out one of these days! This was a good time to escape, so she got up quietly, remained bent over, walked quickly for a few yards, then ran rapidly out of sight.

When she got to the maples near home, she sat down and leaned against a tree for fifteen minutes, making sure she couldn't be seen. Good Lord, she thought. What have I just been privy to? Sally, the proud Swaynes' daughter, engaging in wild romance, rolling in the grass on a hilltop with an Irishman?

Sally was Submit's own niece and Let's cousin. With Sally's beauty, keen intelligence and sparkling personality she could entice anyone into matrimony from the best families of New Haven, Boston or New York. Now such a blue blood is mixing it up intimately with an Irish lad, Dennis O'Neill of the Tavern O'Neills? Gads! What if Sally gets pregnant?

"What influence," said Julia to herself, "can I possibly have where such powerful primeval passions are involved? Was she a witness only to sexual frenzy or was it an expression of love between two individuals who deeply cared for each other? Could they remain happy against all the icy anger which will be hurled violently against them when word gets out in such a biased town? Why is life so checkered, so full of perilous adversities alternating with moments of such beauty and joy?"

A cool breeze came across the purple shoulders of Castle Rock into the valley. Darkness was descending over what had begun as an afternoon of shimmering wonderment but which now Julia, with her special perception, sensed was an unfolding Greek tragedy.

CHAPTER 10

DELUGE

(July 18, 1851)

It had been blowing and pouring for hours. Although it was only mid-afternoon, the sky was so dark between lightning flashes that Submit and Julia were sewing by firelight. They were mending clothes for the missionary barrels which were standing in all their sanctitude in the living room. All leftovers went into the barrels—Let's old shoes, Submit's worn-out scarves and mittens, cast-off petticoats and chipped dishes all righteously packed in the barrels.

Quietly amused by the ritual, Julia kept thinking, be kind to Zulus and Hottentots but hate your neighbors, the Irish, including your own daughter-in-law! Goodness is carefully ladled out by Yankees who eagerly await praise for their generosity from those of their social class.

"What are you smiling about, Julia? That peculiar habit of yours can get quite irksome."

"Oh, I was just visualizing an African man running around in Let's old ragged pants when he's used to running around all naked and happy!"

"What a shocking idea! No one could possibly be naked and happy!"

Ripples of silent laughter ran through Julia. "Dear God!" she thought. "What of love and all its wondrous unity? In what tight wrappings of denial you must have lain on your wedding-night and all the nights thereafter, swathed in long protective flannel nightgowns to preserve your pristine dignity! Poor Albert! How did Let ever successfully battle his way into this world!"

The storm was growing stronger every moment. The line of maples at the end of the west garden tossed their branches wildly. Shutters banged and thunder claps grew louder. Julia went to the window to watch the work of the wind, the slanting silver rain and jagged bursts of lightning. "What a beautiful storm!" she said. "No wonder the Druids used to worship the Storm God."

"You tire me to death with your old Druids. What a nasty storm," said Submit.

There was a loud knock at the front door. Julia rushed to open it. "Come in, oh come in, Lydia." It was Lydia Kinney, wrapped in a long brown hooded cloak.

"Oh Julia. I think the poor people at the foot of Knockmedown Hill must be in trouble. From my house I could hear people screaming and pigs squealing even above the roar of the river. Let's go see what we can do to help."

"I'll put on my rain cape and come immediately."

Submit rose from her chair and glided from the living room in her smooth, noiseless way. "What mad thing are you two planning? No, Julia, not in your condition. You know very well that Let wouldn't approve."

"I'm sure he'd approve. There are people in trouble at the foot of the hill."

"Those people are always in trouble and floods happen every spring. Let them cope by themselves. It's their fault that they intruded into our valley."

Julia didn't answer. She put on her rain-gear and she and Lydia left the house.

"Does she ever approve of anything you do?" asked Lydia.

"Not yet but, as my own dear Mother says, the heavens are full of days."

They were halfway up Pearl Street passing Lydia's house. Because of the afternoon's darkness, Lydia had already lighted the candle lantern that burned all night every night in her front window. She had lit it for several years to light the way for her husband, Llewellyn, who had left for the Mexican Wars with the Ninth New England Regiment in 1846 at the age of twenty-five. He had been reported missing after the battle of Chapultepec. Clark Ford of Seymour, of the same regiment, had returned safely, reporting that Llewellyn had received a glancing bullet wound to the head which had been regarded by army doctors as mild. They were to have been mustered out together but Llewellyn disappeared after behaving strangely.

It was because of this curious story that Lydia had never given up hope. In the meantime she had kept busy with her underground station for escaped slaves. There had been would-be suitors, notably young Dr. Tom Stoddard, but Lydia closed the doors gently on all of them with Penelopean firmness. In spite of her husband's part-Welsh background, Lydia found acceptance in Seymour because her mother was a Beecher and "the Beechers are one of us."

As they passed Lydia's house, clinging arm in arm against the gale, Lydia said, "Doctor Tom has asked me again to marry him, Julia."

"He's a good man, Lydia."

"Yes, he's a dear man and a good doctor but Lew is alive somewhere, still confused from his head wound. It's in the marrow of my bones. I know it."

There was a terrific flash of lightning that seemed to arrow straight down the chimney of Page Sanford's blacksmith shop on the corner of Maple and Pearl, followed by very loud thunder which seemed directly overhead. Both girls started running toward the shop. They burst through the door and were met by a strong smell of ozone. Page lay flat on the sod floor ten feet from the anvil, his heavy hammer beside him. He was unconscious. Lydia knelt down and felt for his pulse.

"He's not dead. Get the bucket of water, Julia."

Julia brought the bucket used to cool the iron. Dipping their handkerchiefs, they wiped his face and arms. His eyes were wide open and glazed. "Most likely it's just temporary electrical shock," said Lydia. "Most people survive with no ill effects."

In a few minutes there was a trembling of the eyelids and a look of perceiving came into Page's eyes. Slowly a slight smile appeared. "Well, with an angel on either side of me, I guess I've been blasted into Heaven."

"You were struck by lightning, Page. Are you all right?" asked Lydia.

"Let's see." He tried to clench his right hand but it was slow; his left was strong. He couldn't lift his right leg off the floor but could wiggle his toes.

"One of us will go for Dr. Stoddard," said Julia.

"No. I'll be all right in a few minutes. Lightning shock often puts parts of your body out of commission for a while. I'm lucky to be alive. You might tell my sons to harness up and come here to take me home in the wagon."

"We'll do that with a heart and a half," said Julia. "If you'll behave yourself and stay quiet, we'll get your sons to help you and then we'll head for the river to see how we can help those who are flooded out."

Julia and Lydia hurried to Page Sanford's house and notified his wife to fetch him. Then they went through the rain and wind down to Knockmedown Hill. They could hear the river roaring like a wild ocean. Above the noise rose unidentifiable shrill sounds like the cries of petrels in a storm. Human wailings or the banshees of Irish folklore, howling into the wind to signify that some family member is about to die?

They could see the river surging across the turnpike and over the newly-laid track of the New Haven and Hartford Railroad. They could see the almost-submerged covered bridge. The swollen Naugatuck swirled past, tawny with mud and froth, full of branches and pieces of barns and houses. A half dozen bedraggled white chickens clung to a coop and a cat grappled a bobbing branch.

To the left of the crossroad where Darkey Hollow had been there was nothing but tumultuous water and the upjutting roofs of two houses that had somehow managed to survive. Above, on the Irish plateau, all was confusion. The water was over the stoops of the shacks. The Irish were evacuating with the help of the blacks who, having lost everything, had turned to help their neighbors salvage something. Further up the New Haven Turnpike, between the Irish settlement and O'Neill's Tavern, townspeople from the hills had gathered to watch rather than help.

By edging along the lower shoulder of Knockmedown Hill, Julia and Lydia were able to make their way across to the Hartigan house where several of Tribulation Cumming's children and grandchildren were helping the family evacuate. Whiddy was there assisting his family, all quirks and idiosyncrasies gone during the emergency. Water was already at the front door.

Above the roar of the river, Mary Hartigan's voice could be heard calling the shrill pitch of alarm, "Heafy! Heafy! Where are you, Heafy?" She rushed back into the house, Whiddy running after her. A shiver ran over Julia with the certainty that something dreadful had happened. Then she heard Mary's wailing cry from the back of the house. Whiddy came running back carrying his little brother in his arms.

"I must get him to Dr. Stoddard!" he cried as he rushed past, his eyes teary.

"He went back into the yard to get his little pet rabbit but the river had already flooded it," sobbed Mary. "He fell into the water, face down. The fence saved him from going down the river. Surely the good Lord wouldn't take a dear little lambkin like Heafy, would He?" Mary began to weep uncontrollably.

Julia and Lydia led her up the road towards Dr. Stoddard's house.

Three black families had been washed away with their houses. The pitiful rescued furniture and belongings of the surviving black families, and of the Irish, were piled along the railroad embankment above the ruined houses. The survivors themselves were standing in the rain.

"This is dreadful," exclaimed Julia. "Is nobody doing anything to offer shelter to these poor people? You take Mary to Dr. Stoddard's, Lydia. I'll see what I can do."

She was not far from the Tavern run by the O'Neills so she hurried up the slope and knocked loudly on the door. Awley O'Neill came to the door. "What's up, Miss Julia?"

"Didn't you know the river's run over all the houses at the foot of the hill?"

"We knew the river was up but we didn't know it was as bad as all that."

"It's very bad! How many families could you shelter, Africans and Irish?"

"We're full up with a convention but we'll gladly be finding places for seven or eight more even if they have to sleep in blankets on the floor."

"Thank you, Awley."

Julia went out the door and saw Mrs. Dunlap's closed carriage approaching. Mrs. Dunlap and Annie were inside and Lazarus was at the reins. Impulsively Julia ran into the street and held up her hands. Lazarus reined in the pair of black horses.

"Oh, Mrs. Dunlap!" cried Julia. "I have a kind favor to ask. The African-Americans and Irish at the foot of the hill have been swept out of their homes by the river. You have a large house. Could you be putting up some of them for a few days?"

"What a question! Money I'll give but there's no room at the Dunlap house for such . . ." Julia gave her such a burning look that she left the sentence unfinished.

"There's the barn, ma'am," said Lazarus.

"I need no suggestions or advice from you, Lazarus!"

"Oh, Mother," Annie urged. "We could easily put up the nice colored people."

"*Nice? Niggers?*" Elvira reached into her chatelaine bag and pulled out a five dollar bill. "Here, Mrs. Wooster, is my contribution. Drive on, Lazarus."

Julia noticed how very red Annie's face had become. Julia shook her head as she tucked the bill into a little silk bag that hung at her waist. She made her plans quickly. She hurried along Pearl Street to call on Reverend Smith for help.

Julia hurried to the Methodist parsonage. The front door was ajar. Julia entered and found Caresse face down on the sofa, crying her heart out.

"Caresse, darling. What is it? What's happened?"

"Oh, Julia! It's too dreadful. I am the unhappiest woman in the whole world! I'm going to have a baby and I should be happy!"

"That's wonderful! What lucky girls we both are!"

"Not I, Julia. My husband will not acknowledge the child as his own, and I am the most faithful of wives. You didn't know, and neither did I before I married him, that Epaphroditus believes in absolute chastity of ministers as well as priests. 'No ministerial servant of God must contaminate himself with a woman!' I might as well be married to a tombstone. I wanted children so much . . . a half dozen at least.

"Well, something happened after we came home from your Thanksgiving dinner. Epaphroditus was wild with passion almost all night long and I still a virgin after five years of marriage! Then he slept from five in the morning until noon. When he woke up he refused to remember any of it, as if it had never happened! I certainly remember it . . . and now I am pregnant! He accuses me of being impregnated by the devil or someone else! He orders me to have an abortion. I wouldn't do such a thing!"

Julia explained how Epaphroditus had become inebriated from spiked eggnog. She promised to tell Epaphroditus when the time was right.

"It won't do any good. You don't know what he's like. He's cold stone and impenetrable iron, without one iota of human kindness or decency."

"Oh, yes, I understand such traits. My mother-in-law is made of similar New England materials which I encounter many times a day. I'm in a rush now because all the colored people and Irish are washed out of their homes on

Knockmedown Hill and I came to ask if you could take in a few."

"I don't dare ask him for anything just now, Julia. He's in an impossible mood, akin to mental illness. He'd probably say he couldn't trust me with strangers in the house, 'not even with niggers.' You have no idea how cruel he is."

Julia rushed up Pearl Street to her home. Submit was sitting in her chair by the window, her head nodding. Julia touched one of her hands gently.

"Oh, it's you," said Submit sleepily.

"The poor people at the foot of Knockmedown Hill are all washed out of their homes. I'll be wanting to put two Irish families into the music room."

"Oh? Without Let's permission? And *mine?*"

"I'm sure Let will consent. I had hoped for your approval, too. The water's still rising and there's no time to be lost."

"The dirty, unbathed Irish? They and all their bugs? Absolutely not!"

Julia picked up her wet skirts and ran out of the house, then walked briskly to Dr. Stoddard's house. A new office and wing with short-term medical care rooms had recently been added. The body of little Heafy Hartigan lay on the examining table. Father O'Laverty was making the sign of the cross over him in the final rites of extreme unction. Whiddy and his mother stood looking down at Heafy, tears flowing from their eyes. The two Dr. Stoddards and Lydia Kinney stood side by side. Julia dropped to her knees and said a silent prayer. Could any sorrow be greater?

Before leaving, Julia had a quiet conference with Father O'Laverty and Lydia, arranging that Mr. and Mrs. Hartigan, Whiddy and the youngest remaining child, three year-old Rosaleen, should be sheltered at the church and that Julia would undertake to care for five year-old Aileen, six year-old

Gavin and eleven year-old Claragh. Lydia would shelter in her barn Tribulation Cumming, Fallopia and all of her kids.

Julia hurried down the hill to assign everyone and make arrangements for others to go to shelters offered by the O'Neills and Page Sanford. Now a train came puffing down the track from the north and came to a standstill at the drowned crossroads. From one of the three passenger cars several gentlemen in tall hats and rain capes came down the steps and walked to where the homeless group was standing. A young man in the lead approached Julia and said:

"It's Governor Seymour and his party. He's surveying flood damage along the river. He would like to talk with you. Your name?"

"Mrs. Letsome Wooster, wife of the copper mill superintendent."

"Mrs. Wooster, this is Governor Seymour."

"Delighted to meet you, Mrs. Wooster. You seem to be taking charge here."

"I'm just assigning various families to shelters kindly offered, Governor Seymour. It's been a little difficult to find the right places because the families in need happen to be either Irish or African. I'm sure you're aware that a cruel prejudice exists in these parts."

"*I'm* aware of it, that's for sure!" exclaimed the tall handsome man with wavy black hair who stood next to the Governor. He released a hearty laugh that seemed to create a spot of sunlight in the midst of rain.

"This is Mr. Alexander Stewart of New York, Mrs. Wooster," said the Governor. "He was in Hartford doing committee work and asked to accompany me."

Julia sometimes seemed to stand in the midst of rainbows. This was the so-called "lucky Irishman" of New York, the wealthiest merchant and importer in America who had won his way through sheer force of ability and charm, not only in business and philanthropic life but even into the sacred precincts of society as well.

"It's a wonderful pleasure to be meeting you," said Julia. "I, too, am Irish, as you may've guessed. I was Julia Sweeney before I was married. God bless you for all you have already done for our people!" Her blue eyes looked at him and she gave him a broad smile. Stewart reached into his pocket, pulled out a thick wallet and handed her three hundred dollars. "Would that be enough to supply food and clothing for all these people for a week, perhaps? You can write to me for more when needed."

"God bless you and a hundred thousand thank yous!"

Stewart and the Governor talked with a few of the unfortunates while Julia went on about her own work.

Whiddy had come down from the Stoddards to look after his brothers and sisters. Page Sanford had sent his two sons down as emissaries and Awley O'Neill had sent Dennis. Julia looked at Dennis somewhat differently since the hilltop episode but quickly assigned the Brodigans and two other Irish families to him.

Julia then took the two youngest Hartigans, Gavan and Aileen, by the hand. Motioning to Claragh, they all walked up to the Wooster house. Julia opened the door and marched them in. Submit, in her taffeta, was there in the hall in a minute. Julia tried to forestall the rush of words with her own. Gently but firmly she said:

"These are Whiddy's brothers and sisters. Their house is half under water. We'll be sheltering them in our music room until the river subsides."

"Oh no, we're not! Take these Irish brats away!" cried Submit shrilly.

Aileen began to wail. Julia kept calm. "These children have lost not only their home and most of their belongings but also their little brother, Heafy, who drowned. They will stay here, Mrs. Wooster. There will be no debate, please."

Aileen wailed louder and Claragh began to cry quietly. Gavan tried not to give way but his small shoulders shook with the effort.

"The barn is nice and warm," replied Submit. "They'll be quite comfortable."

"The music room is mine," said Julia forcefully. "Let built it for me. The children are staying in my music room!"

"I forbid it! I forbid it!" cried Submit, her voice rising to crow-cawing shrillness.

At this moment, Let, home from the mill, opened the front door. "What's all this loud talking? What is it you forbid, Mother?"

"The Hartigans are flooded out of their house, Let," said Julia, "and little Heafy has drowned. I want to shelter these lovely little Hartigan children—Gavan, Aileen and Claragh—in our music room until the river goes down."

"Of course, dear, a wonderful idea."

"I won't have my house over-run with Irish!" exclaimed Submit, her control lost completely. "It's bad enough as it is!"

To Julia's astonishment, Let pierced his mother with the first indignant look she had ever seen him give her and then declared loudly and very firmly:

"This house is shared by the three of us. Julia and I vote for doing the only conceivable Christian option. No further argument is appropriate. Take the children to the music room, Julia, and make them comfortable. You are very, very welcome, Gavan and Aileen and Claragh. As for me," said Let slowly and emphatically, with an adoring look at Julia that made Submit suddenly feel as if she were all alone on Mount Ararat with the cold waters rising around her, "I'm very fond of the Irish and can't think of any group with whom I'd rather be!"

CHAPTER 11

A RIGID HEART

(July, 1851)

Julia set to work making the Hartigans comfortable. Submit could not be persuaded to sit at table with the Irish children and took to her bed with a sudden illness. Julia was delighted that, at last, Let got a full and revealing glimpse at the angry environment Submit created and what Julia was forced to live with on a daily basis. Let seemed quite stunned by his prior blindness and apologized to her several times.

The funeral of Heafy Hartigan took place at Father O'Laverty's almost-completed Church of St. Augustine. The child's body was the first to be consigned to the bleak little cemetery behind the church. Julia and Let stood with the family during the ceremony. Whiddy, with Let's permission, had brought down from the rock-pasture a boulder shaped somewhat like a memorial stone to mark the grave.

"It's beautiful," said Julia to Whiddy, as they turned away from the ceremony, "the stone, I mean. A simple stone is the most ancient and loveliest of all monuments. It's like the Stone of Fame of the old Irish heroes and this one shines with mica, Whiddy. It will shine forever."

"Ah, Miss Julia, you're trying to comfort me. My little brother's deserving of a better monument than that and I aim to get him one some day. A little lamb, you know, or a small stone angel or such. He was a lamb of God himself, Miss Julia, a lamb of God . . . so in love with animals. He died trying to save his pet rabbit." Whiddy's face contorted with grief. Julia took him by the arm tenderly as they escorted each other back to the carriage.

At the house, things were going smoothly and happily except for Submit's sullen bed-riddenness. The sound of children's laughter was a wonderful thing to hear as they played in the house or garden or orchard. At table they were responsive and amusing, adding a nice light touch to the household.

Claragh had taken a liking to Submit and enjoyed helping Julia take tray-meals up to her. She seemed to have forgotten Submit's first greeting to them. She often lingered in the background as Submit ate her meals. Submit even allowed her to reach up and insert into the thick coils of her ash-blonde braids a flower from the little, old-fashioned "tuzzy-muzzy" bouquet that Julia always placed upon the tray. In spite of preliminary aversions, Submit began to behave nicely towards Claragh. Was even granite capable of melting?

Although the cause of Submit's malady was obvious, Let finally insisted on calling in Dr. Stoddard. In spite of Submit's detailed descriptions of headaches and backaches and leg-aches and foot-aches which made it impossible for her to get out of bed, it did not take the old doctor long to make his diagnosis.

"A peculiar form of . . . do you understand Latin, Miss Julia?"

"Oh yes, Doctor, my father began to teach me Latin when I was eight years-old and I had two fine years of Latin in Dublin."

"Submit is suffering from a case of *cor rigido* and *obturatio hibernatis!*"

Julia gave a wonderful look of comprehension to the doctor and tried hard not to laugh. "How can I help her?"

"She is the one who must help herself. You must get out of bed, Mitty, and engage in all normal activities of this home."

"But I can't, Abiram. I can't move!"

"What a pity! I hear your home is now full of the joy of children. Lucky woman! I became well acquainted with all the Hartigans when poor little Heafy died. Hearts of gold. The Mulligans are staying with us."

"Good heavens! How does Sophia like it?"

"She loves it and, believe it or not, she hasn't retreated into bed! If you continue to stay in bed, you will completely ossify."

"Ossify?"

"Yes. Turn to bone and then stone!"

"It's one of those terrible osteoarthritic things?"

"A very unusual form, not often described in medical textbooks." A look of terror came into Submit's eyes. "I will send up some bitters," said Dr. Stoddard, "but to recover, you must return to your normal activities . . . starting *now!*"

"I truly can't, Abiram. Please believe me."

Dr. Stoddard decided to resort to one of those personalized little medical dramas for which he was locally famous.

"Miss Julia, will you please leave the room for a few minutes?"

He threw off his long-tailed suit jacket and began to take off the belt of his trousers while fixing Submit with a passionate eye. "You know you're a very attractive woman, Mitty. If you can't get out of bed, this gives me a wonderful opportunity to get undressed and get into bed with you. I'm a lucky man."

Submit screeched like an eagle and leaped out of bed, wrapping her arms around herself with a look of horror on her face.

"I think I have just witnessed a medical miracle, Mitty," exclaimed the old doctor with a laugh. He got dressed, picked up his pill-bag and left the room.

Julia was not too busy to canvas the town energetically for contributions of money to repair or rebuild houses of the Irish, build a retaining wall along the river, and purchase land for resettling the blacks on higher ground on the west side of the river. She wrote to Alexander Stewart and Governor Seymour for further contributions and assistance. In the course of her philanthropic journeys, Julia came to a halt one afternoon at the door of Epaphroditus Smith. The minister answered the doorbell. He did not look friendly.

"May I come in? It is you whom I wish to see." With obvious reluctance Epaphroditus ushered her into his study.

"How pretty the house looks with flowers in every room, even in your study!" exclaimed Julia, recognizing the touch of Caresse.

"It's a form of vanity," said the minister. "I do not approve."

"Vanity?" Think you that our Lord does not love the beauties of nature?"

"Flowers and beauty, unless devoted to His actual service, are all vanity."

"Oh," said Julia, feeling the icy repelling air of religion gone astray. "I came, dear Reverend Smith, to talk to you about the fund we are raising for the reconstruction of houses down by the river and for the purchase of the Castle tract across the river for resettlement of the African-Americans."

"Who are 'we'?"

"Well, chiefly Lydia Kinney and myself," replied Julia, deciding not to mention Father O'Laverty. "Selectman Daniel Holbrook and Treasurer Burton Smith are backing us and I have just received a second $300 check from Alexander T. Stewart and a fine letter of encouragement from Governor Seymour."

These prestigious names had a positive effect on Epaphroditus. "What do you want me to do?"

"Well, Dr. Smith, on the next two Sundays would you announce that part of the collection plate moneys would be devoted to our local community?"

"H-m-m-m," muttered the Reverend, tapping a blue pencil on his desk. It might be a good opportunity to make the Governor aware of him and his church.

"I'll bring it to the attention of the Board."

"I'm so glad that you and dear Caresse are going to have a baby."

The Reverend became an instant cockscomb red and abruptly jumped up. "Who told you such a thing? It's monstrous! It's not true!"

It was now or never. "Do you remember, Reverend, the Thanksgiving dinner at our house? As a joke, someone strongly spiked your eggnog with rum.

"When you left, you were quite inebriated and needed help walking. Caresse told me you made fervent love to her that very night, not once but several times."

"That is a complete lie, a fabrication! I did no such thing!"

"Yes you did, as you should have done long ago. As you well know, the Bible mentions marital love more than once. You must not falsely accuse your devoted, completely faithful wife of carrying someone else's child."

Julia thought the minister was going to have a stroke or strike her. He towered over her, speaking in a slow fury: "You must never say this again! I will have God smite you! Never again say that Mrs. Smith is going to have a baby!" He rushed wildly past her and raced out of the house.

A weeping Caresse immediately appeared in the hallway. "I heard it all. How can he claim to be a man of God? Your wording was wonderfully accurate and firm. Thank you, Julia, but you see what I am up against."

"Yes, quite hard to believe if I hadn't seen it with my own eyes."

"I'm beginning to think he is actually insane. Oh, Julia!"

The sound of a piercing sweet horn came from the street. "It's the French vendor—Marcel Boudreaux. We need a little fun. His goods are marvelous."

"I know," said Caresse. "I simply adore the lovely French things he sells but, of course, Epaphroditus makes a fuss over spending anything on frills."

"I always manage to buy something although Submit never fails to accuse me of base extravagance and lewd frivolity."

Julia beckoned to Marcel to bring his wares. Though burdened with two immense valises from his cart, he moved happily up the tarred gravel. His navy blue beret was pushed jauntily back over waves of his curly black hair.

"Set down your wares in the front parlor, Marcel," said Caresse. "We're in a good mood to be buyers today but we can't promise to buy very much."

"Bon! Bon. What luck for Marcel to find you two lovely young ladies to whom to show items straight from Paris. You will feel, Mesdames, as if you were walking down the Champs Elysées on a midsummer day."

The young merchant opened up one of his large bags. There were white satin slippers and bronze leather boots and kid gloves, white and black. There were lace-edged handkerchiefs, French perfumes in gold bottles and rose waters and colognes in little wicker bottles. There were silk, velvet and taffeta ribbons, plain and moirée, in all colors of the rainbow. There were yard-long samples of exquisite materials including muslins, poplins, eglantines and silks.

"Oh, how beautiful!" exclaimed Caresse in French, in which she was fluent because her French family spoke it at home. "How it makes me want to visit Paris and dress à la Parisienne! You're a dangerous young man, Marcel."

"I should like," answered Marcel in English but with a French gleam in his eye, "to be dangerous to you, Madame!"

Caresse's eyes touched his for an instant with a surprised look. No one had ever said to her the romantic, witty words her Gallic heart longed to hear. She had married a man with a frozen heart, brain, tongue and pelvis.

"What would you like, Caresse?" asked Julia. "I will give it to you."

"I'd like it all!" answered Caresse with a merry laugh. It was good for her to emerge, thought Julia, from all of her Epaphroditus-enforced suppressions. "Let me see. It must be something small that I can stow away out of sight."

"Why out of sight, Madame?" asked Marcel. "Are these wares not worthy of the lamp of light?"

"Of course, Marcel, but my husband searches my bureau. To him these things are worthless trivialities, baubles of sin, kickshaws of the devil."

"Do I look like the devil?" teased Marcel with a grin.

"Only slightly, Marcel, and it adds to your charm! I'd love this little bottle of perfume but, if I put on a single drop, my husband will call me Jezebel!"

"*Mon Dieu!* A pretty Frenchwoman like you having to live like a Cagot!"

"Why not this narrow little lace-trim?" suggested Julia. "You could use it on a dress for the baby."

"Ah, is Madame going to have a baby? *Bon! Bon!* My felicitations! Let me give Madame as a gift, then, five yards of this lace-trim."

"Oh no, no Marcel . . ."

"Yes, gladly. I insist."

"Thank you, Marcel, but please, I beg of you, tell no one about the baby."

"As you wish, Madame."

"And, please, Marcel, as my gift," said Julia, "this lovely handkerchief which Madame Smith can tuck away behind a book in the library. For me these two velvet roses for my hair, the white one and the rose one, and this embroidered linen collar which I will give to my mother-in-law as a peace offering."

"My husband may be returning home at any moment," said Caresse. "He's in a particularly bad mood today and I'm beginning to get anxious."

"We wouldn't want him to see my Wagon of Sin in front of his house," said Marcel but was not fast enough in packing up and leaving.

Epaphroditus strode into the house saying in a loud voice, "I thought you knew I didn't countenance these frumples and fandangos." Turning to Marcel, he said: "Out of my house, you piddling peddler, you Paris guttersnipe! Don't ever come within a mile of it ever again or I'll smash you and your wagon to bits!"

"Excuse me, Reverend Smith," said Julia, "but it was I, not your wife, who invited Mr. Boudreaux into the house and it is I who have done the buying. You will, I am sure, give me time to pay for, and collect, my purchases?"

Epaphroditus had been about to order Julia out of the house but he remembered in time that her husband was one of the nine Trustees of the Church, that it was Mr. Wooster who had given the first thousand dollars towards the new church building, and that it was he who had donated the pipe organ.

With a wink and a smile, Marcel gave to Julia her purchases and those of Caresse. He closed his bags, bowed to the ladies and left. Epaphroditus was pacing up and down the small reception parlor like an angry mastodon.

"Be of good cheer!" Julia whispered to Caresse as she left. "Life is full of beauty for those who can overcome life's inevitable barriers." As she walked down the porch stairs she could hear Epaphroditus shouting at his young wife, "Now I know who got you pregnant!"

CHAPTER 12

RED-HAIRED NEWCOMER

(August, 1851)

One of the loveliest of all earth scents, the aroma of rain-wet grass, wafted into the Wooster house on a lovely now-sunny day in August, 1851. The distant noise of the Naugatuck River could be heard cascading over its rocky bed. It was a good day for a child to be born.

Julia lay back against the deep-hemmed pillow, relaxing in the quiet troughs between the crests of pain. Let had already rushed down the street for Dr. Stoddard and had also left a message for Mary Sweeney to come up to the house soon. Let had developed a further affectionate admiration for his mother-in-law during the past week. She stayed only a few hours each day and then returned to the Inn. How those two did laugh together! She accepted only one meal invitation, to Sunday dinner. Submit repeatedly objected that this was a typical Paddy invasion into their home—is nothing sacred?

Let was becoming more aware of Submit's negative influence but seemed utterly unable to do anything about it, a son's steadfast loyalty in the raptorian grip of his mother. Horace, from time to time, offered to take Submit off his hands but she squashed the idea immediately, as if unwilling to give up the pleasure of her daily venomous attacks on the

Irish colleen in her midst. A black widow spider, after all, gets accustomed to its Epicurean delights.

Mary brought joy and comfort to Julia. When Mary had come to dinner, Submit sat like a statue at the other end of the table. When Let called Mary Sweeney "Mother Mary" and remarked that it should be spelled "Merry," Submit's face twitched and her head went back like that of a horse with its halter pulled.

Submit put in an appearance as soon as Let told her that Julia was in labor but Julia said, "All is fine. No need for you now." Submit glided away to reread obstetrical paragraphs in *The Popular Cyclopedia of Modern Domestic Medicine*.

Soon increasingly strong pains occurred at regular intervals. Let sat quietly by the bed, holding Julia's hand, with Mary next to him. Submit looked in and a storm crossed her face. So Julia could endure Let and Mary but not her! She lifted her chin proudly as Julia said gently, "Oh, do come in, Mrs. Wooster."

"No, no thank you. I'll go see that Eliza is keeping the water kettles hot on the stove. Someone has to do the work around here."

"Ouch!" said Mary, winking at Julia. "That was meant to hurt but somehow it doesn't hurt at all, at all. I just feel pity for her."

In a few minutes Dr. Stoddard arrived. "It's getting time now for us to make ready for the delivery. Submit, you take charge downstairs and see that warm cloths and bowls of hot water are regularly fetched up." Little did Submit realize that the boiling of water and keeping cloths warm was a time-honored medical strategy designed primarily to keep interfering relatives out of the way. "You can really help best that way, Mitty," said the doctor, using the nickname for her middle name of Mehitobel.

Julia let out a long moan. Submit commented, "The Lord said to Eve, 'In sorrow shalt thou bring forth children'."

The red blazed in Mary's cheeks as she said, "The Lord of the Hebrews said that to a cruel world. The Lord Jesus Christ said, 'Verily I say unto you . . . that your sorrow shall be turned into joy.' The spirit of our Lord Jesus Christ should be in all our hearts in this room of birth, not sorrow but joy and love!"

Submit opened her mouth to speak, then shut it. "I think, Mitty, if you and Let will wait nearby we'll have some news for you presently."

"Did you ever hear the likes of it, Let? That immigrant woman reeling off her Papist sermon to me. I know ten times the medicine that woman knows."

"Mary isn't Catholic, Mother, and what she said wasn't Catholic."

Ten minutes later a daughter was born and named Alice, a name belonging to neither family. Submit was deeply offended but thanked God they didn't choose a Celtic name like Sinead, Siobhan or "Druida". She was particularly upset when she heard Let say, "She looks like you, Julia darling. Her hair must be from County Cork—it's red! I couldn't be more pleased!"

Julia smiled happily, hoping that Alice's heart would be as warm as an Irish peat fire and not as cold as an Ice Age New England glacier.

Julia's own mother said it for her when the two were alone together with the baby: "I'm thinking she'll be a dear treasure to you, Julia. I feared, how I feared, she might be a living replica of Granny Submit but she's not! She shows the touch of a magical Gaelic wand. How Let could have come from the icicle loins of that woman I shall never understand. By

St. Patrick, she must have her good points but I don't think I have enough years left to go dredging for 'em!"

They both laughed and continued to laugh frequently until Mary said her goodbyes and went back to Waterbury a proud and happy grandmother one week later.

CHAPTER 13

A CHANCE ENCOUNTER

(September, 1851)

Julia couldn't get it out of her mind that Whiddy wanted a real tombstone for Heafy's grave. She remembered that at the end of the Dunlap garden the family had buried the children's pet animals, marking the graves of several dogs and two pet lambs with semblances in stone. Could she induce Mrs. Dunlap to part with one of the stone lambs? She decided to walk up over the hill.

It was a lovely early fall day and she took joy from the mica-glinting boulders, the daisies and ferns. She stopped at the summit and appreciated the view. The breeze blew her blue-black hair. Julia climbed the board fence and crossed the pond meadow past the six cows. She sat on the stone wall marking the boundary between the Dunlap and Wooster properties. The Dunlap pasture sloped down to the barn some two hundred feet lower.

Lazarus Jones was behind the barn washing the carriage with a sponge and bucket of water. Annie Dunlap was standing close beside him, talking to him animatingly, now and then touching his shoulder. It was a surprisingly intimate gesture. Suddenly Lazarus wiped his wet hands on his trousers and seized Annie in his arms. Her arms went around him with equal zeal. Julia was amazed and was about to jump back into the meadow when, over Lazarus's shoulder, Annie spotted her. She waved to Julia and happily beckoned.

"Well, Julia," she said. "You caught us!"

"I didn't mean to intrude but do you two know what you're doing?"

"Yes, we do," said Annie. "We love each other."

"Have you thought it all out? A fling is one thing but . . ."

"We do love each other," said Lazarus, "and it's a good love. Is there no place for us to go, no sympathetic place for us just to be happy and left alone?"

"Yes, but you must choose carefully. Are you intending to marry?"

"Yes, of course," answered Lazarus.

"Your family would disown you, Annie. You know that."

"Yes, I know."

"Why not go away alone to New York, Lazarus, and give your relationship time either to cool off or prove itself?"

"It gets stronger all the time, Miss Julia. It wouldn't cool off."

"How about Cuba? You could easily pass for a Spaniard, Lazarus. Or somewhere in the West Indies, perhaps."

"Wonderful ideas, Miss Julia. I would enjoy being a Spaniard!"

"You won't tell anyone about us will you?" said Annie.

"Of course not. I want the best for you both. Now, Annie, let me change the subject. I came here to ask your mother if she would consider letting me have one of the little stone lambs at the end of the garden. I want to give it to Whiddy Hartigan for his brother's grave. How would you feel about that?"

"Fine with me. They don't matter anymore. You can tell that to Mother."

"Thank you, Annie. Now don't do anything impetuous! Plan carefully!"

Julia walked to the front of the Dunlap house. She pulled the bell-rope and a starchy German maid responded. "Yes, Mrs. Dunlap is at home." Julia was led into the reception room. It was done in pale rose and white striped satin with rosewood furniture and a French Moquette rug, clearly arranged by New York decorators influenced by Paris.

In a few moments Mrs. Dunlap, in chestnut taffeta, rustled in. Her large blue eyes were glassed with the studied look of indifference. There was exquisite lace and a strand of pearls at her smooth throat. Julia was not impressed. She felt only sadness for the proud, overdone swan who always tried too hard.

"How do you do, Mrs. Wooster," she said, extending her cool fingertips.

Julia responded, "I do very happily, thank you, Mrs. Dunlap, and you?"

Momentarily startled out of her confident equanimity, Mrs. Dunlap gave Julia a sharp look and replied, "I do not take the simple greeting, 'how do you do?' as a presumptuous inquiry into the details of someone's personal life."

Julia suppressed a laugh. Her father had taught her the original meanings of greetings and farewells, so she, advised by her elf, answered:

"Too bad that so many lovely old phrases seem to have lost their original warm friendly meanings. 'How do you do?' or 'how is it with you?' is not presumptuous surely. 'Good-bye,' how lovely when it was 'God be with you,' and 'farewell' when it was 'fare thee well.' In Gaelic, a hostess welcoming a visitor into her home says, 'A hundred thousand welcomes!'"

Evaluating Mrs. Dunlap's icy stare, Julia quickly shifted tack. "This is a charming room. I am sure there is no other so lovely in all the Naugatuck Valley."

Mrs. Dunlap's eyes unfroze a trifle. "Yes," she said. "I had it designed after the latest Paris fashion by Pothier of New York."

"I became very fond of this décor while staying in the Dublin home of my uncle, Dr. John Canty. He has a beautiful home in St. Stephens Park and his reception room is an almost exact copy of yours."

Mrs. Dunlap paled and a bright red, round area appeared in the center of each cheek as if someone had slapped her twice. "In *Ireland?*" she said.

"Yes, Dublin is a magnificent city and for centuries there has been much commerce between Dublin and Paris."

Julia quickly shifted the subject again because, with Mrs. Dunlap, everything seemed to lead to adversarial interchange. Julia was no longer willing to be perpetually trampled in their conversations. She would be calm and courteous but, when necessary, stand her ground. "I came down the hill through your beautiful garden a few minutes ago. How lovely it is with all the flowers."

"Yes, I think Lazarus did very well with the marigold path."

"Lazarus?"

"Yes. Hans, our gardener, left us for a job in Bridgeport. Lazarus loves flowers and he's now doing double duty as coachman and gardener."

"Lazarus seems a very fine man," Julia ventured.

"That's a strange description of a negro servant."

"May not a negro be a fine man?"

"Hardly." She always seemed so defensive to protect her vaunted space in the world. Poor woman, thought Julia. You're about to have him for a son-in-law!

"As I came through the garden, I noticed the little stone lambs and dogs near the barn. Would you be willing to give one of the little statues away?"

"What are you trying to say, Julia?"

"Whiddy Hartigan's youngest brother, Heafy, had to be buried with only a granite boulder to mark his grave because the family is so poor. Would you be willing to give one of those little stone lambs to the Hartigans?"

"Well, I never! Steal from the grave of a lamb to mark an Irish boy's grave!"

"Are the Irish less than animals, then, Mrs. Dunlap?"

Mrs. Dunlap sputtered incoherently, like frying pan grease spilt on a hot iron griddle. Julia continued. "I spoke with Annie a few minutes ago and she said that the statues don't mean anything to her any more."

"Where did this conversation with Annie take place?" asked Mrs. Dunlap.

"Out near the garden."

"That's odd. She told me an hour ago she was going to walk over the hill to choir practice. Did you see Lazarus?"

Julia decided not to answer the question. "Would you consider giving the little stone lamb as a gift from her to the little dead boy? Annie wants to do it."

"Don't be ridiculous! I'm sure my daughter does not wish to have any dealings with such people, alive or dead, who are so far beneath her."

Oh, what a lovely incongruity, thought Julia. If Mrs. Dunlap only knew of the situation-in-the-making! She will, she will . . . and soon!

Shaken with laughter about to erupt, she made for the door. Then she turned around. "There is kindness within you, Mrs. Dunlap, so if you change you mind, let me know. In the meantime, if ever you must face an unexpected crisis of sorrow, I will always be available to help in any way I can."

After Julia had left, her words reverberated very strangely in Mrs. Dunlap's mind. It had been whispered that this Irish girl had an uncanny intuition about impending events, too often to be by sheer chance. What did she mean by "an unexpected crisis of sorrow"? What did she mean?

CHAPTER 14

RIPPLING POND

(September, 1851)

The next morning the Dunlaps' German maid came to the Woosters' back door and asked Eliza Hull to tell Mrs. Julia Wooster that Mrs. Dunlap wanted to see her at once and to please keep it confidential. Julia smiled and hurried over the hill to the Dunlap house. Elvira, red of eye, was waiting in the front parlor.

"What do you know of this?" She placed a note in Julia's hand.

> Dear Father and Mother,
>
> I am planning to marry Lazarus Jones. We have left town to seek a place with less racial prejudice. We will not be locatable.
>
> I am very happy except in the thought of your unhappiness.
>
> Lazarus gives me constant love and approval. You always seemed ashamed of me and gave all of your love to Gunn, the dashing handsome son. Julia and Lydia know what I plan to do.

The day will come when no one needs to be ashamed to marry someone with a little greater sunburn. I shall always be your loving daughter.

Goodbye,
Annie

Mrs. Dunlap had been watching Julia closely. "You knew about this?"

"I became aware of it only yesterday when I happened to meet Annie and Lazarus on my way here to talk with you."

"Why didn't you tell me? Don't you think a father and mother have every right to know of such a dreadful thing happening to their only daughter? It might have been stopped! Oh-h-h . . ." She gave way to a prolonged wail.

"They swore me to secrecy. I keep my pledges. I don't think what they have done is dreadful, Mrs. Dunlap. Difficult, yes, very difficult."

"You approve of this disgusting, degrading alliance? You *would*, of course," she added, with venom in her eyes.

"Would Jesus have disapproved? It was Simon of Cyrene, a man of dark skin, who helped Jesus carry his crucifixion cross. If Jesus were here, I believe he would lay a hand upon your shoulder and say, 'Give them your blessing.'"

Mrs. Dunlap poured a new torrent of tears into her lace handkerchief. "Oh no! I can never give them my blessing and Mr. Dunlap will disown her. We will never be able to hold up our heads if what has happened becomes known. I want you never to speak of it to anyone. This terrible thing must be kept quiet!"

"Isn't it more important for your daughter to be happy?"

"You will not help me? I can ruin you more than your Paddy-ness has already ruined you! And Gideon can ruin your husband!"

"Are you threatening me, Mrs. Dunlap? You forget that I have the real weapon in my hand, namely the truth. I am not a vengeful person but no one is given the privilege of threatening either me or my husband. Please understand this fully. At this time I choose to keep Annie's secret, not for you but for her, until she decides to reveal it to everyone. Neither she nor Lazerus is ashamed of their relationship. They are both happy with their love. Lazarus is proud to be part-African. He is half-white and is proud of that, too. And Paddies are proud as kings to be Paddies. Many of their ancestors, like mine, were Kings and most of them have kingly souls."

Julia, smiling to herself over all the accumulated ironies, rose to leave. Mrs. Dunlap remained seated and silent. Julia let herself out. She decided to go home by way of the hill. With all of its beauty, the hill had become for her now almost an Irish hill, its scintillating spirit lifting her own. It was indeed a *Mullach na Sidhe*, an Enchanted Hill, of which there were so many in Ireland.

Behind the Dunlap's barn, the carriage stood where it had been receiving its bath. The pail of water and sponge were there, as if Lazerus and Annie had immediately decided to leave after their conversation with her. Julia had a strong feeling they would surprise those in Seymour who will be disgusted at their inter-racial marriage. They had love, energy and determination. They would succeed.

The early morning sun was warm. She found herself walking rapidly. Then an inexplicable panic swept over her, like a dove suddenly aware that a falcon is diving on her. She trusted her senses and knew something vital was wrong nearby. She climbed over the wall and scanned the whole circle of the meadow. There was no sign of disturbance anywhere. The cows were grazing peacefully. There were no visible people or wild animals.

Her eyes traveled to the pond, over which unnatural ripples were moving to and fro. She stared at it, seeing or feeling an indigo shadow, a gleam of liquid over flesh-color. She raced the short distance and saw a body face down in the water. She plunged in and half ran, half swam to the body. She clutched at clothes and arms, pulled, hauled and, with great effort, brought the heavy bundle to the bank and set it down among the cress and arrow-root. It was Caresse Smith, clothed only in a nightgown.

With a sobbing cry, Julia turned her over, head to one side, forcibly opened her mouth and began to press upon her back strongly and rhythmically, as she had once seen some men do to a drowned boy in Waterbury. Initially some water spurted out, then only air moving in and out with her rhythmical pressurings. She concentrated totally on her task except that she also prayed in rhythm—to God, to the Mighty Essence and to the Spirit of the Hill. "Oh, let her beauty flow back into the stream of life . . . flow back . . ."

There was no sign of returning life. She then saw Whiddy striding across the pasture towards the cows. "Oh, Whiddy, Whiddy!" she called loudly. "Please go get Dr. Tom as fast as you can. Mrs. Smith fell into the pond. I'm trying to revive her but she's not breathing on her own yet. Run! Run!" Whiddy ran swiftly across the meadow and down the hill.

Julia did not feel panic. With dramatic urgency she continued to work coolly and methodically, concentrating on rhythmically compressing the rib cage, using her body weight to add pressure. Shortly there was a small choking sound and she could feel spontaneous breathing beginning.

She stopped her pressing. Several strong coughs occurred and she could feel the rib cage expanding well.

Soon Dr. Tom and Whiddy arrived, running. Dr. Tom examined Caresse quickly and nodded approvingly at Julia. He turned Caresse over on her back. She opened her eyes and began to clutch at her belly, her face grimacing in pain.

"I'm afraid she's going to have a miscarriage," said Dr. Tom.

"Oh! Could my pushing on her back have done it?"

"No, no Miss Julia. You saved her life, there's no doubt about that. I suspect she was a minute or so from death. It's the lack of oxygen, everything. We've got to get her down to my office."

Whiddy put her over his shoulders and carried her down the hill to the Stoddard annex. Old Dr. Stoddard examined her and said to Julia, "I think her husband should be sent for. Will you go fetch him, Miss Julia?"

"I think we should wait until Caresse expresses the wish to see him."

Out of the mists of her pain, Caresse cried out, "Don't get him! I couldn't stand his un-Godly fierce admonitions!"

After a half hour, Dr. Tom came to Julia in the waiting room. "She wants to tell us something. Will you come please, Miss Julia?"

"She lost her baby?"

"Yes."

Julia leaned over the surgical cot and said, "I'm so very sorry, Caresse."

"It's better this way, Julia. There was so much anger . . . so much hate . . . so much Old Testament vilification. I must tell the three of you, who are my friends . . . exactly why I tried to kill myself."

She took a deep breath. "Epaphroditus never wanted a child. I thought perhaps when the child came, he might learn to love it but he was bound and determined that the child *should not* be born. At about four this morning he wakened me. It was still dark and he said, 'Caresse, I have a terrible pain in my stomach. Go down and brew me a cup of hot tea, will you? Hurry, please hurry!"

I rushed down the stairs and was saved from the fate he had planned for me by a God-sent ray of moonlight coming through the hall window. He had piled heaps of books on the stairs for me to tumble over, whether to cause a miscarriage or kill me I don't know. I avoided the books and walked out into the night. I wandered the hills despairing, praying. How could I return to a house with such malignant hate in it? How could I bring a child into such a vile home? I must have fallen asleep next to the pond. When I awoke, I felt very peaceful. The pond looked so inviting as if the solution lay within it. I walked into it and fell face down in the water. May God forgive me for killing my baby."

An expression of indignation crept over Dr. Tom's face. *"You* didn't kill the baby. Epaphroditus did and he almost succeeded in killing you, too. This is attempted murder and he should be brought before a court of law."

"Oh no! I couldn't openly accuse him but I never want to see him again!"

"We will protect you, Caresse," said old Dr. Stoddard. "Have no doubt about that. You're going to stay here until you decide on a long-term solution."

The doorbell rang. Young Dr. Tom went to answer it. In a moment he was back with a strange expression on his face. "You're wanted at the parsonage, Father. Mrs. Humphreys just found Reverend Smith lying at the foot of the stairs.

They say he must have been carrying a load of books because there are books scattered all around him. They're pretty certain he's dead, apparently of a broken neck, but they want you to confirm it."

CHAPTER 15

Au Revoir, Seymour

(October, 1851)

On medical grounds, Dr. Stoddard forbade Caresse Smith from attending the funeral of her husband. Julia sat in the church with Let and Submit, listening to the pastor of New Haven's First Methodist Church dispense eulogies about "this dear devoted husband," "this Godly minister of our most holy Gospel," etc. Julia felt like walking to the front and detailing the truth of his ungodliness.

After a few days, Caresse needed to go to the parsonage to pack up her belongings for her return to New York City to live with her parents and sisters. Now she could turn from all the evil and try to infuse her life with new meaning.

Julia picked up Caresse at the Stoddards'. As they entered the parsonage, they met Perrins, the church janitor, who remarked, "Mrs. Humphreys, as Head of the Women's Committee, came yesterday to fix up the house. Everything is in good order, Mrs. Smith."

"There was something unholy about Mrs. Humphreys' devotion to my husband and his to her," said Caresse to Julia. "I'm not sure what went on between them but I never liked it. They met under the sanctified guise of church committees. Perhaps they should have married, uniting their multiple aberrations. She probably snooped over all of Epaphroditus's things and mine yesterday."

"She will now cling even more desperately to poor Helena," said Julia. "She's nearly succeeded in making her a permanent invalid."

"Yes, I know. Can anything be done to rescue the poor girl?"

"My brother, Kevin, likes her very much. Helena, Lydia and I have gone shopping several times in New Haven, overcoming strong opposition from her mother. Kevin has met us and taken Helena on walks across the green or carriage drives. The two seem to be falling in love. What do you think Almira Humphreys will think of that—her darling daughter possibly marrying an *Irishman?!*"

"Well, Julia, your Irishness and my Frenchness aren't very welcome here in Seymour, are they? Have you ever wondered why I married Epaphroditus?"

"Yes, many times but I didn't want to ask."

"My father believed in arranged marriages to avoid 'youthful mistakes.' He met Epaphroditus in New York and liked his seeming honorable virtues. I was only seventeen but I consented because I respected my father. Epaphroditus lied through his teeth to me about having children and never told me that he didn't believe in marital relations. My mother seemed pleased that I hadn't run off with some fool but I married the biggest and most cruel fool on the planet! I think I'll marry a Frenchman next time."

"Or a Paddy?"

"Great idea!" The girls were in the middle of a good laugh when the doorbell rang. It was Almira Humphreys. "Well," said she, "I didn't expect to hear laughter in this house of death." Her eyes were red and sleepless.

"I suppose I should thank you for putting my house in order."

"It was a great privilege to come into this house made holy by a great and good man. Oh, how we shall miss him," she sobbed. The doorbell rang again and Caresse welcomed Lydia Kinney. "Dear Lydia," sobbed her kinswoman, Almira. "We have lost a true man of God, a saint."

Lydia responded, "I'm sure that dear Caresse will go on bravely."

"I am sure that Caresse will soon have many men friends." Almira had a special gift, like Submit, of creating conversation-stoppers. After a tense silence, she added, "I see that I will not be needed here today," and she left.

"Now, Caresse," said Lydia, "what may we do to help you?"

"Help me get some boxes from the cellar and start packing my things." The three young women busied themselves for several hours. The afternoon was almost over when they heard the musical horn of the French vendor. Julia ran down the stairs. "Come in, Marcel!" How wonderful to see you!" Then, in a lower voice, she added, "The minister is dead, you know."

"Ah, yes, I know. Miss Sally told me. And the little one?"

"Caresse has had a miscarriage, Marcel."

"May I, dear Madame," said Marcel turning to Caresse, "offer my sympathy and my consolation?"

"Thank you, Marcel. You have a good heart."

"And merry merchandise!" said Julia. "What have you brought today?

"Ah, such gloves and fans, so fashionably French!" He took out two fans and began to manipulate them with wristy flourishes.

"I'll take a fan!" cried Caresse.

"*Bon! Très bien!* Which one, Madame? This charming one with cherubs?"

"No, this one with ladies and handsome gallants in the garden. I am going back to New York to live. The French colony there is very lively socially."

"Madame, I am delighted to hear that you are moving to New York. I am opening a little shop at 21 Park Avenue to be called *Biloux de Paris*. No more wagon-wandering for Marcel. I am to be a merchant, *vraiment*. Madame, a notion strikes me. Would you consider working with me? You are lovely, you articulate well and your fluency in French will make you irresistible to my customers!"

"What a fascinating idea, Marcel! I accept at once your kind offer."

"Glorious! I can imagine no one who would lend a more gracious French charisma to my shop!" He reached for her hand, bent forward and kissed it. "We will meet in New York on September first and open *Biloux de Paris* the next day!"

"This calls for a celebration," exclaimed Caresse. "'Juices of the devil,' as Epaphroditus called all wines and liquors, were never permitted in this house. However, he kept his ciders long enough for considerable fermentation to take place in the cellar. I believe I can find a bottle of such devilry for our celebration."

While she was gone, Marcel effervesced like champagne. "Oh, what a lucky man is Marcel!" he said, jumping in the air and clicking his heels like a ballet star. "My fortune is made this day! My little shop will soon be the rendezvous of all fashionable people of New York! What incredible good luck!"

Caresse returned and said, "I have discovered several bottles of old cider which smell intriguing." The four sat around the table sipping fermented cider and amiably chatting. Caresse forgot for a little while the darkness of ponds, the loss of her baby, and her dismal marriage with an insane husband.

"I must be going," said Marcel. "Such a happy time you've given me, Madame Smith, and such a wonderful promise of help in my new adventure." In the hall Marcel clasped Caresse's hand with *"À bientôt, Madame!"* As he slapped the reins on his horse's back, he began to sing the new Gautier-Gounod song:

> *Dites la jeune belle,*
> *Où voulez vous aller?*
> *La voile ouvre son aile,*
> *La brise va souffler . . .*
> *Dites la jeune belle,*
> *Où voulez vous aller?*

As Julia and Lydia went down the walk a moment later, they could hear Caresse softly singing: *"La voile ouvre son aile, La brise va souffler . . ."*

The will of Reverend Smith was read the following week in the private office of Attorney Luzon Morris. Soon the news spread that he had not even mentioned his wife in the will, had left all extra moneys to the church and all personal possessions to his most helpful parishioner, Mrs. Almira Humphreys.

The parish was amazed. A will always mentioned a legitimate beneficiary. Had she been a faithless wife? Probably, being French. To the four who knew, the non-mention was in itself incriminating. The Reverend must have compiled this handwritten will the day before he had piled books on the stairs.

Caresse refused to sue. "I want none of his money or possessions. I am beginning life again completely afresh. Our relationship was not a marriage."

A few days later, Dr. Tom, Lydia and Julia saw Caresse off on the two o'clock train. It made talk for many days in Seymour that the widow was not wearing a touch of black anywhere. She was flaunting a pink flowered dress, a pink bonnet and, worst of all, a happy smile.

Julia let Lydia drive off with Dr. Tom who was still pursuing her from the matrimonial standpoint despite her lack of encouragement. She was still completely loyal to her husband, Llewellyn, now missing for five years.

Julia walked home, reveling in the fall colors. When she entered the house, she was greeted by Submit with a stern look: "The baby has been crying."

"Well," replied Julia laughing, "we'll soon have the darling happy! We Irish don't remain sad for long."

CHAPTER 16

DEATH REINED IN

(April, 1852)

Alice had grown into a full rose of a baby with bright red cheeks like Irish babies after their daily "walk" in a baby carriage in the brisk climate of Ireland, seen so often by Julia during her two years there. Alice's deep orange hair was striking, inherited from Julia's father, William. Her bright blue eyes twinkled with charm and she tended to laugh rather than smile at the slightest prompting, reminding Julia of her own mother, Mary Canty Sweeney.

After nursing the baby, Julia lifted her up, took a blanket from the cradle and a white woolen cap from the bureau and carried her downstairs. Submit was mending one of Let's shirts which she flourished in front of Julia, waving it like a banner: "Let is hard on his clothes. I'm glad I'm here to attend to them."

"So am I," answered Julia with the sweetest of smiles. "I'm going up on the hill now, taking Alice with me. It's time she began to know the loveliness of hills."

"It's no place for a child. Bugs and beetles, thorns and thistles, and . . ."

"And robins and rabbits, fawns and fairies!" said Julia happily with Alice in her arms and an elf on her shoulder as she danced sprightly out of the room. There was a cool late afternoon breeze and little gray-white clouds scudded across the sky. The red of new-born leaves was beginning to show on the maples and there was a fresh scent of new life permeating the air.

Julia's spirit always mounted with the rising slope. She moved towards the high plateau under the tall oak and maple trees where Let had built the pavilion for her and little Alice. She walked past the pavilion and up the slope to introduce Alice to the magical fern she had planted in the granite boulder. A new sprout was just unfolding through the meager soil.

Julia returned to the pavilion. She seated herself on the top step so she could drink in the lovely scene. She then spread the blanket on the floor and put Alice gently on it and folded the blanket over her. In spite of the several serious dramas the hill had backdropped in the brief two years she had come to know it, there was always a spirit of sustaining beauty to lessen the impact of all human-induced shadows.

She began to think of the hills she had loved best in Ireland. Cashel of the Kings with its quaint white cluster of castles, round towers and Celtic crosses; Cave Hill high above Belfast, reverberant with the sword-clashing legends of Finn and Ossian; glorious Knocnares Mountain, tall above Sligo Bay, with Queen Maeve's immense tomb-cairn of boulders on the summit. She recalled the far-spreading view of the Blue Stack Mountains, Mac Sweeney's Bay and old Mac Sweeney castles which make a ring around Donegal, and high Ben Gulban where Finn Mac Cool caught up with the escaping lovers, Diarmuid and Grainne. She began to hear the galloping hoofbeats of Finn as he raced up the hill . . .

Julia quickly lifted her head and saw a horse and rider rapidly approaching. Sally Swayne and her bay horse came racing wildly over the meadow, took the rail fence in a high leap and landed hard. Catching sight of Julia, Sally slowed the horse, rode towards her and dismounted at the pavilion.

"Oh Sally, what a high flyer you are! I was so relieved to see you sail over the fence safely! Isn't that rather dangerous. Your horse is all in a lather."

Sally looped the reins of her horse "Lobster" around a maple tree branch and sat down beside Julia. There were deep shadows under her green eyes. "Oh, Julia, Julia, I'm in such deep trouble! Can I trust you with a secret?"

"I know what the secret is, Sally dear."

"But *nobody* could know. It's true, then, that you were born with the caul? You sense people's thoughts and future happenings?"

Julia decided not to share at this time the vivid wherefores of this particular knowing. She remained silent.

"What shall I do, Julia? What shall I do? You guessed, then, why I rode so hard? Why I've been riding so hard every day?"

"To ride your baby to death."

"Oh, don't put it that way! It's not yet a baby," and she began sobbing.

"But it already has the shape and soul of a baby, Sally. What prevents you and Dennis from getting married?"

"Heavens above! You even know that Dennis is, is . . . the one? Does anyone else suspect?"

"I doubt it."

"I'm wild about Dennis but for a husband, I'm not so sure . . . he being poor and Irish. It would absolutely kill my family."

"Does Dennis love you, Sally?"

"He does but he sees the difficulties. He'd like to start a career and make some money before marriage. It's really been fun just to go on making love and letting all problems go hang. I haven't yet told him about the baby."

"Don't you think you should?"

"I was hoping to lose it . . . Now, I'm not so sure. Let me hold your baby."

Julia placed Alice in Sally's arms. A gentle expression flowed into the pregnant girl's face. "I think you should tell Dennis and your family, Sally. The shape is beginning to show. You can't keep the secret much longer."

"Speaking of secrets, I saw Kevin and Helena walking together as I came over the stone wall a few minutes ago. Does Almira know about that?"

"No, heavens no! So please keep that secret as I shall keep yours, Sally! Almira will fight tooth and nail to prevent her darling daughter from marrying *anybody* and especially, oh most especially, an Irishman!"

"Dennis and Kevin have it all over the Dunlap, Goodyear, Beecher and Johnson boys of Seymour, as well as the Bacons, Whitneys, Goodriches, Days and Daggetts of New Haven and the high mucky-mucks of New York and Saratoga. I've had my taste of a few of them. It's the Irish who have the charm, wit, dash and love-making. Ah, the love-making! To hell with those who criticize the Irish! Rub their faces in the dust of scron, say I. Here's your darling half-Irish baby back again, Julia. I'd like one just like her . . . including that lovely red hair!"

"If you stop your hectic riding, Sally, your wish may well come true!"

"It must have been God's will that I found you on the hill today." Sally gave her a warm hug, untied Lobster's reins and walked over the summit.

A young buck leaped past Julia and bounded gracefully over the fence. She walked home with a light step, carrying baby Alice over her shoulder. As she entered the house, Submit asked what in the world she and the poor child had been doing up there all the chilly afternoon.

"Communing with the hills and getting at one with Nature—feeling its spirit and letting the hill's magic work its wonders."

CHAPTER 17

A Farmer's Wisdom

(Spring, 1852)

Julia and Let realized that it was no use discussing any news events when Submit was present. Let and his mother never saw eye to eye on important issues whether local, national or international. Current events were so closely related to the incendiary issues of foreign immigration that Submit inevitably responded with negative comments and insinuations.

Let was slow to realize how often these represented actual attacks upon Julia. He seemed to be in a state of constant denial regarding his mother. He gradually became more concerned by her inability to temper anti-Irish rhetoric but never found the courage to take an important stand. He had been brainwashed by his mother for too long a time and from too early an age.

In April, 1852, William Sweeney wrote one of his "lecturing letters" to his daughter. He had few other opportunities to give a hint of his broad knowledge and understanding of local and national issues.

Dearest Julia,

Please forgive my spouting off a bit today about immigrants. The Puritan has never tolerated the immigration of any other segment of humanity with a truly Christian grace. Yankee behavior in the presence of dispossessed Pequots, refugee Acadians, escapees from the French Revolution, and Irish refugees from the recent Irish potato famine have been openly hostile—hardly compatible with their lofty wording in the Declaration of Independence.

The feeling has been particularly strong against the Irish because of their Catholicism and their supposed 'domination by a foreign power,' namely the Pope. Their frequent lack of education has forced the Irish immigrants to take the lowest paid jobs and their resultant poverty often leads them to create shanty towns. Competition for jobs exacerbates the problem and often leads to cruelty towards everyone alien, all who do not 'belong'.

Of course it is our personal bad luck that the amazing fertility of the seven septs of Clan Mac Sweeney has cast upon America's shores so many of our tribe that the saying 'Tell it to Sweeney' has become a popular taunt.

As for myself, I get along well at the Waterbury Brass Works. I have congenial assistants in my laboratory and my scientific services are appreciated.

Our whole-hearted love is with you. Our kindest regards to your very good husband and many a warm embrace for Alice.

Ever devotedly,
Your affectionate father

Julia learned from Let that he was fourteen when his father, Albert, died at the age of thirty-six of typhoid fever. His older brother, Horace, was seventeen, Henry was twelve and Emma was ten. No funds were available for the two older brothers to go to college so at sixteen Let went to trade school, concentrating in metallurgy, as had Horace. Let got a job at Waterbury Brass Mill at the age of seventeen and was floor manager less than two years later through brightness, talent, engaging personality and energetic hard work. With their own money, he and Horace were able to send Emma and Henry to college.

Let became a voracious reader and his eager mind seized on new ideas. Julia rejoiced that he shared all his thoughts with her. Allusion to any new ideas always turned Submit wrath-scarlet. It was remarkable that Let could welcome new concepts growing up in such an intellectually restrictive environment.

Let did have a wise grandfather, Levi Wooster, who took in Submit and her four children after her early widowhood. Levi was a kindly, compassionate, wide-horizoned man despite his own lack of advanced education and his occupation as full-time farmer. He had lived all his adult days in a rather small, two-story house on a low hill in Prospect, five miles southeast of Waterbury, tilling the land and thinking deeply as he grew his crops from the rocky earth.

Julia finally knew why Submit never mentioned to her various society members that her father-in-law was a farmer and her late husband a shoemaker. Hardly occupations which "armigerous gentry" would proselytize.

Many a wise old saying that Levi had addressed to his grandson had taken root in Let's heart. Some were older cultural wisdoms, some Levi's own:

"Don't snurl up your nose at anybody and never let anybody snurl their nose at you. You're God's son, too."

"I'd a sight rather have you be a good, savory small potato than a large overgrown pumpkin."

"Draw it mild and don't put on scallops. On the other hand, don't eat humble pie or truckle to anybody. If you have made an error, stand up and acknowledge it with a firm voice."

"Hoe your own row and don't be beholden to anybody for anything."

"Fine words butter no parsnips. It's what you do that counts, boy, what you do."

"Never judge a man till you can turn his soul inside out—and only God can do that."

"Don't throw taunts at Old Indian Crazy Sam. His skin and his heart hurt just like yours and his craziness makes sense to God."

"Odd fish and ninny hammers all have their place, even a jackass who swims across a river to find a drink of water. Don't make fun of them. Get your good wholesome fun otherwheres."

"Love is a capsheaf of every harvest," and he practiced it.

Levi managed to get along with Submit in the same house until Let became floor manager at the mill and was able to rent an apartment in Waterbury for him and his mother.

Captain Levi, a former revolutionary fighter, had once taken his grandson down to Derby Landing to see the brigs sail in after long voyages from the West Indies. This was the first time that seven year-old Let had laid eyes on a black man. The Jamaica blacks working on board as ordinary seamen were helping unload casks of sugar, rum and molasses from the islands.

'Why, Grandfather, are those people black?" the boy asked.

"Why does your skin get brown in the summer? Sun, my boy, sun. It says in the Bible: 'I am black but comely . . . I am black because the sun hath looked upon me.' Ebony, my boy, is as beautiful as ivory. Never notice how people differ from one another but how they resemble one another. We're all God's children."

Captain Levi had once said a thing about hills that Julia would have loved him for: "We live on a little hill, Let, but it's as close to God as Tabor and Hermon. All hills are holy. This small hill of Prospect and all the beautiful things it looks at, the far-spread fields and orchards and sea, are part of your blood and bone. You should grow up to be a tall-souled and wide-hearted man, my boy."

So he had, thought Julia, fulfilling every aspiration of his grandfather. He was worthy of all that had gone before, of Reverend Robert Lenthal, the first schoolteacher at Newport; of Edward Wooster who had so courageously gone into the Housatonic wilderness and cleared away the timber, wolves and catamounts to found a settlement; of all the simple ancestral soldiers, farmers, magistrates, merchants, weavers and innkeepers of the family who had helped create New Haven, Milford, Farmington, Hartford, Seymour and Waterbury.

Old Levi had taught Let to be particularly proud of his great-grandfather, Levi's father, Sergeant Walter Wooster who, with his men, had destroyed twelve ships and taken ninety prisoners at Sag Harbor in 1777 and who had himself been the first soldier to enter the enemy fort at Horse Neck, Long Island, to tear down the British flag.

It wasn't Let who was constantly talking of his forebears. It was Submit who, conveniently forgetting her own ancestors who were farmers, shoemakers, drapers and tailors, was forever drumming away about her "first family" Chatfields and the "aristocratic" Gunns, Alsops, Hotchkisses, and Pardees.

One day when Submit had boasted of her ancestor, General Disbrow, who had married Jane Cromwell, Julia had spoken up:

"If you had seen, as I have, all the beautiful castles in Ireland which were battered into ruin by Cromwell, and all the graveyards filled with the men, women and children he massacred, you might not be so happy about General Disbrow. He permitted his men in Drogheda not only to slaughter the garrison after they surrendered but to spike babies on their lances and hold them up and laugh."

Submit was set back on her solid heels for a moment but quickly recovered. "I've always been proud of him for doing his duty to England."

Julia said softly but firmly, "Cromwell called the Irish 'wretched primitives' and recommended that they be exterminated."

"A dutiful Englishman is among the world's best breeds."

Julia felt she had to respond. "A good breed may only be judged by our Lord. I am as proud, Mrs. Wooster, of my ancestors as you are of yours. Some of mine walked the green hills of Ireland centuries ago with the gold of kings upon their heads. Far back in history, the armored Mac Sweeneys were known for never giving one inch before the enemy. As Anthony St. Leger reported to Henry VIII, Mac Sweeneys 'died exactly where they stood on the field of battle.' It's a proud and gallant race and I love being Irish."

Submit looked over her spectacles at Julia. How odd that the Irish could really be *proud* of their race. "Well, Julia, to each his own," she said.

"Oh, dear Mrs. Wooster, let's never again make any negative comparisons. Our dear little Alice has all of these ancestors joining hands in a circle in her tiny body and soul. Why can't she and her lovely personality be the gentle reconciler of us all?"

"She's getting to be quite pretty," responded Submit.

CHAPTER 18

A WANDERER RETURNS

(April, 1852)

On a sunny spring afternoon in April, Julia had raised the shades in the living room to the top when her mother-in-law walked in and refused to allow it. Why Yankees were opposed to fresh air and lovely views was not clear to Julia. Submit always declined to explain. New Englanders never raised the shades above the median line, this representing the definitive demarcation between refinement and cultural depravity. Those in the proper class just knew such things; those who grew up in hovels didn't need to know.

Julia was making a Gros Point crochet lace cape for the baby. Submit could not help admiring Julia's skill in crocheting although she had been vocally critical of her in most other domestic skills. It was a talent with which Submit could not compete, having had to concentrate on creating their basic clothing needs such as knitted jackets, blankets and stockings for herself and Let. During her premature widowhood, she had lived through lean years with her four children and no inheritance. She was at work today on a little knitted vest for Alice.

"Your cape is getting on very well," Submit said with an unusual hint of commendation. "Alice will look well in it. Where did you learn the pattern?"

"It has an interesting history," replied Julia. "It's the old Gros Point floral lace pattern of Venice, brought two hundred years ago into Cork by Italian nuns. Our Cork ladies added the three-leaved shamrock to the six-petaled rose, resulting in this charming rose-and-shamrock design. My grandmother created a variety of floral designs which she taught to my mother and she taught me."

"You do it very well," said Submit and even developed a small smile.

There was a thud against the front door as Freddy Butler delivered *The New Haven Courier*. Julia laid aside her needle work and went to get it. Alice lay asleep in her well-padded wooden cradle by the hearth and Julia paused to look down at her as she passed by. A beautiful child with hair as orange as Queen Maeve's, and cheeks like the apples of Avalon.

Julia gave the paper to Submit according to their customary afternoon ritual. She now read aloud the headings and main sentences of chief articles:

"Anti-Slavery Meeting in Boston. Wendell Phillips speaks. Mazzini writes on the duties of democracy. Schooner *Chateau de Paris* arrives at Dock 27 with shipments of goods for Altman's and the popular new *Bijoux de Paris*, the chic boutique successfully operated by Monsieur and Madame Boudreaux."

"Oh!" exclaimed Julia. "Do you know whose shop that is? It's the French goods peddler who used to come through Seymour. You know his wife."

"I know his wife? What are you talking about?"

"She was known to you as Mrs. Epaphroditus Smith."

Submit gasped. "Don't tell me the wife of a Methodist minister demeaned herself by marrying a mere peddler and in so short a time interval?"

"Monsieur Boudreaux is a very fine and charming man, Mrs. Wooster, and is now a successful New York merchant. He will make Caresse far happier than did Reverend Smith who was almost insane and a very cruel husband."

Quite suddenly, an overwhelming yearning to go up to the hilltop took possession of Julia so she said, "I have a very strong desire to walk up the hill for a few minutes to catch the sunset. Would you watch the baby for me?"

"Of course, Julia. I am getting to enjoy being with her."

Without waiting to put on a scarf or shawl, she went out through the side door and found herself walking rapidly towards the pavilion. She seated herself on the steps and inhaled the beauty, highlighted by a golden sunset. She scanned the scene and noted a shadow of motion to her left. A man was climbing over the fence from the pool meadow. He started walking in the direction of the pavilion. His dark blue clothes were rumpled, he carried a small cloth-roll under his arm and he wore a blue rimmed cap. His hair was tousled chestnut with a long rough beard and sideburns. His eyes were far-gazing. He was passing right by when Julia spoke. "Good evening!"

"Oh, good evening! I didn't see you." He stopped directly in front of her.

"Where am I, will you tell me, please?"

"Where are you? You are crossing Deer's Delight Hill in Seymour."

"Seymour?" His brow furrowed.

Julia wondered, was this some madman escaped from the asylum in Hartford? He did not look insane, only vague. His voice was gentle and sad. "Won't you sit down on the steps and perhaps we can figure things out."

Then Julia remembered that the town's name was new. "It used to be called Humphreysville after General David Humphreys."

The young man put both hands up to the side of his head and closed his eyes. "It sounds familiar . . ." He laid his head upon his knees and mumbled "Humphreysville" over and over again, ending with a sigh.

She touched him gently. "Would it help to tell me your troubles?"

He looked at her, his gray eyes teary. "I will . . . if I can. You see, it's all confused in here." He touched the red-brown mop of his hair. "There's something that hurts in here. My story isn't clear to me. A long time ago I went away from where I was. I think there was a battle and a bullet struck my head . . . Oh, who am I? Tell me who I am. Do you recognize me? Do you know me?"

He grabbed her wrists and looked at Julia with an imploring gaze. There was no threat or terror in his voice, only a tone genuinely asking for help.

As if the hill had spoken to her, Julia suddenly said: "Lydia! Lydia! You are her husband! You are Llewellyn Kinney!"

The man dropped her wrists. The vague wild look faded. His eyes moved back and forth as if searching his brain for answers. After a few moments he said, "Yes . . . I think I am Llewellyn Kinney." Then, after another long pause, he said, "Yes, it makes sense. Where then, is my wife, Lydia? Is she still alive? How long have I been gone? Did she wait for me? Does she love me still?"

"Wait, Llewellyn, wait. Go slowly, go gently. Try not to get too excited. You shall see her in a few minutes. She still lives at your home at the foot of this hill. She loves you, I know that for a fact. You have been gone for almost five years. She has waited for you, certain that you would eventually come home. Do you feel well enough to see her now, this evening? I am Mrs. Let Wooster."

"Well, good for Let, breaking away from that Mother of his! Is Dr. Stoddard still across the meadow from our house? He can help me."

"Yes, old Dr. Stoddard is still here and I'm sure he'll help get you to the right doctor, perhaps in New Haven or New York. Take my arm, Llewellyn, and let's walk slowly down the hill, but first look at the sunset which is rejoicing with you in gorgeous gold and orange. Isn't it beautiful?"

She slipped her arm through his and together they walked along Pearl Street to his and Lydia's house. With a few yards to go, Julia let go of his arm and said, "This is your home. Lydia is waiting for you."

He began to run. Julia watched as Llewellyn knocked loudly on the door. Then she heard a loud scream from Lydia as they embraced eagerly in the open doorway and remained that way for many spellbinding moments.

As Julia watched, her vision became obscured by tears as she deeply savored this miraculous return. She walked slowly home, shaking her head in wonderment as she felt joyous elves dancing up and down on her shoulders. The sunset changed to deep pink and brilliant scarlet and she was sure the surrounding hills were rejoicing also.

CHAPTER 19

COMMENCEMENT

(June, 1852)

Julia's brother, Kevin, was graduating from Yale Law School on the tenth of June, 1852. Let and Julia were going by carriage into New Haven for the event, accompanied by Helena Humphreys who had received permission from her mother to go shopping in New Haven. Kevin's family would be coming down from Waterbury by train. Julia decided the time had come to admit her husband into the secret of Helena's and Kevin's developing love. Let was delighted but, like Julia, he had significant concerns about maternal complications.

The three drove into New Haven in the handsome new carriage that Let had bought along with a pair of bays. There was increasing demand for Let's metal products from his factory, of which he was now one-fourth owner and General Manager although he was only twenty-two. Rising sales were stimulated first by the Mexican War, with its need for brass and copper casings for guns, then by growth of railroad lines in New England and finally, increasing popularity of some of Let's metallurgical inventions such as his new German silver alloy for silverware, now popular in Europe as well as the United States.

Let was becoming increasingly affluent. Such matters were important to the Yankees of Naugatuck Valley. With a touch of Celtic amusement Julia became aware of a slightly increased level of acceptance by the self-appointed social elite of Seymour. The vulcanized rubber Goodyears, the paper mill Days, the Mayflower Johnsons, the sugar mill Dunlaps, the Widow Humphreys and the Chatfield Swaynes occasionally smiled at Julia when they remembered. Sometimes they even emanated rays of grace towards her under which her Irishness *almost* seemed to be forgiven and forgotten. The upper crust ladies might say, "She's pleasant but she's not really one of us, but her husband is," with Let's "Wooster Pedigree" going back to the mid-1600s in Connecticut.

Julia and Let looked very handsome as they drove to New Haven, Let in a dove-gray suit, tall gray top hat, gray gloves and canary vest. Julia wore a blue silk gown with a rose-wreathed straw bonnet, rose gloves and rose parasol. To look like the shopper she had told her mother she was going to be, Helena was wearing a black taffeta gown and black bonnet with small pink flowers.

They drove to the New Haven train station to meet Julia's parents and younger sister, Maggie. The carriage was left at Kelham's Livery Stable while the six walked across the Green to the graduation benches behind the Law School.

This was not the first time that Helena had met Kevin's family. As the friendship had developed into romance, Kevin had induced his family twice to come down to New Haven from Waterbury. They approved warmly of Helena.

Two happy surprises were in store for Kevin. During the ceremonies he was presented with the second highest scholastic award, the Kent prize. He also received written invitations to join two fine New Haven law firms. One was an all-Irish group, Kelly, Monahan and O'Brien. The other was a corporation of young New Englanders with sufficient vision to see that a bright young Irishman would bring to Daggett, Farnham and Whitney more business than he would alienate.

After the ceremony Julia, Maggie and Kevin's mother, Mary, kissed Kevin's cheeks. Julia was amused that the "best families" of Seymour were quite unable to stop the onrushing Irish, God bless 'em! *Erin go Bragh!* Let was very proud of his smart, good-looking, bound-to-succeed brother-in-law.

"I think Kevin's honors call for a celebration!" said Let. "Why don't we all walk over to Tontine House for some refreshment, liquid and solid, my treat!"

"Great idea, Let," said Kevin. The seven broke up into twos and a three and crossed the old New Haven Green. As they approached Chapel Street they noticed a crowd gathered around a loudly shouting street orator. Such outdoor haranguing had increased greatly with all the debates over slavery, the Fugitive Slave Law, temperance and the acrimony over increasing foreign immigration.

An anti-Catholic ex-priest, Gavazzi, had come to the United States and soon began to gather large crowds. Also denouncing Popery as well as slavery was Hector Orr, the odd character known as "Angel Gabriel" because he blew a long brass trumpet to lure crowds. Street orators were causing riots in New York and Catholic church-burnings in Brooklyn and Newark.

Kevin's group had to pass the crowd on the corner of Chapel and Church Streets to reach the Tontine. It was obviously the long-haired Angel Gabriel giving the harangue, flourishing his long brass horn as he spoke. His words rang out distinctly: " . . . the ignorant rabble, the off-scouring of Europe, coming down upon us like the Gothic hordes of old, the depraved and illiterate Irish . . ."

"Wait a minute!" Kevin urged his family. "This requires rebuttal."

"No, Kevin, no," said his father. "Lawyers must choose the proper occasion to make their mark. This isn't the time or place."

Angel shouted, "Do you want your religion toppled by a Papal Conspiracy, your politics dominated by ignorant Irish fit only for booze and brawls?"

"Get your facts straight!" Kevin called out. "What about President Andy Jackson, all Irish, and Presidents Madison, Monroe and Polk, part Irish?"

"Shut up, you damned Croppie!" cried someone from the crowd.

"I demand to be heard! Rebuttal is a justified part of every debate."

En route to Angel's soapbox Kevin was stopped by the crowd. A townie picked up a bottle lying on the street and threw it, bouncing it off Kevin's right temple. Blood began to roll down his cheek. Fisticuffs began between local Irish and non-Irish listeners. The police arrived as Kevin's family walked him towards the Tontine. Helena applied pressure to Kevin's laceration and wiped blood from his face and neck with her lace handkerchief. It looked worse than it was.

Kevin sat down in a chair in the hotel parlor and tried to regain his composure. "You all made me fly the pit! I wanted to nail a few lying radicals."

"Enough is enough," said his father. "It's no use prodding rattlesnakes."

"I know the medicine you need," said Let, finding a quiet corner table and ordering a scotch for Kevin and William and sherry cobblers for the rest.

Helena pressed Kevin's arm. "I love you so much, Kevin," she whispered close to his ear, "and I'm so proud of your law school accomplishments."

"God bless you, Helena. I can feel my laceration healing already! In the past you've only hinted at loving me. I didn't know I'd have to shed blood to make you say it. So you do love me, then?"

"With all my heart," replied Helena.

"Then," he whispered, "I have a wonderful idea." He sipped his scotch.

"I'm listening," said Helena.

"Drink your sherry cobbler first and then I'll tell you."

"This is my first alcohol ever, so I must sip slowly, but I feel wonderfully free with you next to me and mother far away. Must I finish it all right now before I hear your new idea?"

"We both must both finish our drinks to the last drop!" They sipped silently for three minutes.

"I'm beginning to feel the sherry so I must be ready!"

"Do you love me?" asked Kevin.

"Very much."

"Can you visualize marrying me?"

"Some day that would be very nice . . . I think . . . if I'm asked."

"Well, then. I've graduated and I have a job. The family is all here. Let's walk over to The Center Congressional Church and ask Dr. Leonard Bacon to marry us right now! I need a full-time nurse to help heal my wounded head!"

Helena smiled. "That's so exciting, Kevin, but what about mother!"

"She'll make a terrible fuss whenever you marry and whomever you marry! It's time to cut the cord. This is our life. Ours and our children's. Marry me now!"

"Oh, Kevin!" She kissed him full on the mouth.

Heads were already turned in his direction when he said, "Listen, everyone! Helena and I invite you to our wedding!"

"Oh, wonderful! When?" asked Julia.

"Right now if Dr. Bacon will marry us. One more round of drinks, on me! We can have a big lunch afterwards. I might even go Dutch treat with Let!"

It devolved upon Letsome and Julia to break the news to Almira. They drove their carriage back to Seymour after the simple wedding, stopping in front of her house. Almira quickly opened the door.

"Where have you been? Where is Helena?"

"Let us come in, Mrs. Humphreys, and I will explain everything," said Let.

"She's not hurt, is she?"

"Oh, no indeed. It's good news we have, not bad."

Mrs. Humphreys marched ahead of them in her black muslin and opened the door into the reception room. The shades and curtains were drawn. She lighted the naphthalene lamp, motioned them to maroon plush chairs and sat down on the maroon sofa, her back rigid. She glared expectantly.

Let decided to make the scalpel-cut swift and definitive: "Mrs. Humphreys, Helena went this afternoon to the parish house of Dr. Leonard Bacon in New Haven and was married to new Attorney Kevin Sweeney."

"No! You can't mean it!" screamed Almira shrilly. "You allowed this terrible, this wicked, this disgraceful thing to happen? I shall annul it, of course."

"Helena is of age so it can't be annulled by you," replied Let. "It's a very fine marriage. Kevin just graduated from Yale Law School, received the Kent Prize with the second highest grade average in his class and has had an offer to join the distinguished New Haven law firm of Daggett, Farnham and Whitney."

This stopped Mrs. Humphrey for a few seconds. She found it hard to understand how an Irishman could have succeeded at Yale Law School. "No! It can't be! It *must* not be! My darling girl married to a low-down Irishman!"

"Mrs. Humphreys, I must request an apology. You are speaking of Julia's brother."

Almira immediately went into her well-honed hysterical routine, moaning, screaming, clutching her chest and finally writhing off the sofa onto the floor.

"Let," said Julia softly, "You go get Dr. Stoddard." She fetched an afghan from the foot of the sofa and laid it over Almira. "Dear Mrs. Humphreys, I know this is a great shock to you but I am quite sure that Helena and Kevin are going to be very happy. Surely what you and we want is Helena's happiness."

"It will kill her! Marriage will kill her! And to that man! That will kill me! . . . Oh . . . Oh, my heart, my heart," and she grabbed her chest again.

Julia ignored the remarks and stroked Almira's forehead. As soon as Let and Dr. Stoddard arrived, Almira began the drama all over again.

Dr. Stoddard stood over the figure on the floor and said, "Get up, Almira!"

"I can't, I can't, Abiram. Oh, my heart!"

Dr. Stoddard resorted again to one of his unconventional measures for which he was famous throughout Naugatuck Valley. He briskly removed the afghan, took hold of Almira's high-button shoes and tilted her legs vertically so that her skirts fell back in a swirl of white eyelet-embroidered petticoats, revealing linen pantellettes from top to bottom. "Mercy!" shrieked Almira.

The doctor let her feet fall to the floor with a loud thud. Immediately Almira bounded up, rubberball-fast. As she dropped back on the sofa, he took his place beside her so that she could not stretch out piteously. He felt her pulse and declared: "Perfect! Now, Almira, I have some remedies to prescribe." He reached into his pocket, brought out a prescription pad and small pencil and gave them to her. Please copy these prescriptions as I dictate them, Almira."

"Prescription one. Before you go to bed tonight, mix three scruples of sulfur with three of milk of magnanimity and drink slowly while you swallow your pride. Then sit at your desk and write a gracious letter to your daughter's new in-laws, the William Sweeneys of Waterbury, telling them how glad you are to welcome their fine son into your family. You will then write an affectionate letter to Kevin and Helena as soon as you know their address."

Almira began to splutter. Dr. Stoddard put up a silencing hand.

"Prescription two. First thing in the morning, take one tablet of antipathy dissolved in three drops of mercy and two drams of ginger and treacle and then walk, not drive, to the office of the *Seymour Record* on Main Street. Hand to Mr. Sharpe for publication an item reading somewhat as follows:

"Mrs. Almira Aurelia Humphreys is happy to announce the marriage of her daughter, Helena, at the parish house of Center Church, New Haven, Dr. Leonard Bacon officiating, on July eighteenth, to Attorney Kevin Sweeney, who won the Kent Prize at Yale Law School graduation ceremonies and has been invited to join the prestigious New Haven Law Firm of Daggett, Farnham and Whitney. He is the son of industrial chemist William Sweeney and his wife, Mary, of Waterbury and the brother of Mrs. Letsome Wooster of Seymour. A large reception is planned for the young couple upon their return from their wedding journey."

Mrs. Humphreys waved her arms in protest in the old doctor's face but Dr. Stoddard fixed her with his indomitable gaze.

"Prescription three to go into effect in two days. If you are still suffering from bile, gall or flux, mix one scruple each of nux vomica, quinine, cascarilla, Epson salts and strychnine with one glass of ass's milk and drink it slowly."

Julia brought her handkerchief to her face to suppress a loud laugh.

"You will, day after tomorrow," continued Stoddard, "get busy on plans for the reception. You will make it the biggest and best which Seymour has ever seen. Music, superlative food and abundant spirits. The whole caboodle.

"You will buy new clothes with cheerful colors, making you as handsome as you were in your twenties, it's not too late for you to attract a handsome widower."

"Prescription four. When all these prescriptions have been accomplished, mix oil of roses, honey and sauterne and drink as many glasses as possible. With no responsibilities except to yourself, you must start living it up!"

Almira said, "You old fool," but Stoddard went on:

"These remedies, Almira, will give you health of body and mind and engender a new esprit. If you decry your daughter's husband at this or any other time, you may lose Helena forever. If you follow my prescriptions carefully, you will be a very happy woman surrounded by friends and a fine new family." Dr. Stoddard placed a comforting hand on her shoulder. "In addition, to relax at night, I'll send up some bottles of port from my cupboard. Take a glass every night before going to bed. Would you like anyone to stay with you?"

Almira Aurelia began to feel the challenge of the new situation. Her pride, her character, her reputation were on trial. She straightened up.

"Abiram, I appreciate this advice which came from the heart of a lifetime friend, not just a doctor. I'll be too busy taking all those bitter pills you've prescribed to need any company but perhaps you could send over a bottle or two of that port wine right away."

CHAPTER 20

LOVE EXPLORED

(June, 1852)

The next day Julia fed Alice, burped her and put her to bed. She then walked to Sally's house and invited her on a walk up the hill. After sitting down on chairs in the pavilion, Julia told Sally how she had been trapped into listening to her and Dennis making love. Julia said she was surprised at the duration of the love-making, especially the preliminaries, and didn't understand all the activities.

"You stayed behind the fence and listened to *everything?*"

"I didn't mean to, Sally, but I didn't think I could escape without being seen so I thought it better to hide and not interrupt such a happy tryst. I do admit that the excitement helped ensnare me."

Julia explained that she and Let were extremely close and had a happy romantic life but they never discussed sex and seemed at a standstill, stuck in an unchanging marital routine. "The only advice I ever got," said Julia, "was from my mother who said 'Be natural, relax and enjoy it,' which isn't very helpful."

"No it isn't. As I've found out, sometimes to my temporary astonishment, there's a lot more to it than that!"

Julia told Sally she felt potentially very passionate but never seemed able "to get there". She wanted to learn more, with details and specifics. If Sally would explain techniques, tricks and subtleties, she would be very grateful.

"I have no problem with describing everything to you, Julia. I wish someone had informed me before I was hurled, at a young age, into the cauldron of love without any foreknowledge. I matured by the age of twelve, felt strong sexual urges by fourteen and started having sex at fifteen. I was incredibly clumsy and so were my boyfriends. We didn't have a clue how to make love, just the final stage which was much too quick and unsatisfactory."

"How did you avoid getting pregnant?"

"I demanded premature withdrawal which caused all kinds of problems. One summer I sneaked off and sought older men, most of them married, and asked them to teach me. I was fairly attractive and they readily agreed. I told them they could have sex with me only if they taught me everything they knew, including how to please them. That was a busy summer experiencing love's intricacies with half a dozen men but I learned a fantastic amount and have put it to good use. Why not? It's gotten better and better and is a vital part of life!"

"Give me an example of what you learned."

"A whole new world opened up. I discovered I had immense sexual potential which I didn't even know existed."

"Like what?"

"Like multiple orgasms. Wow! Sometimes beyond belief!"

"I've never even heard of that! I'm lucky to have one. I'm getting excited just talking about it! Please share everything with me, Sally. I can then work on it with Let. We're the perfect couple to experiment and improve because we love and admire each other so much and we try to share everything."

"First of all, Julia, you and Let have to agree that anything, and I do mean anything, is all right during sexual intimacy as long as you both desire it. The only way to get better is to experiment and be free and open about it all."

For two hours Sally held forth on a variety of techniques and tactics. Julia asked a myriad of detailed questions. She found herself increasingly fascinated and aroused by this new world. It all seemed so natural, a lovely physical and emotional connection which so rarely reached full potential even in marriage.

"People, even loving couples," explained Sally, "are so often shy or overly self-conscious, or have been taught that it is dirty or a duty to be tolerated, not enjoyed, or are just too embarrassed to discuss sex with their husband. So they never improve. It's absurd! I know a number of married women who have never experienced the joy of orgasm during long decades of marriage. Hard to believe."

Julia finally found no more questions to ask. She enthusiastically thanked Sally and promised to tell no one about their conversation except Let.

"You mean you're not going to share these details with your mother-in-law?" asked Sally. They both laughed.

At Julia's suggestion, they then sat in silence for twenty minutes looking at the view, watching insects cavort and frolic, listening to the diversity of bird calls and songs, and inhaling the many lovely fragrances of the adjacent meadow and nearby trees. As they stood up to leave, Julia thanked Sally again for opening her eyes to so many new and wondrous facets of life.

Sally responded, "Julia, you are so delightfully different from most people here. I wish we had met earlier in life. Now you have taught me the silent joy of communing with nature, letting all its beauty seep pervasively into one's soul. I will no longer take such beauty for granted. This is truly an enchanted place."

The following evening, Julia told Let about her discussion with Sally. She asked for some alone time with him to explore the situation further. She insisted, however that they choose a place where they couldn't possibly be interrupted.

"Sometimes you amaze me, Julia, but I am always proud of you. You are an incredible wife and I love you more all the time. I do think that's a good topic to discuss but I think I need a few days to build up my courage!"

Three days later, they asked Submit if she would take care of the baby while they went out for a carriage ride and picnic. She was about to object when Let said that every couple needed alone-time. It was a beautiful summer day. Eliza had prepared a lunch of chicken sandwiches, potato salad, hard-boiled eggs, sweet pickles, applesauce and cider.

Whiddy arranged the carriage for them, including picnic blankets. They headed south along the Naugatuck River for about three miles. At a bend in the river, they found a nice grassy area under a large oak tree seventy-five yards off the road. The river cascaded gently over smooth granite rocks, making a soft gurgling sound. Julia suggested that they get in the mood for their discussion by relaxing and eating first. They spread a red and white checkered blanket on the grass and got out the sandwiches, pickles and potato salad.

While eating, they watched a belted kingfisher sitting quietly on a branch overhanging the river and diving intermittently, getting a small fish on three out of four dives. It had lovely dark blue coloring, a shaggy crest, white neck band, bluish band around its upper chest and smaller russet band below, one of the few species which featured more beautiful color patterns in the female. Julia loved watching birds and was teaching Let how much fun the hobby is.

Julia then asked, "Am I a good physical partner for you, Let?"

"Of course you are! I love being with you."

"I love being with you, Let, but we aren't nearly reaching our potential. We both can improve greatly, especially me. I want us both to be completely open and honest with each other in this important arena of life."

Julia went on to describe her whole conversation with Sally. Let got more into it as time went on, asking many questions, often quite detailed, which Julia encouraged. Sometimes one or the other would blush or choke up a little and sometimes there were brief silences.

After an hour and a half, Julia said, "I seem to have run out of information. Is there anything else we should talk about? Do you have any other questions?"

"I think that pretty much covers it, Darling. I'm so glad you decided to pursue this! I wonder how many married couples have such discussions?"

"Very few," replied Julia. They ate their applesauce silently while watching insects flying and hovering over the river bank. A great blue heron joined them on the other side of the river, staying still for a minute or two, then wading slowly upstream for a few feet, then stopping and waiting. Suddenly the heron darted his head downwards and came up with a very surprised, struggling frog.

"I need to talk with you about something else, Let. I've held back for more than a year but now is the time to bring it up. I hope I won't offend you."

"We promised to be free and open in our discussion, Julia. Go ahead."

"I'm sure you have noticed, Let, that from time to time I become quite inhibited when we make love, at times almost 'frozen in place,' attenuating my part of the interaction and urging you with my touch to complete things."

"Yes, I've noticed that. I tried many times to figure out what had happened but never found a common denominator."

"I hesitate to tell you, Let, but after you and I go into our bedroom, Submit frequently opens her door and listens to us. If she hears early sounds of love-making, she often walks slowly over to our bedroom door and listens to us."

"I don't believe it! Are you sure?"

"I have very good ears and the hall floor gives out subtle creaks in different tones. I have tested it out myself and know exactly where each creak comes from. There is absolutely no doubt about it."

"My God. I wish you had shared this with me earlier.'

"There are many things about your mother you may not realize, Let dear. Without being disrespectful to either one of you, I don't think you will truly believe what Submit does until you see it with your own eyes."

"It sounds as if you have a strategy. Please go on. This is a problem which must be solved, and soon!"

"All right. Tonight we will leave the door slightly ajar. I want you to stand by the door where you can see out into the hallway through the narrow crack. Then you and I are going to make noises as if we were beginning to make love."

"What next?" asked Let.

"You wait until she walks down the hall and stops by our door. I don't want you to open the door and catch her red-handed. I want you to move back out of sight and I will taper my little noises."

"You don't think I should confront her?"

"No. Then she will be angry with me and accuse me of trapping her. To preserve my tenuous harmony with her, I must leave this important issue to the two of you. You can discuss it with her sometime when I am out of the house."

"With your tactical brain, you should be an Army General! Please continue!"

"We are more affluent these days, isn't that right?"

"Yes, definitely."

"I think it's time to remodel our house. We both want more children. I think we should get an architect and turn the entire upstairs into our space. Change Submit's large upstairs bedroom into three bedrooms and move outward the entire west wall of the house facing the river so all three rooms will be of comfortable size. Since we have never had live-in servants, the two bedrooms downstairs can be changed into a lovely bedroom for Submit with big windows overlooking the Naugatuck. We can also enlarge the music room."

"Excellent ideas!"

"The entire upstairs will be just for our family. That will make me very happy, Let, and I'm sure it will once and for all release the inhibitions which have blocked my responsiveness. Oh, Let, I can't wait!"

"I can't either, Darling. What a wonderful picnic! Perhaps next time we can find an even more secluded spot!"

"Oh, you!" she said and pushed him backwards on the blanket, then kissing him hard. She slid off of him and said, "We haven't seen a human in more than two hours. Why don't you bring a little extra joy to an excited and exciting Irish colleen? I'm not bashful in front of a kingfisher and a heron!"

"If we're going to make uninhibited love in front of two birds," said Let, taking off his shirt, "I want to know whether those birds are male or female."

"Female!" she said and they burst out laughing.

CHAPTER 21

HATE UNBRIDLED

(July 3, 1852)

Almira Aurelia Humphreys, after some anxiety-laden days of wrestling with her mind's indwellers, began to make progress planning the fulfillment of Dr. Stoddard's wise prescriptions. A visit from Helena and Kevin just before they took off on their honeymoon, in which Helena's joy and Kevin's wit and charm were very disarming, finally convinced Almira to go ahead with all plans.

The wedding announcement was sent to all regional newspapers. The reception to meet Mr. and Mrs. Kevin Sweeney was set for Saturday, July third, the day on which Independence Day was being celebrated. Almira's friends began flocking to make a social call before the party to see how she was adjusting to Helena's sudden marriage to a bog trotter.

Almira was quick to observe, unhidden among all the flourishes of courtesy and swishings of taffeta, the little contumelious upcurl of eyebrow and downcurve of lip of her gentry friends. The greatest comfort came from an unexpected quarter, from Elvira Gunn Dunlap, whose once towering pride had been brought to the depths by Annie's unspeakable decision to marry a negro.

Almira had fully expected that Amy Swayne would give her the hardest time. On the contrary, Amy repeated several times that Almira was fortunate to have a Yale graduate for a son-in-law, if Irishman it had to be, especially one who was a Protestant and who had a promising career in the offing.

Almira could not help wondering why Amy, of the unimpeachable Goodwins, was so complimentary and pleasant. She did not know that Amy was going through her own particular kind of hell, for she had just found out about Sally's condition. She had been helping Sally into a tight corset and Sally had cried out, "Not so tight!" and had dropped to the floor in a dead faint. Amy had called Dr. Stoddard who quickly diagnosed the pregnancy. Sally confided the whole story to him. Amy could not tell her husband but had been unable to carry the burden of the terrible secret alone and had confided it to her son, George.

Saturday the third of July opened auspiciously, a clear warm day. A holiday spirit was in the air. Members of the Order of United Americans, with their banner showing a hand gripping the neck of the coiling snake of foreignism, gradually assembled in the early afternoon as did members of the Mechanics Lodge of Odd Fellows. Town officers and committeemen arranged platforms and benches on the large grassy space in front of Tingue Opera House. They also placed brands and pitch barrels to light torches for the evening ceremonies. The ladies decorated tables with flowers and prepared the bowls of lemonade and switchel, the old haymakers' drink of honey, molasses, brown sugar, ginger and water. Hartigan's Saloon was doing a brisk business.

In and out, like a ribbon of flotsam on a clear river, circulated the wilder town elements, teenagers on the loose, unemployed mill hands and the violent nativist fringe looking for damned Irish, damned Germans, and damned-anything-different-from-me to confront and beat up.

Towards the home of Almira Humphreys the town's elite converged in their carriages, on horseback and on foot. Almira had belatedly risen to her duty and had invited the father, mother and sister of the groom to the wedding reception. She had not been able to invite them to stand in the receiving line where they just didn't belong. William was wearing a dark blue suit and green tie and cut a handsome figure. Mary Sweeney's clothes were comely but unadorned, lacking the spangles and embroideries which served to differentiate plutocrat from peasant. Even the lovely Irish crochet lace around her wrists and throat could not prevent her from being, in Almira's eyes, "just a plain Irishwoman."

Helena, in white silk with white roses in her dark hair, and Kevin, in olive broadcloth with fluted white shirt, made a strikingly handsome and happy pair.

Almira received her guests with every semblance of feigned pleasure.

Bandstand musicians played behind the usual array of potted palms, bushes and flowers. Butlers and maids from New Haven refilled the temperance bowls with benign fruit drinks and the intemperance bowls with brandy smash and whiskey punch. Also served were silver salvers and tureens of duck and shore birds, fried chicken, terrapin stews, oysters, shrimp salad, cheeses, frosted pound cake, floating island meringue, ices and bon bons.

While the social leaders from Seymour and neighboring cities passed dutifully down the line, most of the young men avoided it with the exception of more respectful immigrant families such as Llewellyn Kinney (part Welsh), Luzon Morris (part Irish), Will Gardener (German, the family having quickly changed their name from Baumgarden) and Dr.

Tom Stoddard, whose father had taught him to like everyone without favor or fear, scoff or sneer.

Young Benny Johnson, Gunn Dunlap, George Swayne, Philo Buckingham, George Bungay, Tim Clark, Yelverton Perry and their friends skipped all lines and went directly to the copious liquor bowls. They circulated through the rooms and gardens pursuing pretty petticoats, dancing, cutting up and getting higher and more reckless in their behavior as the afternoon progressed.

At sundown, Revolutionary cannon thundered the opening of Independence Day ceremonies of speeches and fireworks. Many of the flush-faced, loud-voiced young men, at the boom of the cannon, began searching for wilder adventure.

The program on the green began with brief speeches by Selectmen Sharon Beach and Harpin Riggs. The featured speaker was Wilphalet Todd of New York, a rabble-rousing emissary of the United Order of Americans. He had enjoyed the free rum barrels at Odd Fellows Hall and his tongue was already thickening. Instead of keeping to the planned topic of positive patriotism he moved rapidly into the dark tributaries of vituperative negatives:

"The great mainstream of majestic pure Americanism is constantly being sullied, blackened and muddied by endless tides of unwashed immigrants—the dirty, ignorant, Pope-driven hordes."

"Hear, hear!" cried some in the crowd, exhaling their alcoholic fumes.

"The hordes," continued Todd, "are bent on the overthrow of this great country. Foreigners are the spawn of the Devil, storing their arms in houses, fields and those rallying-places of the forces of Hell, the Catholic Churches!"

Wilphalet took from under the podium a glass supposedly filled with water but actually with gin and tonic. He took a healthy swig.

"I hear this town has just allowed such a structure to be raised to the Prince of Dark Dogma, the Foul Fiend of Vatican-land. You may be certain that in the cellars, yes, even under the praying benches of that Catholic Church, you will find guns, sabers, clubs and knives to be brought out on the day appointed by the Man of Rome, weapons by which you, your wives and precious children are to be maimed and killed wherever you may try to hide."

Waves of emotion stirred through the crowd and some headed in the direction of Father O'Laverty's church. Selectman Beach, a Justice of the Peace, leaned forward and admonished: "Cool it down, Todd, or we'll have trouble."

Todd didn't understand what he had said wrong. He meant every word. "Let's sum it up, my fellow patriots, America Forever and down with foreigners!"

Spreading his arms wide, he bowed, retrieved his gin and tonic and sat down.

Selectman Beach instantly went to the podium. "Please do not disperse yet. Kindly return to your seats for the Grand Fireworks Display." It was too late. A quarter of the audience was already on its way to the church, including the hoodlum fringe and well-liquored refugees from Almira Humphreys' bash. Many had plucked torches from their standards and were waving them as they moved along, creating long streamers of saffron smoke wafting in the breeze.

The crowd came to a yelling halt before St. Augustine's Church. In the torch-light, the fresh golden cross on top of the church gleamed serenely. To the right of the adjacent cemetery rose the high iron fence dividing the property of Chatfield Swayne from Church property. His large maroon-colored house with two candle-snuffer towers resembled a French chateau. All the first floor windows cast oblongs of light on the extensive front lawn. A single room upstairs, Sally's room, was lighted, as noted by her lurching brother, George.

Moral indignation quickly arose in George's mind over Sally's foul impregnation at the hands of a lower class Irish rapist. With his thoughts incendiarized by Speaker Todd, his anger quickly found targets not only at all Irishmen but all Catholics, all foreigners—everyone who wasn't solid New England, like Swaynes and Chatfields, by God.

Someone cried out, "Let's break down the doors and get at those guns in the basement!" Other cries erupted, "Yes, break down the God-damned doors!" "Foul conspirators!" The crowd pushed and shoved into the church and began to overturn pews and tear up the missals. The plaques of Stations of the Cross were ripped from the wall as if they were uniquely Catholic symbols. Since no guns or weapons of any kind were found, the altar cloth was ripped off, with no weapons or ammunition found underneath.

The sanctuary door was locked. Ah, ha! That must be the hiding place! The heavy candelabra from the altar were used to break down the door. Cupboards were opened and folded garments, books and sacred vessels were thrown on the floor and trampled. Vestry tables were overturned. Pictures of saints were yanked from the walls. No guns anywhere. In the tool room the mob helped itself to hatchets, axes, claw hammers, shovels, hoes and rakes. They broke windows, including the large stained glass window. Someone shouted, "This is the House of the Devil. That cross on top must come down!"

Yelverton Perry, a scapegrace member of one of Seymour's old families, armed with an axe and crowbar, was hoisted up over the door archway by his friends. He ascended the clapboarded roof to the vent-boards of the tower, up to the spire and began to hack away at the cross.

Father O'Laverty, walking up the hill, heard the sound. He could see the flare of torches and the crowd of black figures. He picked up his pace. Thoughts of martyrs who had summoned their courage for historical ordeals gave strength to his spirit and speed to his feet. Just as he reached the church grounds, Yelverton Perry gave a shout and the golden cross came hurtling down. To Father O'Laverty the black figure of Yelverton against the constellation of the Serpent was the Devil's figure, the crowd below a pack of fiends. He hurried forward into the very midst of them, carried by a mighty indignation. In a voice louder than Savonarola's, he cried, "Give me that cross!"

In answer to the imperious voice, the startled multitude parted and Benny Johnson and one of the town ne'er-do-wells who had hold of it, dropped it.

"How dare you bring down the holy cross of God? Is it not also the symbol of Christ's crucifixion to you who call yourselves Christian Protestants? Shame on you who are destroyers of this most sacred cross!"

He stooped, lifted up the cross where it lay in front of the door and stood with it before the Church. "Go home, all of you," he cried. "There are many houses of God. This is one of them. You have heard multiple lies about Catholics and the holy Catholic Church. This is sacred ground. Disperse now from this holy place and sully it no further. May God forgive you."

George Swayne, Gunn Dunlap, Benny Johnson, Philo Buckingham and Dave Bungay slowly moved off, but rougher elements shouted curses and obscenities at the priest. The throng moved towards him threateningly. Then, through the open church doors, flame and smoke issued from the sacristy. Some of the townies had set fire to the prayer books and vestments. In a matter of moments the whole room and surrounding areas burst into flame and smoke.

Yelverton Perry scrambled quickly down the roof. Wind carried burning church documents and fragments of wood-embers to the Swayne house, to the curtains at Sally's open window and the roof-clapboards. The volunteer fire company soon arrived but the church was already destroyed and the Swayne house was aflame. Sally was in her night-robe at the far edge of their lawn.

There was a small commotion in the corner of the yard where George Swayne and Dennis O'Neill were now pounding the daylights out of each other. Returning from work at the Inn, Dennis had seen the church fire and had raced up the hill. Seeing Sally on the lawn, he was begging her to move farther away from the flames when George had spotted him. Angry over the family scandal, George had rushed full-swing at Dennis. His friends had gathered around the fighters, yelling encouragement to George. The fight continued for several minutes of fisticuffs and wrestling. Then Yelverton Perry shouted, "Let's tar and feather that damned paddy! Just beating him up is too good for him. There are plenty of tar barrels and torch sticks down at Tingue Park."

Local hoodlums and George's friends grabbed Dennis and pinioned his arms. Then Benny Johnson cried out, "All the O'Neills should be tarred and feathered! We don't want immigrant tavern keepers around here!"

"Yes, all the damned O'Neils," shouted a townie. They carried a struggling Dennis downhill to the park. The boys heaved the half-empty pitch barrels to their shoulders and moved towards the tavern only a short distance away.

"For God's sake!" entreated Dennis. "Do what you want with me but leave my family alone! What harm have we ever done you? Leave my family alone!"

"You've hurt my family enough," shouted George, his face bloody. "Nothing is too bad for you and your family, God damn it, nothing!"

George, Gunn and Yelverton held Dennis. The rest stormed into the tavern.

In the kitchen, Maeva, Moira and Awley were finishing cleaning up after a busy holiday. The young men quickly overpowered Awley, trussed him up and dragged him outside. After stuffing their mouths with cloth napkins, they hauled Meava and Moira to an upstairs bedroom. They discovered old Patrick in his bed, dumped him on the floor and snatched the chicken-feather pillows. They tied the women to bedposts and told them they would return later to entertain them.

They dragged a struggling Patrick out to the park. Behind the woodpile, kettles were brought from the kitchen in which to liquefy the pitch. Dennis, Awley and Old Patrick were stripped bare, their mouths stuffed with washcloths.

Old Patrick felt that his hour had come. He remembered the long line of his ancestors, the Northern High Neills of Donegal and the Southern High Neills of Tara, and the chiefs and princes of Tirconnel and Tyrone. He began to repeat St. Patrick's "Dear Cry" song of bravery to himself in old Gaelic as he lay face upward on the ground while the brave boys spread warm pitch over his body:

> Christ shield me today
> Against poison, against burning,
> Against drowning, against wounding.
> Christ with me, Christ before me,
> Christ behind me, Christ above me . . .

Awley and Dennis were full of fury. Dennis was swearing eternal vengeance. If this was what Sally's damned brother was doing to him and his family, to hell forever with her and her relatives. With laughs of exultation, the group smeared pitch over the three men, back and front. then slit open the pillows and covered them with chicken feathers. They stood the three men on their feet, hands now tied behind their backs and began making crude witticisms and laughing loudly in the dim light.

At this moment Whiddy Hartigan passed by on his way to the O'Neill Tavern. He heard the laughter and saw figures moving in the yard. He could just make out the three strange, whitish, statue-like figures. He moved closer behind the trunk of a maple tree and heard some of the talk:

"Now we'll ride 'em out of town! Maybe we should kill 'em."

"Don't ever set foot in Seymour again, you damned potato-immigrants!"

"We'll send your women after you, sure enough, after we've had a little fun with 'em! May take us awhile."

"There are horses in the barn. Hitch up a wagon!"

Whiddy realized who the three feathered men were. My God, what had they done with Moira and her mother? Whiddy walked rapidly to the tavern. No one was downstairs. He climbed the stairs and opened the bedroom door. A hall lamp offered just enough light to make out two women roped to the bed posts.

"My God. Whiddy's here, never have a fear. Poor miss Moira! Poor Mrs. O'Neill." He removed their gags and cut the ropes with his pocket knife.

"God bless you, Whiddy," said Moira.

"Come quickly, I'm taking you to Dr. Stoddard for safe-keeping."

"What's happening to Dad and Dennis and Grandfather?"

"Not good things. Let's get out of here." They rushed downstairs, climbed out a back window and walked fast to the Stoddards' house. He told them what he had seen and they planned their strategy to rouse the town. Whiddy fetched Let Wooster, Llewellyn Kinney and the blacksmith, Page Sanford, then hurried to the Methodist, Congregational and Episcopal Churches to have their bells rung, signaling emergency volunteers to gather at the firehouse. Tom alerted the Selectmen to assemble a posse. Men came tumbling out of their houses. Loud whistles of the Brass Mill soon joined the cacophony of bells.

By this time the tar-and-feather boys were rocketing along the river road towards Pines Bridge. Yelverton Perry, at the reins, lashed wildly at O'Gallop, the O'Neills' horse. For the first time, fear entered into him and the rest of the gang. The alarm bells meant that the whole town would soon be after them.

"Let's dump 'em here! Stop, Yelve! Let me out," shrieked Dave Bungay.

"We're almost at the bridge. Hold on!" Yelverton shouted back.

"I'm leaving! Skin your own skunk!" said Dave, leaping off and breaking his leg. Yelverton slowed the wagon. The town boys jumped off, rolling in the dirt.

The wagon was now past the main part of town. Yelverton drove over the small plank bridge on Little River that separated Seymour from Pines Bridge, then drew rein. The seven boys now remaining, George Swayne, Gunn Dunlap, Benny Johnson, Philo Buckingham, Yelverton Perry and two of the boys from the mills, Otto Schmidt and Eb Danelson, jumped from the cart.

George, shocked into a growing sense of the gravity of what they were doing, cried out, "Let's cut them free! For God's sake, we must let them go!"

"Hell, no!" exclaimed Gunn. "Get them out of sight down the bank!"

"Yes, hurry! Then let's get out of here fast!" said Yelverton.

Gunn and Yelverton heaved the victims out. Yelverton let fly a few kicks at the Paddies, then they pushed them down the bushy bank. They heard the splash of one of the O'Neills hitting the water but ignored it.

"Now, let's make a dash for Waterbury," cried Yelverton.

"You are fools," said George. "If you run away, you convict yourselves. I'm walking home. We've had our Fourth of July fun."

"Listen, you O'Neills," called out Yelverton, "if you squeal on us, we'll cut your throats! Do you hear, you filthy Irishmen? The rest of you, are you coming with me? If so, climb in and be quick about it! If not, to hell with you."

"Otto and I are out of here," said Eb, and they ran off.

"You coming with me, Gunn?"

The sound of galloping horses and human yells was now distinct and torches were reflected in the river to the south. Gunn jumped back into the wagon and Yelverton whipped the horse along the road towards Waterbury.

"Let's get going," said Benny to George and Philo.

"Wait," urged George. "Let's cut the O'Neills free before we go. We've scared the hell of them and taught them a lesson. Enough is enough."

"For God's sake," Benny said with fear in his voice. "The whole town is coming. We've got to get out of here." The three ran.

When Let, Llewellyn Kinney, Page Sanford, Dr. Tom and Justice Beach came riding up ahead of the posse, a strange figure stood signaling them in the middle of the road with a cloth burning on a stick. It was old Eunice Mauwehu, the Indian woman, daughter of Chief Mauwehu. She had been fishing at the meeting-place of the rivers near where the wagon had stopped.

Old Patrick had landed in the water ten steps away but the river moved him away from her. She had clambered over the rocks with some difficulty and finally hauled him out of the water but had known at once that he was dead. Then she found Awley and Dennis on the bank, had taken the gags from their mouths and had cut the ropes that bound them.

The five riders and, shortly, the throng behind them on horses, carts and on foot, came to a stop. Eunice indicated where the three men lay. Awley and Dennis and the body of old Patrick were carried up the bank and laid in the cart which Whiddy had driven from Let's barn. Whiddy drove the victims back to the Stoddards' home-infirmary. Dr. Tom worked on old Patrick the whole way but Patrick had already joined his ancestors in the invisible green fields.

Then they turned their attention to the tarred bodies of Awley and Dennis. It took them all night to gently remove the tar layers with kerosene-soaked wash cloths, soap and water, followed by gentle plucking with tweezers. No serious burns were present. By early morning, the two O'Neill men were placed in infirmary beds. Dennis's skin and soul were aflame and raging, and he had to be given sedatives. Maeva and Moira were already in sedated sleep.

Late that night it was Whiddy who, before going to his home at the foot of Knockmedown Hill, made a detour to see the burned Church of St. Augustine. There he found Father O'Laverty lying in the bushes in front of the church, holding in one hand the blackened chalice, his other hand resting on the golden cross. His cassock was partially burned, his face black from smoke and red from heat. He was outraged and exhausted but not seriously injured.

CHAPTER 22

Coping Strategies

(July, 1852)

Dennis wanted revenge on all guilty persons. He strongly felt he should shoot George dead and put the houses of Dunlap, Perry, and Buckingham to the torch. It took the combined efforts of all relatives and friends to prevent his holocaust of reprisal and let law authorities decide on appropriate justice.

Dennis decided to leave Seymour. He told his family, "I cannot and will not stay in this town of cruel prejudice any longer. I am going away to make my fortune in a more tolerant society and, by Saint Patrick, come back some day and ram sacks of gold down the throats of these hateful murderers!"

He did not go near Sally to say goodbye or send any word. His feelings were in a wild tumult. She pranced joyously in his mind and she laughed and loved like no other girl. Deep down, he knew she was not of the accursed race of arrogant, malignant New England Yankees who were stranglers of all happiness and ruiners of earth's endless beauty. A curse upon them all.

Dennis waited only long enough for his grandfather's funeral at St. Augustine's Church. Then he departed by train to New York, heading out into the world alone, telling his family they might not hear from him for a long time.

When George was arrested and incarcerated, Amy Swayne could no longer keep from her husband the personal incentives for his son's terrible quarrel with Dennis O'Neill. When Chatfield learned that Sally was pregnant by Dennis, his shame and indignation overwhelmed him and he disowned her. Sally packed up a few belongings and fled to Lydia's house.

After bold surgery in New York to remove a chronic subdural hematoma, Llewellyn Kinney convalesced for a month in the Stoddards' infirmary and then at home. After three months, both he and Lydia felt he had returned completely to normal. Let gave him an accounting job at the Brass Mill in which he performed well. Llewellyn and Lydia happily accepted Sally as a guest in their home.

Two days after Sally's arrival, Lydia knocked on Julia's door and asked her to come over for a serious discussion of what to do with Sally.

"Do the O'Neills know about you and Dennis?" asked Julia.

"I don't know," answered Sally. "Why didn't Dennis say goodbye to me? Has he the same blind fury against me that he must have against George?"

"He went through a dreadful experience. I could try to find out. Do you want them to know about the baby?"

Sally hesitated. "No, not yet but try to find out where Dennis has gone."

"You really love him, don't you" asked Lydia, laying a hand on her arm.

"Yes, against all common sense," Sally said, tears welling up. "I don't care any more about social class or what people think."

"You want to keep your child, too, don't you, Sally?"

"Absolutely, but I can't have the baby here on account of my family. Where shall I go? I'm cut off from all family funding."

"I have an idea. You could stay with my family in Waterbury until the baby is born. My mother likes you, Sally."

"And I like her but it's a lot to ask."

"I'll run up on the train to talk to her this week," said Julia.

"We would love to have you in our home," said Julia, "but Submit clearly is not ready to cope with an unwed impregnation by an Irishman, even though you are her niece. She has had to learn that the Irish are a wee bit above the level of animals. Submit made me feel as if my blood were some kind of gumbo made of snake gizzards and pigpen muck. I believe she now regards me as partly human."

They giggled and Sally said, "Poor Aunt Submit. She already has a half-Irish grandchild. Now she'll have a bastard Irish grand-niece or grand-nephew, too!"

"Your child will have the sound of skylark wings and harps in her soul just like my Alice and, best of all, she will be imbued with laughter!" said Julia. "Most Yankees just don't know how to laugh. When I visit my family in Waterbury, it's laughter from morn till night, till the blessed cows come home!"

CHAPTER 23

Baby Talk

(July, 1852)

Julia called on the O'Neills the next morning. She took a basket of eggs to the old tavern. Maeva was in the kitchen baking pies and Moira was shelling peas.

"Sit down, Miss Julia. I hope you don't mind if we go on with our work," said Maeva. "We count our friends very few here now. Perhaps we should've headed out with Dennis but, God willing, there won't be any more horrors here."

"No more horrors, Maeva, I'm sure. That dastardly deed has brought disgrace on the doers and justice will be firm. God is on the side of the good."

"Is He, I wonder, on the side of the Irish? At times He seems to desert us."

"He loves the Irish even though He senses a bit of the devil in them."

"Ah, don't be speaking of the devil so lightly, Miss Julia. He might be listening outside and hop in through a crack in the door."

"He can't function in the middle of laughter! But I came here to talk to you about Sally. You do know about her relationship with Dennis, I feel sure."

"Yes," replied Maeva. "They were more than friends and I sensed she might be pregnant. She seemed puffy. Does her family know?"

"Yes, her mother just let Sally's father in on the secret and he disowned her. She has taken refuge with Lydia Kinney. She truly loves Dennis."

"Are you sure? She was worried about his lowly pedigree. I don't know whether Dennis loves her. When he left he was consumed by pervasive hate for her family, especially George who participated in those hateful crimes."

"Where did he go? Do you know, Maeva?"

"He said it would be far away and it might be years before we heard from him. Oh, dear!" Maeva broke down and cried. "He said that he'd make his fortune and come back and ram sacks of gold down their throats!"

"Sacks of gold," said Julia. "Must be California. Well, all we can do is wait. Meantime, the fate of Dennis's little child—your grandchild, Maeva—is our chief concern. I'm going to Waterbury tomorrow to ask my mother to take Sally into her home until after the baby is born in a nice Irish home."

A whole sequence of gradually softening expressions went over Maeva's face. "And why couldn't it be born here, under its own grandmother's roof?"

"Oh, Maeva, may I tell Sally that? I fear she will not want the child born here in Seymour, so close to her family and the town's inevitable cruel gossip."

"Tell her to come see me as soon as she cares to."

Sally visited that same evening, smiling and extending her hand. "Thank you, Mrs. O'Neill, for letting me come under these circumstances."

"Whom Dennis loves, I should feel kindly towards also."

"You say 'loves'. Oh, if you had proof of that!" Sally began to weep quietly.

"I have no way of interpreting his heart. The poor boy was very distraught. He had to get far away in a hurry. Did he know you were going to have a baby?"

"Yes. Oh, yes! There were no secrets between us. All we knew was that we loved each other and hoped that time would show us the way."

"Didn't you ever talk about marriage?"

"Yes, we did, but there were big boulders in our little stream."

"A stream goes rippling 'round big stones and sings louder than ever."

"Ah, Dennis talks like you—a kind of magical language. Julia does, too."

"It's just the Irish language, which surely puts a dab of whimsy on the English tongue and a note or two of the heart's music."

"Dennis speaks it so well with so much joy! Oh, if Dennis would only come back, I'd marry him tomorrow if he'd be willing, and even turn Catholic for him."

Maeva smiled, as if Sally had said, "And even turn cannibal for him!"

Sally continued. "I'm afraid he'll marry the first girl he sees even though I know he's very loyal to his family here. He is a bit impetuous, as you know, and I'm worried about the impact of the wild West, if that's where he went."

"Would you consider having your baby here under the O'Neill roof?"

"Dear Mrs. O'Neill, thank you so much but I don't want the town to suspect what's happened until the time is right. I think it's best to go and hide in Waterbury with Julia's family. And please call me Sally."

"This home, my dear, and the Sweeney home in Waterbury shall be your two homes . . . until your father unbolts his door.

"I'm afraid he never will."

"A baby is a great softener of stony hearts, Sally."

Putting her hand on Maeva's, Sally said, "It's been wonderful to talk with you. I think I'll be weeping less now."

"God bless you, Sally. Now I'm certain as the saints that you really do love my boy. You seem to have in your heart the tender love along with the passion love."

CHAPTER 24

STAR SPANGLED SNAKE OIL

(Early September, 1852)

The first fall meeting of the Daughters of the Star Spangled Banner was to take place in the Wooster home. Submit suspected that Julia had listened in on a couple of previous meetings from the staircase but the time had come fulfill her own social obligation. She must invite Julia to attend as a guest.

Meetings began with sewing and conversation. There would be plenty of discussion about the upcoming trial and against the Irish who, by merely being in Seymour, were the real cause of all the trouble. Submit was giving the paper today and wanted Julia to hear it but not the preliminary conversation. Having no dignified ancestry of her own, Julia might benefit by hearing more about the gentry of New England.

Julia agreed to come, wondering how many overt or covert insults she would have to endure. The ladies would present a united front, heraldic shield to heraldic shield, in defense of the "pranks" of their sons on Independence Day. Julia was ready when Submit called her. She had put on a Puritan gray wool dress with black braid but had followed her elf's advice to tuck into her hair a lovely pink velvet rose bought from Marcel. She and the elf hoped that Submit's grim friends would regard the flower as reckless frivolity with Satanic overtones.

As a secret talisman against Yankee poisoned arrows she slipped around her neck the gold chain and pendant given to her by her father on her eighteenth birthday. The pendant was a gold and blue enamel replica of the ancient, shield-shaped Mac Sweeney coat of arms showing two gold boars facing each other above two crossed battleaxes and in small gold Celtic letters the motto: *Buailtir buaigh cabirh.* Strike for victory. Julia had never shown the pendant to Submit but her senses informed her to wear it today. She had tucked it into invisibility behind the bright green rick-rack collar of her dress.

As she came down the stairs, Julia tried to infuse herself with the courage of an ancient Irish warrior. The babble in the living room was like the chatter of crows over a dead carcass. She entered with a smile. A sudden hush came over the ladies and fifteen pairs of eyes gimleted her. From her chair Submit introduced her as "Mrs. Letsome Wooster, ladies."

Instead of sinking obscurely into the only empty chair, Julia, like a swan swimming on the River Liffey, gracefully made the rounds, extending her hand warmly to those she already knew—Amy Goodwin Swayne, Almira Aurelia Humphreys, Elvira Gunn Dunlap, Mrs. Abiram Stoddard, Mrs. Mary Davis and Mrs. Henry M. Beecher. Julia also found something nice to say to each unknown, for she already knew them by reputation—the rubber plutocrats Mrs. Austin Goodyear Day and Mrs. Charles Goodyear, the mothers of Benny Johnson, Yelverton Perry and Philo Buckingham, Mrs. William Gardener of the changed name, Mrs. Franklin Farrell, Mrs. Matthew French and the eldest Miss Farnham, Chary Ann. Julia hadn't been able to resist saying sweetly to Mrs. Perry:

"Oh, how lovely a collar you're making with this Irish printed linen cambric, a material much favored by Queen Victoria as well as Irish ladies." Mrs. Perry had flushed and hastily put the work away as if she had been told that the cambric had been saturated with prussic acid and Paris green.

With a smile Julia sat down in her assigned chair next to Chary Ann Farnham who quite fascinated her. Let had told her how old Deacon Farnham, a man of many notions, took his three daughters every morning, winter and summer, to the woodshed and there doused them, clothed only in their nightgowns, with cold water dipped from a wash pan, to make them sturdy. They weren't allowed to squeal or wrinkle up their faces or show any skin-grooving emotion whatsoever on this or any other occasion. As a result, their faces were as smooth as unblemished marble, without the slightest trace of personality or character. Chary Ann looked at Julia with the unmoving face of a doll. Here was the unlaughterful New Englander personified, sculpted in cold granite. Julia's Irish imp tried in every possible way to make Chary Ann laugh but failed.

Mrs. Johnson called the meeting to order and asked Mrs. Henry Beecher to read her Secretarial Report of the previous session. Mrs. Beecher paid tribute to Almira who had read her paper on "General David Humphreys and the Hartford Wits, a paper worthy in every sparkling line of her inspired ancestor."

Mrs. Johnson, a woman puffed with obesity and ancestral pride, then gave her introduction of "our beloved Submit Swayne Wooster, in whom an entire garden of illustrious ancestors combines in a bouquet of lofty heritage. Her subject is 'The Brocketts, Chatfields and Swaynes.'"

Submit took her place behind Captain Levi Wooster's Chippendale mahogany tabouet table. The paper was, as Julia predicted, a pedestrian account, without any glint of humor, grace or originality, of all those ancestors about whom Julia had heard so often. Submit glozed over the fact that she could not carry the stock of the central Swayne family further than three generations back. The family Bibles and records had suffered "unexplained damage by natural forces, with lost pages and unreadable paragraphs in crucial places."

Submit proudly carried the noble Brocketts far back into their castles and stone manors in Yorkshire, and the Chatfields into their manses in mid-Suffolk and Chichester. Julia noted that she never mentioned her father or husband. Submit ended with the hope that she might "prove worthy of her heritage in England and that we may all carry forward our sublime New Englandism." The room burst into a flutter of applause and a warble of approval.

"And now, after this charming history of Submit's wonderful family," said Urania Johnson, "we come to the always pleasant portable heirloom part of our program. We'll start alphabetically. Jane Beecher, have you anything to show?"

"Yes, I have, Urania." Laying down her lace on the sofa, Jane smoothed her black silk dress and took from a gray velvet bag that hung from her belt a little silver nutmeg grater that had belonged to great-great grandmother Beecher. There were "ohs" and "ahs" and the passing of the curio from hand to hand.

For the next half hour, many quaint objects were transmitted along the rows of exploring fingers—samplers, silver knee buckles and stock buckles, patch boxes and snuffboxes, flip glasses, brass buttons worn on ancestors' coats in the Revolution, shot moulds, silver pepper-boxes and ivory miniatures.

When Submit's turn came she showed two items. First a pair of white silk-covered slippers which her Grandmother, Concurrence Brockett, had worn at her wedding in 1770. Then she said: "I also want to show you a brooch that has come down in the Swayne family. It has a coat of arms and an indecipherable inscription said to be an ancient Masonic device."

When the brooch reached Julia, she inwardly gasped. There on the shield-shaped brooch were two gold boars above two crossed battleaxes and, in almost indecipherable letters because of attempts to obliterate them, the Celtic words *Buailtir buaigh cabirh.* As she held the brooch, Julia remembered her father saying that Queen Elizabeth had forced many prominent Irish families to Anglicize their names. Mac Sweeneys or Mac Swaneys became Swaynes or Swains. Why had she not realized this before? A little smile of irony curled her lips. She was tempted to point out the similarity to her own brooch but decided she would only make the comparison if significant provocation justified it.

The afternoon was drawing to an amiable close. Julia had distributed cups of plain raspberry shrub and cardamom cookies. The ladies were chatting in groups of twos and threes when Julia heard the words, "Maeva O'Neill" and "those dirty O'Neills" bandied contemptuously by Minerva Buckingham in conversation with Amy Goodwin Swayne.

Then occurred one of those silences which happen at any gathering. Into such a silence plunged Mrs. Buckingham's remarks meant only for Amy's ears but Minerva swept on with the proud propulsion of a scythed chariot: " . . . and I agree with the patriotic Know Nothing Party that the dirty Irish should all go back to their hovels in Ireland! Thank

God our boys had the gumption to do the right thing against these filthy immigrants and teach them a lesson!"

"I agree!" said Amy. "Oh, how I agree."

Julia's cheeks reddened and she became rigid. The time had come. The Rubicon had been breached. From the deep whirlpool of her dismay at such blatant prejudice, lack of grace and grotesquely bad manners, an immense clarity and calmness took hold. She rose and faced the group.

"Ladies," she said firmly. "I ask for just a moment of your time. You have been listening this afternoon to a splendid paper by my mother-in-law and to praises of all her noble New England ancestors. These are praises which make me proud too, for they are now the ancestors of my little daughter, Alice. My child has other ancestors, too, Irish ancestors, of whom I am equally proud.

"You ladies constitute a group devoted to history, yet you and most of your fellow New Englanders have a dangerous misconception of the Irish. You see our impoverished potato famine immigrants but rarely see our brilliant writers, poets, artists, musicians and statesmen, our beautiful women of the aristocracy.

"You forget that Ireland was the cradle of culture long before England grew out of savagery. Ireland has been known for almost two thousand years as 'the island of scholars and saints.' Out of her monasteries and great schools went the missionaries and scholars to bring culture to the European continent during their Dark Ages. It was they who Christianized a large part of Western Europe when your Saxon ancestors were still worshipping idols and spattering the blood of human sacrifices on their altars."

Julia took breath. The women looked at her motionless, as if entranced by her gentle soft voice, her lilting musical tongue and her tranquil composure. "You seem to think the

Irish countryside consists only of shacks and pigpens. Ah, no! It is beautiful, with stone-carved cathedrals and abbeys, stately castles and great cities. The castles of my father's people are all around the seacoasts of Donegal and in the beautiful green hills and meadows of County Cork.

"Have you read of the Hill of Tara and the great palace that stood there in the Third Century when there were no English people at all? Three hundred feet long it was, with fourteen great doors, a hundred and fifty goblets of pure gold in the Meal Hall and the air resounding with songs of minstrels. Nowhere was gold more wondrously wrought than in Ireland.

"Perhaps I've given you enough, ladies, to show you why I am proud of Ireland and why you, who are of English descent, should also be proud since you have taken so much of our beauty and splendor into your history, literature, and sometimes, without knowing it, into your very blood.

"You speak of your Star Spangled Banner and your patriotism. Where do you think your country would be without the loyal Irish who fought with George Washington? When your own soldiers were deserting by the hundreds, it was the Irish who stuck with him and won your country away from England!

"Three of your Presidents have been of part-Irish descent, James Madison, James Monroe and James K. Polk. Andrew Jackson was totally Gaelic. Many of your Generals, your signers of the Declaration of Independence and the Constitution were Irish. The music of your two patriotic songs, 'My Country 'Tis of Thee' and 'Yankee Doodle' are based on old Irish folksongs and airs.

"Every day you use Irish words and phrases without knowing it. When Mrs. Buckingham, a few minutes ago, remarked she was glad that your sons had the 'gumption to do the right thing,' she was using an Irish word. Gumption to tar and feather? Gumption to murder? Would God approve of such gumption?

"My mother-in-law conspicuously left out of her talk any mention of her father, Joseph Chatfield of Waterbury, where I was born and brought up. Why did she omit her own father, I'm wonderin'? Well, he was a full-time farmer, a respectable and honest profession requiring hard work, knowledge and skill—just as honorable as that of my father who is an industrial chemical engineer.

"Have you wondered why Submit never mentions her husband, Albert, who so tragically died of typhoid fever at the age of thirty-six? Could it be because he was a simple artisan of leather, a shoemaker? He was a handsome, fine man and excellent at his craft but Submit has been deeply embarrassed all of her adult life by what she regards as a lower class way of making a living.

"You yourselves might want to look further into Irish history, perhaps starting with the greatest of all Irish families, the O'Neills. It is a family celebrated for fifteen hundred years in history and legend. For six hundred years the O'Neills were kings. Every person of that name descends from High King Neill of the Nine Hostages in 400 A.D. and can trace his ancestry much further back than any Englishman or any New Englander. It is the oldest family of proven descent in all of Europe, one of the proudest family clans on earth! The name 'Niall' means 'noble knight.' I am proud and happy to be living on the same hill with a family of O'Neills and to have some O'Neill blood myself. And such a dear, loving, gracious, witty family you will rarely find! The idea that the O'Neills are filthy scum is not only erroneous but displays a great unawareness of history and genealogy.

"This being an historical society, it might behoove you to learn more about family names and their derivation. Many Irish landowners were forced by Queen Elizabeth to take English names. Several of you in this room bear, unbeknownst to you, an Irish name turned English. One in particular, just proven to me beyond reasonable doubt, I find most exciting. Mrs. Wooster, will you hold out your brooch which has just reached you again? I'll be coming to get it."

Julia took the brooch, unclasped her own necklace and held up the brooch and pendant together. "This locket of mine has come down in my family for generations. It shows the old Mac Sweeney heraldic shield which goes back six hundred years to the great Chief of Tirconnell, Mac Sweeney of the Battleaxes, Marshall and Standard Bearer under the Earls of Tirconnell, to whom he was related by blood. The emblem, showing two boars and two crossed battleaxes, is absolutely identical with the crest of the Swayne family. The inscription is Gaelic, still legible though attempts have been made to obliterate it. *Buailtir buaigh cabirh*—Old Irish words meaning, 'Strike for victory'! A valiant creed!

"They are identical because these Swaynes are actually descendants of some of the Irish Mac Sweeneys whom Queen Elizabeth forced to change their names to an English form. I am happy to know that my mother-in-law and I descend from the very same illustrious old Irish stock. The same," she added looking straight at Amy Swayne, "holds true of the ancestry of Chatfield Swayne, who actually carries a distinguished Irish name." Julia stopped, feeling she had provided the group with an ample dosage of genealogical infusions for one day.

Amy Goodwin Swayne rose quickly and made for the door without saying a word. Submit Swayne Wooster leaned her back on the antimacassar with a pale face and cold perspiration. The ladies began fanning her and administering eau-de-cologne out of a filigree bottle pulled from a velvet sash-bag.

Julia put on her Mac Sweeney locket and went for a long walk on the hill, her steps bouncing sprightly, her face embroidered with a happy and contented smile. She hoped she had been sufficiently courteous, polite and respectful but also well-informed and confident. She did not feel unkindly, just factual. The Irish, at last, had held their own today. There is a time to stand. The elf on her shoulder, dressed entirely in green, was jumping up and down shouting "*Erin go Bragh*"—Ireland Forever!

CHAPTER 25

TRIAL FOR MURDER AND TORTURE:

PROSECUTION

(September, 1852)

The State of Connecticut versus the killers of Patrick O'Neill and tar-and-featherers of the O'Neill family came to Court on September 24, 1852, in New Haven. The Prosecuting Attorney had opted out of the case because of "conflict of interest," presumably because of his known prejudice against the Irish.

The law firm of Daggett, Farnham and Whitney had been consulted by the State of Connecticut and had sent into the fray their young associate, Kevin Sweeney, as Special Prosecuting Attorney *pro tempore*. Kevin had briefly hesitated to undertake the case, concerned that Submit Wooster's cousin, George Swayne, was one of the defendants. The opportunity to plead the Irish cause, speak out against flagrant prejudice, advance democracy and defend the O'Neills proved too great a challenge to resist, especially when encouraged to do so by senior members of his firm. The opportunity was exactly what Kevin had hoped for but he had not expected such a break so early in his career.

Kevin had already gathered a wealth of material on the nativist movement and the history of immigration in

Connecticut for his undergraduate thesis and his law school debates. The subject was now one of his favorite hobbies.

When Julia had recently brought him the news that the Swaynes were indeed ancient Mac Sweeneys and that George Swayne, therefore, was part-Irish by descent and name, the final link of irony was forged in his management of the trial. He was not overawed by that fact that the Swayne, Dunlap, Perry, Johnson and Buckingham families had hired as Attorney for the Defense, Henry Tomlinson of New Haven, a well-known, competent defense lawyer whom Kevin suspected of being a member of the Know Nothing Party whose membership was limited to Protestant English males who hated foreign immigrants, especially Irish Catholics.

Kevin discovered that Tomlinson was from an old Connecticut family and a second cousin of Submit Swayne Wooster. He was twice Kevin's age, a tall and husky, now somewhat obese, former Yale tackle who relied on his powerful baritone voice, spread-eagle gestures and banner-bright platitudes to overwhelm his opposition. In court he showed not one iota of humor, subtlety or intellectual adroitness. Some of his courtroom ploys displayed questionable ethics.

The charges in the case were straightforward but the underlying issues of ethnic prejudice, immigration and social class were highly inflammatory and could easily lead to a hung jury. Neither side wanted that, nor did those under indictment, so it was agreed to dispense with a jury. The Judge approved by both sides was firm, fair and reasonable Robert Munger of New Haven.

Dave Bungay had been released from the case. The O'Neills had not recognized him and he had voluntarily dropped off the wagon before Patrick was rolled down the bank. The mill boys and other Seymour townies had disappeared.

Since the case was a dramatization of the conflict between "true native citizens" and Irish immigrants, it attracted a great deal of press attention in New York, Hartford and Boston. Irish and anti-Irish factions crowded into New Haven to add their bias, loud voices and fisticuffs to the emotion-laden confrontation.

In his opening statement, Tomlinson tried to minimize the tarring and feathering as a youthful prank with no harm intended at all. He also implied that the O'Neils' Whittemore Tavern was a dark rendezvous for Irish schemers and outright anti-American conspirators. He stated that Patrick's death was unfortunate but that the old man would have died of natural causes that very evening. Tomlinson felt it safe to declare that Father O'Laverty had given extreme unction to Patrick that day because of severe illness. Tomlinson was confident that O'Laverty would not agree to appear in Court because he was recovering from his burns at a Catholic retreat in Albany. Kevin, however, easily induced him to come from Albany to testify. The skin of his face, neck, and arms was still red and scarred from the blistering heat of the church fire.

Although mention of the church burning had been excluded by the judge during pre-trial motions, Kevin asked Father O'Laverty whether he had visited Patrick O'Neill before or after his church had been reduced to a fiery ruin by the same individuals who attacked the O'Neills.

"I saw him just before the church-burning, Mr. Sweeney. I came up the hill to find God's holy cross being ripped from the tower of St. Augustine Church."

"Objection! Objection! Totally irrelevant," shouted Tomlinson.

"Objection sustained," said Judge Munger.

"I saw Patrick at the tavern," continued O'Laverty. "His ailment consisted only of imbibing a bit too much beer which he had done once or twice before in his life." A ripple of laughter swept the courtroom. "That very afternoon he had been dancing an Irish jig with his granddaughter, Moira, at a tavern party."

"Did Patrick, on the whole, seem a healthy person?" asked Kevin.

"He was in superb health in spite of his seventy years. He kept the tavern supplied with firewood and took care of the landscaping. He had wit akin to Irish sages of yesteryear." Father O'Laverty loudened his voice. "He should've lived a hundred years had it not been for his murderers!"

Dr. Abiram Stoddard, whose excellent medical reputation was well known in New Haven, testified that "Patrick was as strong as Joshua Sperry's oxen which always took first prize at the Orange County Fair. He was kicked and then pushed into the river with his hands tied, which are methods of cowards. The coroner reported drowning as the final cause of death."

Kevin now brought the Indian woman, Eunice Mauwehu, to the witness box. She was old, squat and fat, a picturesque figure wearing a long gray woolen gown, a green woolen shawl and two necklaces made of greenish linden seeds. Her gray hair was in braids and there was a fillet of beads around her head.

There was a slight difficulty about swearing her in on the Bible. "Indian woman needs no book to tell truth," she said. "Indian woman tell truth anyway. Her God not hide in book. Her God everywhere." Kevin gently laid her hand on the book and asked her to repeat the words of the white man's oath.

"You are a daughter of Joseph Mauwehu, Chief of the Pequot tribe?"

"Yes, sir."

"What were you doing on the night of July third, last?"

"Fishing. I catch catfish and other things, too, that night."

"Exactly where were you fishing?"

"Under bridge where Little River meets Naugatuck River."

"Will you tell the Court what interrupted your fishing that night?"

"Yes. I hear clop-clop of horse coming along road. When wagon reach bridge, man's voice say, 'Whoa!' I look up. I see seven men jump out of wagon."

"How could you see so much at night, Eunice?"

"By light of wagon lantern and by Eunice's very good sight of eyes."

"What else did you see and hear?"

"Two of men run off. Other five men quarrel. One say loud, 'Let's cut them free! For God's sake, we must let them go!' Other man say, 'Hell, no!' They take three long bundles out of wagon. They drop bundles at edge of road. Then they kick and push two of them down bank."

"They? How many, actually?"

"Two men. They stoop and push other bundle down. I watch careful."

"And what happened to the third bundle, Eunice?"

"Third bundle come roll, roll, roll and splash into water near Eunice."

"How near?"

"About ten footsteps away."

"What did you do then?"

"I hear moan-sound as bundle rolls. I rush along bank but river carried him away maybe thirty more footsteps. I find him caught by willow branch, face down in water. I pull him up on bank. I take cloth out of mouth. Not breathing. Then I go back to other bundles caught against little bushes, not reach water. Two men alive. I take cloths out of mouths. I cut ropes with my knife. Then I put cloths on stick and light them and go up to road to make signal. Wagon has gone away but I hear sound of many other horses, wagons, people coming."

"Did you understand what had happened, Eunice?"

"I understand one kind of white man hate other kind. Hate very bad. Your God not like hate. My Great Spirit not like hate."

"Thank you, Eunice. That is all."

Tomlinson tried to make a laughing-stock of Eunice's witnessing by reminding the Court that, since the beginning in the New World, testimony of Indians had been worthless.

"Objection, prejudicial and irrelevant," said Kevin, immediately standing.

"Sustained," said Judge Munger. "Proceed with care, Counselor."

"I will try to do that, Judge, but it may be difficult in this case."

As the trial proceeded, Kevin brought to the witness box Whiddy Hartigan and Moira, Maeva and Awley O'Neill, in that order.

Whiddy laid aside all his little quirks. He knew Tomlinson would regard him as a dim-wit because his witnesses would tell him so. He would simply testify the truth. Let had loaned him a dark blue suit. He looked calm and almost good-looking as he nodded at the Judge and a seated Attorney Tomlinson.

Kevin began. "You were passing in the vicinity of the Inn that Saturday evening of the third of July, were you not?"

"Yes I was, Sir."

"At what time, Whiddy?"

"At about ten o'clock in the evening, Sir." Whiddy gave unhesitating answers to all of Kevin's questions and presented a clear picture of what he had seen of the tarring and feathering in the Tavern yard, and of how he had found Maeva and Moira O'Neill tied up on an upstairs bed.

When Tomlinson came to cross-examine him, Whiddy met him with a broad smile and thought to himself, "Beware, oh supremely confident lawyer. You don't yet realize it but you're going to meet your match today."

"You live at the foot of Knockmedown Hill, do you not?"

"That's a name, Sir, given to the hill in honor of coal mine fairies in Ireland and Cornwall who were called 'Knockers.' It's really Knockmealdown Hill, named for the hills around Lismore in lovely Ireland."

"We'll have none of your Irish blather! Stick to the point, boy!"

"I'm surprised you could bring yourself to be using an Irish word."

"What word? I certainly did not! What word, you . . ."

"'Blather' is a word brought in by the Irish, Sir, begging your pardon."

There was laughter in the Court. Tomlinson proceeded in a calm, firm voice. "You will answer my questions or I'll call for contempt. Your father, Crotty Hartigan, keeps a saloon, does he not?"

"My father keeps an inn at the foot of Knockmedown Hill. Exactly, Sir, as your grandfather, Henry Tomlinson, kept an 'ordinary' on New Haven Green not five hundred steps from here. It's on record that your grandfather was sent to jail for a year for failing to pay his liquor taxes. My father always pays his taxes."

The whole courtroom laughed, including the Judge. Kevin had shared that item with Whiddy just for the fun of it. Tomlinson's cheeks reddened. "Your Honor, is this not contempt of court?"

"It depends on whose ox is being gored," said Judge Munger. "As I recall, you gored him first by calling him 'boy'." The Judge turned to Whiddy: "You will answer questions briefly and to the point, Mr. Hartigan."

"Yes, sir," answered Whiddy, "and I'm sure I may expect, in return, that Defense Attorney Tomlinson treats me and other witnesses with respect."

"How was it, Hartigan," asked Tomlinson "that, instead of giving the alarm immediately, you went into the O'Neill quarters first. To remove evidence of Irish conspiracy, perhaps? To take away guns and ammunition stored there?"

Kevin chose not to object to this irrelevant innuendo.

"It seems to me, Sir, that you are full of inventings today. There was no conspiracy and there were no guns stored at the tavern or at the church so maliciously burned. The only conspiracy, Sir, is by those in this country towards those who come seeking a refuge. I refer, Sir, to the despicable acts by your so-called 'nativist Americans', including tarrings and featherings and murder."

"Step down! No! Stay where you are. Why, then, did you go into the tavern before giving the alarm?"

"Because, Sir, I wanted to see whether Mrs. O'Neill and Moira were safe or whether they were harmed by those violent, ill-tempered sons of the elite."

"Oh," sneered Tomlinson, "it was the girl you were after? Is she a friend of yours, a close bosom-friend, perhaps, Mr. Hartigan?"

"If you are referring to Miss Moira, I know her only as a neighbor. But if a lovely girl and her fine mother, may be in grave danger, it would be a surly heart indeed that would not do his best to get them out of trouble, wouldn't you agree, Sir?" Right you are, Whiddy, he said very softly to himself.

"Address me, not your foolish self. Had you already made up your mind what poor boys you would accuse of that tar and feather job."

"There was no making up of the mind in advance, sir. I recognized the voices of three of them, Mr. Swayne, Mr. Dunlap and Mr. Perry."

"How could you recognize them?"

"I've done errands at their houses many times and I know their voices. And sometimes they used one another's first names. I didn't recognize any others."

"You didn't recognize any others? How many others were there?"

"Three or four. The only ones I was sure of were those three, Sir."

"You claim you could also see them on a pitch-black night. How was that?"

"The pitch fire was still burning and now and then someone lighted a lucifer match briefly but, frankly, I couldn't make out the faces, only the figures."

"You couldn't make out any of the voices either, for that matter."

"I thought, Sir, that I was the one supposed to do the answerin'. I've sworn on the Good Book, Sir, and I'm not a liar."

"Some think an Irishman's oath isn't worth a clap of air from the back end of a billy-goat."

"Objection!" cried Kevin.

"Sustained," said the Judge, firmly admonishing Tomlinson once again.

"Witness dismissed," said Tomlinson.

There was time left only for the testimony of Moira O'Neill before the lunch break. Kevin asked her only a few factual questions.

Tomlinson took over. She was an appealing witness, young and pretty but he treated her only as an ignorant Irish girl.

"What relation does the saloon keeper's boy bear to you?"

"I don't understand you, Sir."

"Whiddy. Whiddy Hartigan. How well do you know him?"

"I don't know him as well as I would like to know him, especially because of his kind, brave actions towards my mother and me on the night of the horror."

"Answer my question. You're an impudent Miss, aren't you?"

"Impudent? It seems *you* are the one asking rude personal questions, Sir."

"Hurrah! Hurrah for the colleen!" cried someone at the back of the room.

Judge Munger pounded his gavel on the table and warned the audience not to interrupt the proceedings in any way or he would clear the courtroom.

"I have finished with the witness," said Tomlinson, his face wattle-red. These Irish always had some trick up their sleeves, even those who seemed guileless. How did they become so clever with words? Devils with angels' faces.

When Moira's mother, Maeva, came to the stand that afternoon, Kevin handled her very gently for fear she would break down. His questions about being tied up were straightforward. She accurately identified the guilty.

Tomlinson, too, handled her warily, for the mother of a family usually carries a special appeal in a courtroom. Under

Tomlinson's sanctimonious, treatment, however, Maeva fell to weeping. Then he suddenly changed tactics.

"We hear you are a good cook, Mrs. O'Neill. What kind of patronage do you have at the Inn?"

"Very satisfactory, Sir."

"Is it chiefly the Irish who come to Whittemore Tavern?"

"I would not say so, Sir. Most are not Irish. We serve them all equally at the Inn, Sir, mindful of Apostle Paul's words: 'Be not forgetful to entertain strangers, for thereby you may have entertained angels unawares.'"

"You Irish are the greatest gibble-gabblers and bibble-babblers in God's creation! Stick to the questions, woman, and answer with plain 'yes' and 'no'."

"Yes, Sir." Then, under her breath, but audible, she added, "You're a pretty good blatherskite yourself, I'd be thinking." This caused loud laughter in the courtroom, once again including the Judge.

"Hopeless," said Tomlinson. Then he turned quickly upon her. "Wasn't the Inn turned over entirely to the Sons of St. Patrick on St. Patrick's Day this year?"

"By your leave, Sir, no, not entirely. The Inn was open that night, as every night, to all wayfarers. They had the back dining room to themselves, that's all."

"It was a quiet evening?"

"Scarcely quiet, Sir. It was a great let-out entirely. Speeches and singing and Irish jigs, but there was no trouble, if that's what you mean, Sir."

"No conspiring, as far as you know, against this great land of ours?"

"This great land is home to us now, Sir. What could the Irish gain from conspiracy? You're looking under the wrong beds, Mr. Attorney. The beds are your own, with the torches and tar and goose-feathers under 'em."

A deathly quiet came over the courtroom. Suddenly Tomlinson asked, "Did you get along well with your father-in-law?"

"With that grand old man? Of course! I thought of him as my own father, having lost my own flesh-father when I was a child." Tears sprang to her eyes.

"You worked him pretty hard around the place, you and Awley, didn't you, to get your money's worth?"

"He had been an inn-keeper himself in Armagh and he didn't like to be idle. He loved keeping the grounds tidy and chopping wood. He also loved tending the grass and flowers. He was a good man, happy and wise. We all loved him." She broke down and wept. Tomlinson immediately dismissed her.

During the last few days of the trial, the courtroom, corridors and lawn were packed. Alexander T. Stewart of New York and Governor Thomas Hart Seymour were in attendance. Awley O'Neill was the next to be called up.

Kevin's questions of Awley were the expected ones, establishing his whereabouts and activities on Independence Day before he was grabbed for tarring and feathering. Awley had planned to be self-restrained and courteous.

"Your name is Awley O'Neill?"

"Yes, Sir."

"When did you come to this country?"

"Fifteen years ago, Sir, in 1837."

"Why did you come?"

"The tithes had risen so high that few could afford to spend the night anymore at my father's inn. We were near being ruined by constant taxes and interference by the Irish government. We'd heard of 'the land of the free,' and, hoping for better opportunity and happiness, we found our way here."

Tomlinson frowned. "How did you get to Seymour?"

"I did odd jobs around New York for several years. Then, four years ago, I saw Mr. Wooster's advertisement in the *New York Times* looking for an inn-keeper. I took the first train to Seymour and Mr. Wooster offered the job to me."

"Would you say that Mr. Wooster favored the Irish?"

"I would say, Sir, that Mr. Wooster is a true Christian, that he's a good example of Biblical advice: 'He who loveth God should love his brother also.'"

"I didn't put you up here to preach your Catholic sermons to me!"

"We use the same text that you use, Sir, the very same."

"Confound your impudence! Are you trying to make a Catholic out of me?"

"No, Sir. Nor a Christian, either." There was heavy laughter. Alexander Stewart in the front row shook the bench beneath him with loud laughing.

"Is it not true," roared Tomlinson, "that you advertised in *The New Haven Courier* on tenth September for a seditious meeting of Irishmen at your hotel?"

"It was the Secretary of the Robert Emmett Society who advertised a meeting at our hotel and who extended a welcome to all interested persons."

Now Tomlinson was sure he had him. "If memory serves, Robert Emmett was a traitor. A dangerous fomenter of revolution."

"Or a very great patriot, Sir, depending on your point of view. Every American soldier who fought against the King of England seventy years ago was 'a dangerous fomenter of revolution' and a 'traitor' to the country that nurtured him. Are some of your ancestors foul traitors, Sir?"

While Tomlinson was wondering whether to stop the questions and get Awley off the stand in a hurry, Awley continued.

"Descendants of early immigrants love to change their ancestry, it seems, and go on inventin' generation after generation. They love to verbally attack and now tar and feather recent immigrants who work hard and become good citizens of their new country. They even stoop to murder, as they did with my father."

Tomlinson realized he was losing ground. "No further questions."

"You may return to your seat, Awley," said Kevin. Turning to Judge Munger, he said, "The prosecution has no more witnesses, Your Honor."

CHAPTER 26

TRIAL FOR MURDER AND TORTURE: DEFENSE

(September, 1852)

It was time to call witnesses for the defense. Attorney Tomlinson first presented a few members from the leading families to testify to the high moral character of all the young defendants and to the fact that none of them, according to Tomlinson, had ever been in any trouble before. He referred to them with a grand flourish of mixed metaphors, "the finest flowers of the finest families, pure gold, *crème de la crème* of the flock."

Tomlinson started with Benny Johnson and Philo Buckingham.

Tomlinson made much of Benny's Mayflower descent, "the proud posterity of that distinguished, aristocratic man, Governor William Brewster, the best stock this country has to offer, a high-born imbued with great patriotism who cannot bear to see his country over-run with the riff-raff of Europe and Ireland. You were motivated by the highest patriotism, were you not?"

"Oh yes, Sir."

"And you're very sorry it all happened, right?"

"Yes, indeed."

"Have you anything further to say for yourself, Benny?"

"No, you've said it all for me . . . just like you said you would."

Witness dismissed.

Philo was just as unresponsive as Benny and responded to both Tomlinson and Kevin with plain "Yes" and "No" answers.

Gunn Dunlap was also presented by Tomlinson with a genealogical flourish as a scion of two of the most important New England families, the Gunns and Dunlaps. There was no reference to his sister Annie's elopement with Lazarus.

"You had been to a party, Gunn, at a very distinguished home, that of Mrs. Almira Aurelia Humphreys?"

Kevin was sure that Tomlinson wouldn't mention that the reception was given in honor of Attorney Kevin Sweeney and his new wife, Helena Humphreys.

"Yes, Sir," acknowledged Gunn.

"You, ah, helped yourself a little freely at the whisky punchbowl?"

"Who did not, Sir, on that gala day? I remember seeing you in the vicinity of the same punchbowl more than once." Tomlinson visibly winced.

"We were all in a festive mood that day," said Tomlinson. "Now would you say, Gunn, that when you and your friends left the house you were confused?"

"Confused? Why yes, Sir, to an extent, I think we were confused."

"Had anything happened at the party to stir you up particularly?"

"Well, there were some Irish people present and that did stir us up. The idea that the Irish were crashing in everywhere, even into a party given by one of the very best families in Connecticut, made us angry."

"Were you stirred up to the point of wanting to do something about it?"

"No, I think we were only seeking a little action in general."

"Very well. You may have the witness, Mr. Sweeney."

"Mr. Tomlinson referred to your fine ancestry, Mr. Dunlap," said Kevin. "How long have your ancestors been in this country?"

"Why, since the beginning, of course. I mean since Colonial times."

"Can you tell us anything about your great-grandfather, John Dunlap?"

"Yes, he had the great honor of printing the Declaration of Independence."

"Yes, very impressive. From where did your great-grandfather come?"

"England, of course. Famous old English family."

"I am sorry to have to correct you, Mr. Dunlap. My great-grandfather, John Mac Sweeney, happened to be a classmate of your great-grandfather, John Dunlap, at All Hallows College, a Catholic College in Dublin. John Dunlap, printer of the Declaration of Independence, was born in 1740 in Strabane, County Tyrone, in the northern part of Ireland. He came to this country in 1760. He was not an Englishman. Your ancestor, Gunn, was a full-blooded Irishman."

Gunn Dunlap turned an angry pink. "That's not true! It's a base lie!"

"If you wish documentation, Mr. Dunlap, I brought it with me." Kevin drew from his pocket some letters and a book. "Do you wish me to take the time of the Court to read these proofs, or would you prefer to read them later?"

Gunn made a motion with his hand as if to sweep the papers away. Kevin handed the documents to the bailiff and proceeded.

"Moreover, the Gunns are Scottish and Irish, not English. I believe that the tarring and feathering in which you took part was the last that will ever occur here. You admit taking part in the tarring and feathering?"

Gunn was pale and his hands were clinging tightly to the edge of the witness box. "I do admit to taking such a part. I am honest," said Gunn.

"What did you expect to accomplish by such a foul deed?"

"I don't know. It was a wild night and it makes little sense to me now." He kept his head bowed. "It was a very complicated and confused evening."

Kevin quickly asked, "Are those Attorney Tomlinson's words or yours?"

"His but I agree with him," Gunn replied. "The party was strange with lots of people who didn't belong. We took too many drinks to try to forget what was happening to our society. Each person's remarks stirred up the rest and then there was that hell-raising speech. Why hasn't anyone put some of the blame on that speaker? He was the real inciter and instigator."

"Are you implying that there can be inciters among our own natives?"

"I'm not implying anything, I'm just . . ."

"Trying to put the blame on someone else?"

"No! I'll take blame where I have to. I'm no coward."

"Good! Then you admit taking part in the tarring and feathering?"

"Yes, I do." Gunn still clung hard to the edge of the witness box.

"Tell us what happened at the river. You are under oath."

"I don't remember too clearly. I recall the terrible sound of horses bearing down on us. We had to get rid of them somehow and get away . . . so we set them in the grass at the side of the road."

"There's no grass there. It's a steep bank with sparse fern and scrub going down to the river. You say 'we set them.' Who is 'we'?"

"I'll not name them. I set them down."

"You set them down? You didn't give a *push?*"

"I . . . oh, God." Gunn became paler and slumped from view. He was out of sight for a few moments, then was helped out of the courtroom.

Tomlinson now brought Yelverton Perry to the witness stand. Yelverton was a homely fellow, nose too obtrusive, lips too everted, ears that slid into the neck without the articulation of lobes, and a shock of light brown hair that stood up like a brush. He looked upon himself as an amusing and likeable fellow but for the first time, Yelverton realized that it was a deadly game he had played which could yield a death sentence. Tomlinson noticed Yelverton's nervous swallowing. He asked the same questions he had asked Gunn, trying to establish that there was no premeditation and too much whiskey.

Kevin had concluded that Yelverton was the primary force behind the tragic events of July third, imbued with a dangerous mixture of prankiness, irresponsibility, malevolence and inability to admit error. Julia and many in the court sensed that these were the two main adversaries in the trial, the young Irish attorney and the young, fervently anti-Irish Yankee who had activated his hatred into a truly evil force. Whereas George Swayne's hatred was personal towards Dennis, based upon his sister's pregnancy by a lowly Irishman, Yelverton's hatred was diffuse, learned from childhood and all-consuming.

Kevin began, "You started raising cain at an early age, Mr. Perry. Your first recorded act of prowess was with paint at the age of eight. The day before hog farmer Sperry was to exhibit three fat porkers at the Fair, you painted his pigs with green and red stripes. That cost your family a lot, true?" The crowd laughed.

"Yes," answered Yelverton. "An enjoyable childhood prank."

"Your painting habit became a bit more serious when you painted one of Fallopia Cumming's little black pickaninnies white. Dr. Stoddard had a hard time saving the baby from dying of lead poisoning, isn't that so?"

"Sure! I'm an artist from way back." He laughed.

"So you still think it humorous that you almost killed a Negro baby?"

Tomlinson leaped up. "I object to this meaningless past history."

"Past actions may be quite relevant to present behavior," said Judge Munger. "So far we see no necessity of curtailing the prosecutor. Proceed."

"Thank you, Your Honor," said Kevin. "I repeat my question, Yelverton. Do you still think it humorous that you almost killed a Negro baby?"

"I did at the time, yes. Perhaps not now." This time he didn't laugh.

"Later, you took to frightening animals and people. I'm not speaking of releasing a skunk in church one Easter Sunday nor seizing Crotty Hartigan's dog and smearing it under the tail with lye and alcohol so that it ran yelping all over town to your delight. I'm speaking of you at the age of fifteen finding it great fun to hide yourself where the New

Haven Turnpike at Pearl Street in Seymour makes a sharp turn down to the river. You then blew loud horns in order to enjoy seeing horses rear and people fall out of carriages and carts. Is that not so?"

"Yes. No harm done. A boy must have his fun."

"No harm done? Dr. Stoddard treated several cases of broken arms, a fractured collarbone, and a smashed spine that never healed well. Miss Amy Crowfut of Oxford, a very pretty girl, is now a condemned old maid, lying in bed with her crushed spine in an upstairs room at her father's hostelry. High jinks can be carried too far sometimes, wouldn't you agree?"

"Bad things happen. The carriages were badly made," answered Yelverton. Kevin noted that the mood in the courtroom was turning negative.

"More recently you began using fire. Did you laugh heartily when you almost killed Seventh Day Adventists Alex Horbal and his family when they climbed a huge haystack to await the end of the world and you set fire to it?"

"I thought it was quite a clever prank. They were stupid people telling everyone that the end of the world was coming."

"Perhaps it was even funnier when William Meserve invited everyone in Stratford to watch how his newly-invented fire extinguisher could put out the blaze of a large pyramid of branches and timbers assembled on the village green. You had, I believe, emptied out the dousing fluid and filled the extinguisher with kerosene, causing such astonishing flames that it almost set fire to the whole town of Stratford. Did you find that humorous also? Most townspeople didn't."

Yelverton remained silent. He avoided Kevin's eyes.

"Would you agree, Mr. Perry, that it wasn't funny when you climbed to the top of Father O'Laverty's church to proclaim to the world below, 'Look at me! Ain't I the devil?' Then you tore down the golden cross of God and encouraged the destruction of the church by fire which almost killed the priest."

"I object!" shouted Attorney Tomlinson. "Irrelevant and immaterial."

"Prosecutor Sweeney will come to the point," said Judge Munger.

"Very well, Your Honor. We have here a person given to dangerous deeds from an early age, with malignant habits constantly increasing in scope, without a scintilla of care for human injuries or even potential death. Without the slightest remorse, he found no reason to stop. How old are you, Mr. Parry?"

"Just twenty."

"Are you proud of this record of accomplishments?"

"Well, I'm not ashamed of it. I reckon every man in this room has played his pranks, even you attorneys. A man would have to be made of straw and rags, like a scarecrow, if he hadn't cut some capers in his time."

"Pranks are one thing, Yelverton. Destruction—and murder—are quite another. Your wild pranks led, step by step, as if the devil himself had built the stairway, to the actual taking of life without the slightest hesitation. Did you have any qualms when you dragged old Patrick O'Neill from his bed?"

"No! We could have killed him then and there, and Awley and Dennis, too—the whole damned Irish family—but we didn't aim to kill."

"Just like you didn't aim to kill Fallopia's baby, which you almost did. What did you aim to do, exactly, with Patrick?"

"Rid the town of them, the O'Neills. Cleanse the town!"

"Had they ever done anything reprehensible to the town?"

"Yes! Just by being there! Dirty Irishmen in a fine New England town!"

"What do you mean when you use the word 'dirty'? Were they dirty in their personal habits? Was the Inn kept in a dirty manner?"

"You know what I mean."

"The witness will answer the question," said Judge Munger.

"No, they were not dirty in that sense but you can see what a mess the Irish have made of Knockmedown Hill!"

"Have you ever been inside any of the houses in the Irish community?"

"No, but look at the pigs and chickens and laundry hanging on the line."

"Wouldn't wash on the line indicate cleanliness rather than dirtiness?"

"They're dirty Irish just the same! We don't want them here!"

The Judge rapped on his desk to silence the courtroom mutterings.

"So, you are angry with them for fleeing starvation and certain death in Ireland? You took it upon yourself to override the official invitation of the United States government and teach them a lesson? You thought you were doing a great patriotic service to the community and to the United States, was that it?"

Yelverton's cocky expression had long since disappeared. He wanted to get out of the witness box quickly. "I don't think we thought it out exactly."

"So you dragged an old man from his bed, tied up two women and threatened them with rape, tarred and feathered three innocent Irishmen, took them to the river and drowned one of them? Did you find that exciting and fun?"

"Maybe. I'm not so sure but they deserved it, damnit!"

"The witness will be careful of his language," said Judge Munger.

"Who rolled Patrick down the bank?" Kevin asked suddenly.

"We all did."

"You are under oath, Yelverton. All eight of you rolled them?"

"Three had run off. There were only five of us left."

"You don't take personal responsibility for rolling them down to the river?"

"Why should I?"

"Why should you? Although your four companions have attempted to protect you, we have evidence from the two living victims that it was *you* who dumped them. It was *you* who did the kicking and the rolling. Do you deny it?"

The courtroom was tensely silent. Yelverton's ruddy complexion turned pale and the freckles seemed to be protruding from his cheeks.

"I deny it," Yelverton said, looking downwards and swallowing hard.

"Who, then, did kick and shove them?"

"It was dark. How could I know? We all did, all except George."

"How do you know that George didn't, if it was dark?"

"Because he turned pigeon-livered."

"Did he say anything to try to stop you?"

"Yes. He said, 'Let's cut them free!'"

"That's what the O'Neills say, that you and Gunn were the ones who did the pushing and you did the kicking."

"We had to. We had to get the hell out of there. The town was coming!"

"Thank you, Mr. Perry. So it was you and Gunn who actually gave the fatal shoves which sent old Patrick to his death in the river."

Yelverton was silent for a few seconds, then said "Yes" in a quiet voice.

Kevin now placed into evidence the five pairs of shoes the boys had been wearing during the assault. The heavy semi-boots of black leather belonged to Yelverton and fit the wounds found on Patrick and Awley. Yelverton agreed that the boots were his. He left the stand with sagging shoulders and head down.

George Swayne was the last witness. His voice was subdued but he answered Tomlinson's questions readily. Kevin chose not to question him in detail at all, trying to avoid any mention of Sally's pregnancy. George made only a brief appearance and conducted himself well, including obvious remorse.

Julia noted how much less up-chinned his parents looked after three devastating blows to their family pride—their daughter's pregnancy by an Irishman; the discovery that Swayne and Sweeny were the same name in their genealogical history, and George being brought to trial on such serious charges.

On the day of final summations, the court was packed. Tomlinson stressed the sterling backgrounds and blue blood of the boys, their high patriotic motives which became confused by alcohol and crowd behavior. The harm done was accidental, not with malice aforethought. Their families are prepared to make generous amends to the O'Neills. Let them off, Judge, from severe penalties which would accomplish nothing.

Kevin knew that he, as prosecuting attorney, represented an unpopular Irish minority. It was his job to try to stop the hateful evils of ethnic prejudice by setting an important precedent. He must appeal to the concepts of liberty and justice on which the country was founded, not just for a few self-appointed upper crust elites whose credentials were so often fraudulent.

"This is no longer a country inhabited only by descendants of those who fled to this continent on *The Mayflower, The Fortune, The Increase, The Lyon* and other ships that followed in their wake. Most of these people were simple craftsmen, not second-son English nobility as is so often claimed.

"Such origins are nothing to be pompous and superior about. Many of the later and recent immigrants—German, Polish and Irish—are of a background fully as fine as that of the so-called 'native stock.' Such artificial divisions should not matter in a new country like ours. Let everyone start over and prove themselves by hard work and good citizenry.

"In God's eyes, we're all of Adam's race. It behooves us to welcome the newcomer, accept him, incorporate him with kindness and encouragement into the body politic. You can't send him back home. You can't burn him out, flood him out, shut him out or kill him. He's here to stay.

"There are now four times as many Irish in America as there were Yankees in the original Thirteen Colonies. They fought admirably with General Washington to break England's stranglehold and have given us four Presidents—Andrew Jackson, totally Irish; James Polk, Scottish and Irish; James Madison and James Monroe, partly Irish.

"Many other generals and statesmen were Irish including Major General John Sullivan and General Montgomery of the Continental Army. Also Charles Thomson, Secretary of the Continental Congress, Stephen Moylan, aide-de-camp to

General Washington, Commodore John Barry and a number of signers of the Declaration of Independence.

"Most of the accused are friends or kinsmen of my wife, Helena Humphreys Sweeney, and of my brother-in-law, Letsome Wooster. As the designated Public Prosecutor, however, I serve the bereaved O'Neill family and the cause of an oppressed minority. Our community and our young nation must be protected against similar barbarous assaults in the future. It is not the Irish who are on trial. They have all behaved admirably, with restraint and Christian charity.

"These young men must not be permitted to go unpunished. To condone what they have done would only multiply such assaults, such savageries as covering a man's stripped body with pitch and chicken feathers, and murdering one of them in cold blood without any inciting cause whatsoever.

"Tarring and feathering is considered by civilized societies a completely unacceptable form of humiliating feudal punishment, a form of mob vigilante justice akin to lynching. It is totally antithetical to all human values and to the basic precepts upon which our country was founded.

"You have heard, your Honor, the cases of Philo Buckingham, Benajah Johnson, Jr., George Swayne, Gunn Dunlap and Yelverton Perry. It is clear from the evidence that George Swayne pleaded at the river for the release of their victims. He can, therefore, be considered non-implicated in Patrick's death but not exonerated in the torture of the innocent three Irishmen.

"We urge and request, your Honor, in this important and exemplifying case, a verdict of guilty for all five defendants. We recommend for your consideration a less severe penalty, because of mitigating circumstances, for George Swayne, Philo Buckingham and Benajah Johnson.

"It is clear that the two most violent and unforgivable behaviors were those of Gunn Dunlap and Yelverton Perry who actually caused the death of old Patrick O'Neill. They have admitted their guilt and their leadership in these dastardly crimes. As punishment and as a warning to all would-be torturers and murderers of the oppressed who have sought our shores, and as a blow struck against hatred, acrimony and prejudice, towards the making of that distant society where fellowship, humanity and goodwill may ultimately prevail, and where the only remaining prejudice will be a prejudice against prejudice, we advocate the verdict of guilty and application of the maximum penalty."

Kevin had spoken forcefully in a ringing voice, far more impressive than the smug and less convincing oratory of Attorney Tomlinson. No one could deny that Kevin was an effective and spellbinding prosecutor at a young age. He had directed his summation not only to Judge Munger but also to journalists covering the case throughout New England, New York and adjacent states.

A recommendation for the death penalty for Gunn Dunlap and Yelverton Perry had been unexpected. Kevin had reached his decision after long and thoughtful rumination, hoping that the shock of his request as disseminated in the public press would stimulate a reassessment of ethnic prejudice by the average American citizen and, in the long run, lives would be saved and maimings prevented. He knew that Judge Munger's sentences would be more lenient.

The next afternoon, Judge Munger reconvened the Court. "I have given the deepest consideration to this challenging case. Our society's interests must be protected against grievous assaults by those who harbor ill-considered ethnic and racial prejudice. Yet here we have moderating influences. The youth and immaturity of the accused were affected adversely by alcohol, mob behavior and ill-advised parental bigotry instilled in them since earliest childhood, not yet tempered by the moderating influence of adulthood."

My God, thought Julia, he's going to exonerate them. Kevin is going to lose his case entirely despite his brilliant prosecution.

"Although all five defendants are found guilty, the case pleads for a balancing of the scales of justice, for moderation in our sentencing.

"We therefore decree that Philo Buckingham and Benajah Johnson shall be sent to the penitentiary for six months and George Swayne for two months as accessories to the crimes committed and proven in Court. If, after five years, they commit no further offenses against the State of Connecticut or any other State, their names may be removed from the State's lists of felons.

"Gunn Dunlap and Yelverton Perry shall each serve four years in the State Penitentiary for manslaughter, affliction of bodily harm and inexcusable torturing. Because of a notable lack of remorse, the sentences must be served completely, without parole. Each defendant will be considered a felon by the State of Connecticut for the rest of his life."

CHAPTER 27

BAFFLING BLAZE

(October, 1852)

The trial caused significant debate among citizens and in newspapers and magazines throughout the eastern United States about artificial social tiers, fraudulent genealogy, immigration, unnecessary social discord and the evils of ethnic prejudice.

No longer could "best family Yankees" broadcast their arrogant superiorities which, it turned out, were often based upon complete fictions created deceitfully by previous generations. Claims of impeccable aristocracy could never again be made by Johnsons, Buckinghams, Perrys, Swaynes or Dunlaps. The contamination of these supposed pure blue-bloods seemed to touch with a blight many rigid old Colonial families of New Haven County and drove them into embarrassed social silence.

The verdict marked the virtual end of tarrings and featherings, cowhidings and tribal-hate conflagrations in Connecticut, as predicted by Kevin. Such outbreaks occurred elsewhere in the country, however, until the gathering pre-Civil War currents created more widespread conflict of broader import.

Kevin had aroused, even among anti-Irish Yankees, grudging admiration for his effective bearing, outstanding preparedness, courtroom skill and oratorical abilities. The Partners in his law firm, without exception, congratulated him. Several had been present at the summations.

Kevin and Helena had to become more flexible in their social interactions in their new home of New Haven, never quite sure from where their invitations would derive. Their glowing relationship and interesting conversation, with Kevin showing increasing moderation in tone and content, made their company widely sought except by the most bigoted.

Governor Thomas Hart Seymour, perhaps at the prompting of Alexander T. Stewart, appointed Julia as Woman's Chairman of an Accord Committee which he created and staffed with some of the most forward-looking members of various mixed ethnic communities throughout Connecticut. It became a dynamic and distinguished committee, sponsoring lectures on foreign cultures, social meetings of racially different groups, entertainment of prominent visiting foreign dignitaries and many projects for more harmonious living. Julia's prestige mounted with the success of the Committee and with the many invitations extended to her and her husband from the Governor's Mansion in Hartford.

At home on Pearl Street, after catching Submit listening at their bedroom door, Let had had a frank discussion with her about such intrusive behavior and her frequent tactless, often cruel, verbal assaults on Julia. He told her a remodeling of their home would begin soon. She would have an even larger bedroom on the first floor with a sweeping view of the Naugatuck Valley. He and Julia and their enlarging family would occupy the entire upper floor.

Submit, who had been very worried about being transferred to the care of one of Let's siblings, agreed without a peep. She promised to try to decrease the demeaning content of her conversations with Julia but she had little success in doing so. Her beliefs and behavior were just too deeply ingrained.

Let was the middle son of Submit's three sons and had always been her favorite, which is why she chose to live with him rather than with Horace, the oldest, who had a growing family but whose wife was sickly. Henry and Emma lived with Horace and were still in school. Horace was working in a supervisory capacity at a mill in Waterbury. Let was still in his early twenties, the same age as Julia. The three brothers got along very well and hoped to become owner-partners of a mill in Seymour some day.

Let as General Manager of his mill was so bright, hard-working, efficient and popular with his workers that the owners, all over fifty-five, were determined to entice him to stay. Therefore they had given him an option to buy into the ownership of the company over a five-year period with an incentive that they would match his contribution with stock if he made certain production goals. He always easily exceeded those goals.

After Julia had mentioned, at the Daughters of the Star Spangled Banner event, the true profession of Submit's father as a farmer and her husband as a shoemaker, Submit had had a flashback to the final days of her husband's struggle with severe typhoid. Two days before his death, during a lucid interval when he was less febrile, Submit had accused him of not trying to get well.

"You've given up, Albert. I can see it in your eyes."

"Perhaps you're right, Mitty. I think the typhoid is going to win and I am too exhausted to fight much longer."

"You can't desert me, Alfred, with three young boys and a daughter! You've got to conquer this illness. Think of me!"

"Maybe I'm tired also, Mitty," responded Alfred after a moment of silence, "of defending my profession against your constant assaults. You've never understood how good I am as a shoemaker. Shoes have fascinated me since I was a little boy. I have a special feel for leather and an unusual knack for creating shoes, the way Mitch the farrier has with iron and horseshoes. It's easy to be good but not so easy to be the best. I see the possibilities of leather craftsmanship intuitively, like a sculptor, and think I have become the finest leather artisan in all of Connecticut. Everyone tells me that."

"My God, Albert, any lower class male can make shoes. What could be simpler?"

"I've made a good income, Mitty. We have a simple but very nice house. We have four wonderful children and we've lived well. We've even had money left over for you to buy antique furniture but you've always been deeply embarrassed by my profession and your father's also. How did you come by such ideas, that we have humiliated and mortified you with our honest ways of making a living? You've been nagging me almost daily now for fifteen years to go back to school and become a lawyer so we could have better friends and take our place in high society. How can you like such false and arrogant people?"

"Is it really asking too much, Albert? Just a few more years of schooling and we would be as good as anyone! We could move to another town and start over, immediately assuming our rightful place among the gentry. What's wrong with that? We *belong* there!"

"I'm getting weak with arguing, Mitty. I'm not a book person. I'm a happy craftsman who, like your father, gets his joys from his family and from a close relationship with nature. I loved you almost from the first moment we met as teenagers and I continued to love you for many years, Mitty. But the constant haranguing has driven love from my heart, especially after you refused to have marital relations any more after Emma was born."

"We had enough children, thank you, and there was no further purpose in such embarrassing activities. There are many other reasonable ways for husbands and wives to express their affection and leave their dignity intact."

"Well, that unilateral decision on your part was the final tarnishing of my spirit and my soul, and I'm quite content now to exit our beautiful planet before my time. I think my fever is beginning to rise again. I'm so sorry I have deeply disappointed you for so many years. Since we first met, I have always tried my best to please you. Goodbye, Mitty. Be kind to our children."

"There's still time for you to change, Albert! Don't you dare leave me all alone. You can't do this to me!"

Albert slipped into coma that evening and died the next day. No further words were exchanged between them.

Thinking over those final hours of Albert's life, she brought herself back to the present by shaking her head in angry remembrance. After watching him take his last breath, she had sworn a solemn oath that no man would ever leave her again. She had many times repeated that oath to herself, mainly with reference to Letsome. By God, he would never leave her, no matter how tightly his peasant wife wrapped her serpentine coils about him.

Within two months, architectural plans for 28 Pearl Street had been drawn. The upstairs would have four bedrooms. Submit's new bedroom, as promised, was created out of the previous two servants' rooms at the southwest corner of the first floor, enlarged by pushing the entire west wall outwards. A bigger music room was designed similar to a room in the Palace of Versailles with high narrow windows, including two of stained glass. A much larger fireplace was built featuring smooth granite rocks and pebbles from the river. The wide verandah was extended half way around the house with balconies above. A porte-cochere was added at the front for carriages to unload, protected from rain and snow.

The residence was now large, not big enough to be called a mansion but all agreed that it was one of the handsomest homes in Seymour. It ranked with those of the Gunn Dunlaps, Charles Goodyears, Austin Goodyear Days, Henry Beechers and the fire-damaged, now rebuilt home of the Chatfield Swaynes.

Let and Julia continued to show their interest in the community and in every type of person inhabiting it from plutocrats in their cone-towered houses on Washington Hill down to the Irish of Knockmedown Hill and the blacks re-established in safer homes across the river. Everyone knew they had a genuine interest in those less fortunate. Theirs were clearly not the mere self-promotive activities of those who sought admiration through benefactions.

The old complacencies of Submit Swayne Wooster had been shaken. After reflection, however, she decided that she didn't really want to change, although she would try to be kinder and more understanding with Julia. After all, Submit concluded, her own values were tried and true. The gentry always maintained their long-validated standards, come what may, or society would inevitably deteriorate. It was the lesser social classes who must do the adapting.

It was extremely difficult for her to have anything but contempt for the Irish. She was unsure where these feelings came from; not from her parents or any other family member. Whenever she tried to analyze her beliefs about the Irish, modify them or get rid of them, she just couldn't. She was horrified when the O'Neills drove jauntily by in their new buckboard, usually laughing. This particularly offended Submit because she thought it unseemly to laugh in public.

Whiddy Hartigan, the Woosters' coach driver, assumed a new air of confidence since the trial. The town heard about his clever retorts to arrogant Attorney Tomlinson, giving him a good Irish whupping with his savvy repartee. Some Seymour townspeople began waving at him and smiling as he drove by.

This time Julia informed her mother-in-law of her second pregnancy as soon as the diagnosis was confirmed by Dr. Stoddard. Julia and Let were greatly looking forward to the arrival of their second child in less than six weeks. On a September morning when Let had gone to Bristol on a business trip, Julia had just finished putting Alice to bed when she heard Submit scream from the lower hall. She ran along the upper corridor to the stairway.

Looking down, Julia could see flames streaking up scarves and coats on one side of the coat-rack. Submit had been using a camphene lamp despite there being plenty of light in the house. The metal lamp had fallen about four feet from the rack. There were small flames around it. Submit was sitting on the floor staring as if transfixed, making no effort to move or put out the flames.

Julia rushed down the stairs, stumbled and fell down the last six steps. She picked herself up with a wince of pain, grabbed umbrellas from the door stand and used them as pincers to remove burning coats from the rack and hurl them out the door onto the cement driveway. She extinguished the flames around the lamp by throwing a coat over them. All flames were out in less than two minutes. Submit was now sitting on the stairs muttering to herself.

Julia sat down in a soft easy chair in the music room as her abdominal pains got worse. Eliza had heard the commotion and came into the hallway. Julia asked her to go get Dr. Stoddard and tell him that she had fallen and gone into premature labor. Before he arrived, Julia wondered whether the fire represented a conscious or subconscious attempt by Submit to express her hostility at Julia for getting her kicked out of her bedroom, or for revealing the truth about the professions of Submit's husband and father. Why was Submit using a camphene lamp during the day? How did scarves and coats catch fire when the small camphene flames were at least four feet away from the coat rack? Why was Submit, usually so efficient, sitting unmoving on the floor? It was a strange sequence, hard to decipher.

Julia's pains worsened. Doctor Stoddard did all he could but hemorrhaging was profuse. The baby boy was born and survived only a few minutes.

Submit now sat in her chair, repeating over and over: "Oh, Julia. I don't know how it happened. I just don't understand what I was doing with that lamp."

Julia repeatedly reassured Submit that it was only God's will but Julia had difficulty convincing herself of that. When Let put the details together, he said he likewise didn't understand the sequence at all, especially why Submit had lit the lamp in the first place, which she had never done before during daytime. At Julia's urging, they decided that further pursuit of the strange fire's causation would not be productive of harmony at 28 Pearl Street. She told Submit repeatedly that she completely forgave her. No apology was ever forthcoming.

In October, when Julia was well again, Let decided to take her to New York for a holiday to help her forget her grief over her lost baby son. She rarely spoke about the miscarriage but her eyes often misted with tears. Although Submit had been behaving nicely recently, Julia insisted on taking Alice to the

Sweeney home in Waterbury during their week's vacation in New York. Submit objected but was not given any option.

Julia and Let stayed again at Irving House where they had spent their honeymoon. The next afternoon they went to the magnificent Fair of the American Institute at Castle Garden with its mechanical and agricultural exhibits, its dahlias, grapes, sixty kinds of pears, textiles, telescopes, agricultural implements, fire engines and drawings of Fisher's patent steam omnibus which could well be the prototype of steam energy of the future and fascinated Let.

They saw a fine performance of *Hamlet* with famous actor Edwin Forrest. They attended Henrietta Sontag's beautiful concert at Metropolitan Hall. At Niblo's Gardens they saw the celebrated French dancers in *La Fille Mal Gardé*.

One day they went in search of Boutique de Paris at 21 Park Row. The shop's window was filled with lovely creations in bonnetry of silk and straw, fancy basket lace, and double-ruffed satins. "They have lovely hats here, Julia. Buy whatever you want!" said Let.

"I shall just be so happy to see Marcel and Caresse!" There were three clerks and a dozen customers moving about the shop. The clerk nearest the door, very pretty and very pregnant, uttered a squeal and rushed for Julia.

"My darling!" said Caresse loudly. "I knew you'd come to see us some day! How is everything with you and the old town?"

"All goes well but we miss you terribly. You're expecting a child! How wonderful! You look very happy."

"Marcel and I are incredibly happy! He's at the wharf to meet a consignment of goods from Paris. We now make most of our own hats."

"You look so well and happy, Caresse," said Let. "How about the green ruffled silk hat with the pink rose, Julia?"

"It would look like a dream on her," agreed Caresse. "How about coming to supper with us tonight at our little apartment on Courtland Square?"

The evening couldn't have been more pleasant. Marcel and his wife were obviously very much in love. Caresse cooked a fine supper of French onion soup, veal with mushrooms and capers, and peas graced with herbs. They sipped French champagne for hours and talked until well after midnight.

During the evening Julia thought that here, far away in New York, Sally might be an excellent worker in their shop. So she began to tell Sally's story with no names attached. Before she had gone very far, Caresse exclaimed:

"It's Sally! You're speaking of Sally Swayne. It couldn't be anyone else."

"I think she could hide out in New York, don't you, Caresse?"

"Perhaps, but everyone finds you here sooner or later. Every woman in Seymour, with a purse of any size, has been here."

"In January," said Marcel, "we plan to open a little branch shop way up at Fifth Avenue and Forty-Second Street. The town's bound to push up that way. Miss Sally is most attractive and articulate. Why couldn't she be the manager of that shop, Caresse, instead of Mme. Rokard, or have you asked her already?"

"No, dear, I haven't. *C'est bon!* A wonderful idea! If she would like the job, we'll take her and she could stay with us until she finds a place of her own."

On the last day of their stay, Julia and Let visited Alexander T. Stewart's office on Fifth Avenue. Let carried a cardboard box which Julia had filled with beautiful hand-crocheted laces by her and Maggie, Maeva and Moira O'Neill and several other Irish ladies from Seymour. All were done in the lovely County Cork style with shamrocks and roses, some with Venetian point, others with delicate picot filigree. There were pieces for tables, chairs, piano tops and other furniture. They left the box with Stewart's Executive Secretary along with a note:

Dear Mr. Stewart,

You helped the Irish and other inhabitants of our town when we were down and out after that bad storm. You brought smiles to our faces at a difficult time. Colleens don't forget such kindness!

These little crochet items were all made by the Irish ladies of Seymour and their elves, using old Irish patterns and made with our love. We hope they will remind you and your wife of Ireland and the indomitable spirit of the Irish which you represent so well.

Cordially,
Julia Wooster

They walked to their carriage and asked to be driven to the Irish Shanty Town which began at Fifty-Ninth Street and extended to Mount Morris Park, where some five thousand Irish squatters lived in poverty. They presented the picture by which the anti-Irish stigmatize all Irish immigrants—pigs, goats, cows and chickens, washings on the line, dozens of unkempt children and small, poorly-constructed shacks.

Julia stopped to talk with a number of the inhabitants, quickly finding their simple wisdom, resiliency and genius for laughter. Her Irish lilt plus a few words of Gaelic to the older ones, immediately won them over. Let asked a middle-aged man lounging in a broken chair tipped back against his shack, "How goes it?"

"Foine, Sir, foine."

"You look happy."

"Happy? I am that, Sir. I can't find a good job but I'm happier than a king. Happier than Alexander T. Stewart, bedamn! Do you think he can take his ease in the mid-day sun, smoke his pipe, stroke his dog, drink his glass of poteen and dream a dream or two? Ah, no! Poor man, he'll get a stomach ulcer soon. He can have a hundred beds in his mansion down there on the avenue but he can sleep in only one of 'em, just like the likes of me! I'll not be envying him."

On the way back Julia and Let talked of New Englanders' and New Yorkers' driven sense of achievement and the contentedness of so many Irish in meager circumstances. If the aim of life was "the pursuit of happiness", who was more successful? Julia kept laughing over the many Irish witticisms she had just heard.

"A doughty race it is," Let said, also laughing because Julia's laughter was so infectious. "I'm glad I married an Irish girl! They seem so much happier than most other ethnic groups."

"That's what we believe, Let," said Julia. "New Englanders believe that Life is basically grim and not to be laughed at. They set their chins and lips tightly, clench their fists and work hard to 'succeed,' losing laughter in the process.

"The Irish think Life is a laughing matter. Although we don't always succeed, and Life often includes disappointments and sadness, we look at the elves on our shoulders and start laughing. Yes, even in the face of death like the heroic Irish warrior of old, sitting on the battlefield with a large sword-wound to his gut, his blood blending back into the earth, his orange hair wafting in the wind, spending his last moments laughing at Life's ironies.

"I truly enjoy being Irish," continued Julia, "and I do think we have more fun no matter what difficulties we encounter!"

CHAPTER 28

THREE YEAR MONTAGE

(1852-1855)

The rivers of human turbulence in the United States poured into an ocean slowly rising towards the immense surges of the Civil War. The little town of Seymour, surrounded by their hills of Biblical names, looked peaceful on the surface but still manifested its basic tensions. The mansion people went about a little less certain of their status and were more likely to smile down from their carriages at blacks, foreign mill hands and the Celts of Knockmedown Hill.

The Irish a little more sure of themselves, their sense of humor continuing to laugh at life. The O'Neills, confident that through their personal tragedy and the resulting change in attitudes, they would never again be physically attacked. The Irish beginning to get a reputation for patience, humor, forgiveness, gentleness and potential eloquence.

Submit Swayne Wooster, shaken to the bone by all the events which had implicated her friends, her relatives and herself in so many genealogical untruths, lying in bed at night trying to reappraise her life in the Naugatuck valley . . . but unable to do so. New Englanders, her own kin, could be violent and sinful, could take lives but Yankees stay firm and rarely change their minds or their attitudes in hard times or otherwise. Strength is a virtue.

George Swayne sent to prison. Submit, admitting to herself after contortions of conscience that perhaps she had created provocations to try Julia's patience. Not a single word of reproach from Julia over the terrible incident of the dropped lamp . . . how did that happen? Submit didn't know . . . the fall down the stairs, the loss of Julia's baby. Dreadful. It was you, Submit Wooster, who caused the loss of your son's son. Go down, white moon, over the apple orchard . . . leave me in darkness with my thoughts.

Submit, to help assuage her guilt, tells Let and Julia that they need one night a week to be by themselves with their family. She will now be absent from the Pearl Street home every Saturday night, either at the home of Almira Humphreys or Amy Swayne or taking them out to dinner. Julia very surprised and pleased and accepts the offer.

By Christmas-time, 1852, Julia pregnant again and Submit praying to God, hands clasped together in the night, that He would create another son for her son, thus signifying His forgiveness for the loss she had inflicted.

Increasing affection encircling little Alice. Grandmother knitting a fresh red cap for the child's elf-doll, Pooka, created for her by Julia. Grandmother buying pink peppermint so she could slip them into the child's hand. The small red-haired child throwing her arms warmly around grandmother's neck and exclaiming, "Oh, I love you, Gamma." Submit genuinely enjoying the company of Alice and is creative in making up children's games and activities, showing a new side of herself—kindly, thoughtful and playful.

Just before Christmas, Sally Swayne, in the Sweeney household of Waterbury, delivering a son whom she named Dennis Patrick O'Neill, dreaming of a future day when the name might be truly legalized by marriage. Letters announcing the birth sent to the two sets of grandparents.

Quick fervent reply from the O'Neills: "We're marvelously happy. Do bring yourself and little Denny to us as soon as you can and stay as long as possible. God go with you and the bairn. A kiss from us on the top of his little head. Would it be red hair he has?"

No reply from the Swaynes. Amy begged Chatfield to allow them to invite Sally and the baby back for a visit; the answer from Chatfield was "No." A lonely Christmas in the Swayne house, driving Amy to bed with a black headache. George unable to face his post-incarceration mortification in Seymour. Moving to Bridgeport, marrying the first pleasant girl who comes along, a "girl of no consequence," as the Swaynes put it, thus alienating George and his bride.

In February, Sally bringing Denny to the O'Neills at the Tavern, to their unbridled joy, to stay until his mother can find a place in New York and establish herself at the new *Trésorie de Chapeaux* of Marcel and Caresse Boudreaux at Fifth Avenue and Forty-Ninth Street.

In the surrounding world, as the year moved towards 1853, Harriet Beecher Stowe publishing *Uncle Tom's Cabin*, dramatizing the newly relevant cleavages and antagonisms in the body politic. The old nativist hostilities still seething below and above the surface. Ex-priest Alessandro Gavazzi still preaching anti-Popery up and down the East, re-stirring the puddings of hate.

Submit remaining silent most of the time in Julia's presence about the Irish instead of pecking away as often as possible. Julia still heading the Governor's Accord Committee but is a homebody nine-tenths of the time now.

The new little daughter, Emma, born in September, 1853. For the present, then, a God-has-not-forgiven-me granddaughter, thought Submit, in spite of the blonde resemblance of Emma to Let and her own side of the family.

The Know Nothing Party in its final splurge. Victory in New Haven and Hartford. Then their Convention in Philadelphia not only confirming its anti-Irish and anti-Catholic planks but also adopting a Pro-Slavery plank, cutting its own throat in Connecticut and other Northern States.

From Springfield, Illinois, the measured voice of Abraham Lincoln declaring against Know Nothingism in a letter of August, 1855: "How can anyone who abhors the oppression of negroes be in favor of degrading various types of white people like the Irish . . . As a nation we began by declaring that all men are created equal. If the Know Nothings obtain control it will read: 'All men are created equal except Negroes, foreigners and Catholics.'"

Let bringing home liberal magazines and books such as Henry Ward Beecher's *Star Papers*, Arthur Helps' *The Spanish Conquest in America and Its Relation to the History of Slavery*, and Walt Whitman's *Leaves of Grass*. Submit preferring biographies such as Washington Irving's *Life of George Washington* and Rodenhamer's *Diseases of the Intestines*.

Let and Julia, when alone, discussing the new voices, new clamorings, and new tides rising from the dark confluences of increasingly diatribal currents, only vaguely feeling the looming tidal waves of tumult.

CHAPTER 29

Golden Return

(December 23, 24, 1855)

It was two mornings before Christmas, 1855. Maeva was stirring large pots of potato soup and goose gravy in the kitchen. Moira was setting tables and putting a spray of holly at each place while her husband, Whiddy Hartigan, was assisting his father-in-law bringing in the firewood.

Sally, who had come up from New York with little Denny the night before, was adding bright tinsel ornaments to the home-made popcorn garlands and gilded apples already on the Christmas tree in the music room. Three year-old Denny was playing, getting in everyone's way without bringing any scoldings down on his small red head. He had an exuberant personality, abundant zest for life and had brought even greater charm and laughter to the O'Neill home.

Sally had just stepped into the kitchen to say to Maeva, "Oh, do come look at the tree, Mother Maeva!" when the Inn door opened and a loud ringing masculine voice sang out the old Irish Christmas air:

Come buy my nice fresh holly,
And let me home, I pray!
And I'll wish you Merry Christmas
And a happy New Year's Day!

Maeva left the stirring spoons in her pots as she and Moira rushed towards the voice. Sally, feeling her heart race, moved into the corridor leading to inn bedrooms and leaned her head against a clothes rack. She could hear the voice saying:

"Hello! Who be you?"

"I'm Denny!"

"So you're married, Moira, lass?"

Then Sally could hear the joyous sounds as the two women enveloped the speaker with their arms and wild cries.

"Oh, Dennis, Dennis!"

"Don't be crying now. It's only your wayward son returning from the wilderness and coming to spend Christmas with his family. How's Dad?"

"He's fine, darlin'. He's bringin' in the firewood with Moira's husband."

"Who's the lucky man, Moira?"

"Whiddy Hartigan."

"Whiddy? Well, be darned I am! Wonderful that you married a good Irishman! Cute child you've got. Denny he is, is he? Thanks for the naming!"

Sally sank deeper into the clothes hanging from the rack and her eyes became teary. Maeva clutched Moira's elbow and gave her a look which said, "Don't explain anything yet."

In came Awley and Whiddy. Awley was so moved that, as he embraced his son, all he could say was, "God bless you, son, God bless you."

Dennis then gave his hand to Whiddy who looked confident and happy.

"Bring the drinks into the kitchen," suggested Maeva, "so I can get on with my work while we talk. I've got to keep going if the guests are to eat but I'm so bedazed with joy that I'm sure I'll be stuffing the geese with peas and basting the pumpkin with gravy!" Maeva was wondering when and how to bring Sally out of her hiding. She sensed that some kind of a build-towards was needed.

Chairs were drawn around the kitchen table and Awley set down a bottle of whiskey and three glasses, for himself, Dennis and Whiddy. Maeva, her eyes shining now like Christmas stars, resumed her pot-stirring and Moira drew up to the table and started shelling peas. "Well, Dennis," said Awley. "When you care to tell us, we'd be glad to know where you've been."

"Guess!" said Dennis.

"California, we'd be thinking," said Maeva.

"Yes, California."

"You look as if you might have come across a bit of gold dust. That's a pretty good overcoat you're wearing," commented Awley.

"I *have* picked up a nugget or two. I swore not to come back to this damn town until I could cram gold down its throat. Now I have it, by God, plenty, but not from mining. I opened a tavern down by the loading docks in San Francisco and a mighty good tavern it's grown to be. I've saved very frugally. I've come to take you all back to California. It's a grand place to live! My pub needs enlarging and I've built a hotel. We'll run them together. Will all of you come?"

The child caught the excitement. He came up, put his hands on Dennis's knees, looked up into his face and asked, "Denny go too?"

"Why of course, Denny. California's a grand place for a boy to grow up! What a fine broth of a boy he is, Whiddy. Congratulations, both."

Said Maeva quickly: "He's the dear love of our hearts. We all adore him."

"Come lad and sit on my lap," urged Dennis. The child climbed up and began to play with Dennis's gold watch and chain. "It's sunshiny," he said.

"That's good! Sunshiny!" said Dennis.

Dennis gave the boy a sudden tight hug and a thought, deep-hidden, came stabbing up to the surface. What had become of the child that Sally had told him about? She'd aborted it, no doubt, forgotten the whole episode, had a dozen lovers and finally married a rich Yankee. He had learned to avoid thinking about her but it had been no use. Under the scar tissue lay all the warm springs of his tenderness and passion for her and his faith in her finer qualities. "How old are you, Denny?"

"I'm three," Denny answered proudly.

"Three? You can't be three, I'm thinkin'. When were you married, Moira?"

Whiddy blurted it out: "A year and a half ago."

There was a silence from everyone, during which Whiddy tightened his lips and blushed. Dennis smiled. "Well, I'm glad you decided to marry and give the boy a name. He takes after the O'Neills rather than the Hartigans, in spite of you, Whiddy, I'd say. What a cute nephew I have!"

"His name in its entirety," said Maeva, "is Dennis Patrick O'Neill."

"Dennis Patrick O'Neill Hartigan. I'm glad to be figurin' in it with Granddad."

"I didn't say 'Hartigan,'" said Maeva. "His name is Dennis Patrick O'Neill. "

"I don't get it," answered Dennis but his mind was racing.

"Ah, but you're a dumb one," said Maeva tenderly. "You must be Irish!" Everyone laughed. "His father is one Dennis O'Neill and his dear mother is Sally."

Strong emotions flooded through Dennis. He drew a deep breath, then he hugged little Denny so tight that the boy squealed. Everyone held still. The ticking of the kitchen clock became very loud.

"Where's Sally?" asked Dennis.

"Would you be carin'?" asked Maeva.

"I loved her deeply. She was flesh of my flesh and heart of my heart. Then—dear God, I do confess it—I tried to loathe her as I loathed her brother, but I couldn't. I tried to forget. I whirled around with a lot of girls out there but they all turned out to be worthless fluff. Never met anyone like Sally. A wild yet a grand good girl at the heart of her. Damned exciting. Whom did she marry and where did she go after she left Denny here?"

Maeva heard a small sob in the hall. "She hasn't married anyone, Dennis, though she's had her chances, plenty of 'em. She manages a very successful store in New York and the lad stays with her but they come visiting often. Her whole life is centered in the boy and, if I do say so, in the boy's Dad."

"In me?"

"Yes, *you*, you foolish Irish boy."

"You mean . . . she might be lovin' me still?"

"Will you get me my green shawl from the hall rack, I'm a bit shivery."

"Get down, son," said Dennis. He went out into the hall, reached for the green shawl and a coat swayed. He flung it open and there, folded into it, was Sally. It was several long minutes before the two, in happy mussed-hair dishevelment, came sauntering into the kitchen, arms around each other.

After luncheon at the Inn, all the O'Neills, dressed in their best, climbed into a big sleigh, Julia and Let following in their cutter. The group drove to Father O'Laverty's rebuilt Church of Saint Augustine and there the good Father performed the wedding ceremony for Dennis and Sally O'Neill.

Late on the afternoon of the following day, December twenty-fourth, Chatfield Swayne was standing at his living-room fireplace, looking down at the holly-shaped flames. It was the third solitary Christmas Eve since George and Sally had left home. It was nice for Chatfield and Amy that they would be taking Christmas day dinner with Submit, Let and Julia and the two little girls.

Chatfield allowed himself to wonder about Sally. Where was she living now? What was she doing? Hadn't she, after all, inherited her passionate blood from him? There must be, to this day, in Jamaica, a coffee-colored child or two, or rather, grown young people by now, from his pre-marital adventures there in his twenties. Could he ever forgive his daughter for emulating him?

Both joy and direction seemed to have gone out of his life. He thought of the inscription on the tomb of the young Revolutionary soldier in New Haven's Center Church: "His purposes were broken off." What did the gains of the Brass Mill profit him except to put an extra fur tippet around the bejeweled neck of his wife and an extra carriage in the stable? He turned from the fire and headed for his bar to mix himself a mug of Jamaica rum and cider before dinner.

After the first couple of swigs, Chatfield thought he heard a faint knocking at the door. He turned up the whale-oil lamp on the hall table and opened the door. A little boy in a green woolen cap and coat, with a red muffler around his neck, stood there. His green eyes shone in the glow from the lamp as he looked up with a shy smile and handed a letter to Chatfield.

"You Mr. Swayne, awright?"

"Yes. Won't you come in? It's cold and blowy out there."

The child jumped straight up and landed hard on the doormat, the snow on his red-booted feet falling off. He smiled, happy at his little trick. Amy emerged from the dining room at that moment. "Oh, whose son is that? I've never seen him before. Would you like some Christmas cookies, little boy?"

"Yes, ma'am. Thank you."

Chatfield was reading the letter by the light of the lamp. It was written in the swirling dynamic script so well known to him:

Dear Father and Mother,

I was married early this afternoon to my little boy's father who has come home for Christmas all the way from San Francisco. He is the only man I have ever loved. I am very happy but my happiness would be perfect if you felt like welcoming the three of us for a few minutes. It might make it less embarrassing when we all meet tomorrow for Christmas dinner at Cousin Let's. Dennis and I are waiting outside in the sleigh. Just tell little Denny "Yes" or "No". He will give us the message.

Love,
Sally

Tears flooded Chatfield's eyes as he handed the letter to Amy. When she had read it, Amy cried out imploringly, "Oh, Chatfield!"

"My answer is 'Yes!'" said Chatfield.

Amy got down on her knees on a level with the child and took him into her arms. "Oh, Denny. I can't believe it! My grandson!"

"We'll have plenty of time to get acquainted with him and to show him our affection," said Chatfield. "Tell your father and mother, Denny, that we will be very happy to see them. The answer is 'Yes,' Denny. 'Yes.'"

CHAPTER 30

CHRISTMAS DINNER

(December 25, 1855)

Twenty adults sat down at the Wooster table for dinner late on Christmas afternoon of 1855. Six children sat at a smaller table in the adjoining living room—Alice and Emma Wooster, Dennis Patrick O'Neill, Lydia and Llewellyn Kinney's young son, Tristan, and Kevin and Helena's little twin boys. Whiddy Hartigan's mother was called in to supervise this merry, somewhat noisy, table.

Julia noted the immense difference between the atmosphere of this holiday dinner compared to the Thanksgiving celebration in the same room five years before. There was a much friendlier, happier mood and no one spiked the eggnog this time.

Chatfield and Amy Swayne were no longer contemptuous and glacial, their sorrows having leveled their demeanor. Elvira and Gideon Dunlap had directed their personal tragedies inwardly, resulting in personal deadening and artificial smiles. The original humiliation inflicted by Annie was compounded by Gunn's imprisonment and Kevin's dramatic genealogical unveiling of their actual Irish origins. They now heard taunts such as "they're really nothing but Irish immigrants themselves . . . no wonder their daughter ran off with a nigger!"

Contributing to the more pleasant and positive elements of the table were Llewellyn and Lydia Kinney, and Kevin and Helena. Almira Humphreys had died of a stroke in the interim. Julia's parents and younger sister, Maggie, added to the joy of the group, as did Sally and Dennis, Awley and Maeva, Moira and Whiddy. Maggie was two years younger than Julia with a similar joyful face and sprightly sense of humor. She was twenty-three and unmarried. The entire Irish contingent was always happy and brought great laughter to the table.

Julia yielded to ethnic distinctions in her seating arrangement to avoid as much embarrassment and tension as possible. At least Yankees and Celts were all at the same table sharing the same loaves of bread. Julia chuckled inside at the idea of Whiddy Hartigan, the coachman, sitting down at table with Mrs. Dunlap. The Irish imp that so often leaped to her shoulder and whispered in her ear had tempted her to seat them side by side but she controlled the whim. She surrounded Submit, who sat at Let's right hand, with her New England kinsmen, the Swaynes and Dunlaps. She placed the O'Neill and Mac Sweeney parents together. Eliza Hull and two of her daughters served.

The first part of the meal was taken up with Let's blessing, his carving of the geese, and small duo conversations. Let had prepared several topics of benign conversation to avoid anything contentious. The presence of the O'Neills, the tragically injured family, did not conduce to a general feeling of ease.

The superb but embarrassing performance of Kevin at the New Haven trial had not yet been forgotten by the former "first families", recently accentuated by Kevin's being made a partner at his prestigious law firm. His courtroom skill had given a prison sentence to a Swayne and a Dunlap and had probably forever driven them from Seymour. Above all, Let wished to avoid adversarial subjects. Setting down the carving knife, he said in a loud voice:

"Dennis, I think we'd all like to hear some of your impressions of California. You're the only person here who's been to the Pacific Coast. I'd personally like to know what kind of place San Francisco is, what it looks like, what its people are like, whether it's still a rough and rowdy frontier town."

"It's an unusual town, indeed, Sir, the damnedest mixture you ever saw. Wild and elegant at the same time."

"Elegant?" exclaimed Amy Swayne, in a disbelieving tone of voice.

"Yes, ma'am. Elegant. Don't forget that sailing ships bring treasures and people from Europe, London, New York and the Orient. At a ball you see ladies as handsomely gowned, as gorgeously jeweled as any ladies in the world."

"Ladies?" echoed Amy incredulously.

"Yes, ma'am. Fine ladies. Beautiful ladies. I'm afraid you people in the east may think of San Francisco as a small settlement of riff-raff, stevedores and sailors. Not so at all. It's now a town of fifty thousand people from everywhere."

"Fifty thousand!" exclaimed Chatfield Swayne. "Bigger than New Haven! Indeed remarkable in such a short time. Chiefly sustained by the mines, by banking and trade, I presume. Any manufacturing, Dennis?"

"Small-scale, Sir. Peter Donahue has a flourishing foundry and his wife has just bought the first glass coach produced in the city. Shipping and all that goes with it. Huge cattle ranches and farms on the outlying hills. Lots of inns, taverns, theaters, even opera houses. Of course, it's the gold that still stimulates the town. Sixty-five million dollars in bullion shipped out two years ago but there are a hundred thousand men in the mines so that's only $650 per person. That's why I went into the tavern business first and now into the hotel business."

"Is your business already successful, Dennis?" asked Llewellyn.

"It is, indeed. Very rewarding in every way. My tavern, 'The laughing Elf,' which features entertainment on weekends, including dancing girls, is always crowded. My new hotel, 'The International,' has already earned a fine reputation and has a 90% occupancy rate. The city is a wonderful place for people from all over the world to meet on a level playing field. A man is valued for what he is, not for his family's past. It's the truest democracy anywhere in the country."

"Not a bad place for a rising young man," remarked William Sweeney.

"It's the cornucopia of opportunity for the energetic," said Dennis. "There are several men already worth half a million and living in grand style."

"That's interesting," said Gideon Dunlap, rousing himself at last. "Tell us more about the newly rich. Who are they? How did they make their pile?"

"Well, there's James Lick who started life as a carpenter in Pennsylvania, saw the potential of real estate in San Francisco and has already stowed away three quarters of a million. There's William Howard from Boston, a general merchant worth over half a million. There's John Parrott, the shrewd banker, who is now a wealthy land mogul." Dennis hesitated, then took a breath and plunged.

"Another of our leading citizens has made a great deal of money importing and breeding race-horses. San Franciscans are wild about horses and racing. He imports thoroughbreds from Australia, Kentucky and especially Cuba, from where he came two years ago. He and his charming New England wife have a fine home on Rincon Hill where they do elegant entertaining. They are a generous, popular, well-liked couple—Señor Lazaro Santiago and his wife, Annie."

Julia breathed softly and smiled but remained silent.

Gideon Dunlap suddenly asked, "Surely not *our* Annie?"

"Yes, sir."

Gideon's face turned red as he asked, "Are they happy?"

"Indeed, Sir, yes. He has the olive skin of a Spaniard, they speak fluent Spanish and are regarded as a very happy Spanish couple."

"Remarkable," said Chatfield. "Who would've thought a runaway slave with no education could rise so far so fast?"

Elvira Dunlap, who had been doing some of her own gasping and dabbing at her eyes with her handkerchief, now recovered sufficiently to ask:

"Are there any children, Mr. O'Neill?"

"Yes, ma'am. There is one child, a lightly tan little boy, a fine spalpeen."

"A what?" asked Elvira.

"A good lad, ma'am, sometimes a bit rascally. Excuse my Irish!" Kevin threw back his head and laughed.

"You Irishmen are all characters!" exclaimed Sally. "Well, Dennis, you've described a town to my liking—exciting, vibrant, full of new ideas and new opportunities, and an exciting and fun place to live. It sounds great for us!"

"It is that, Sally. It's a grand city but don't be thinkin' it's all good. There's much of the devil there, too, as there is everywhere, even here in Seymour." The group looked around a bit startled but Dennis rushed on. "There are gamblers and drunkards and loose women, 'soiled doves,' they call 'em. There are duels and shootings and cowhidings and murders. That's the other side of the coin."

"That just adds spice to the pudding," said Sally.

"You wouldn't consider settling here, Dennis?" Chatfield put in. "Let and I can make a very good supervisory opening for you at the mill, I'm sure."

"No, thank you, Sir. The West is the place for us. A wonderful area for a new and fresh start, leaving the past behind. That's what I sought and I found it! I'm aiming to make a fortune out there and I'm already well on my way. I'm in the process of planning other hotels. We'll be visiting back and forth, I'm sure. Railroads will soon shorten the transit time dramatically."

"Such visits are good to think about," said Chatfield. "I'd even like to hope the little fellow might be coming to Yale in about fifteen years."

"I intend the best for him and Sally, Sir. I've bought a lot in South Park, the finest new development in the city. I'd intended it for my father and mother but since they've decided to stay here, I'll be building Sally and Denny a grand house there soon. I'll also be buying from Lazaro a pair of horses for riding and, as soon as Sally wants it, a carriage from London. We'll go to horse races, balls, the theater and to the best restaurants in the city. Of all the young women in San Francisco, Sally, you will be the most beautiful and dashing!"

"Thank you, Dennis! It sounds wonderful but I needn't tell you that little Denny and I would go with you if it were nothing but a strip of sand with wolves and Indians peering out of every willow bush!"

"Hear! Hear!" said Let. "A toast to that!" He stood and lifted his glass of Christmas punch and all the company lifted theirs. "A Toast to Dennis and Sally! Their beginning has been somewhat less than they would've wished but they've picked themselves up by the bootstraps and appear to be well launched on a fascinating joint venture! Long may their joy and success continue!"

When dinner was over and conversation dwindling, Let stood up again. "I'd like to offer one more toast, this time to inter-cultural marriages which already are frequent and certainly will become more so, an important hallmark of our wonderful melting pot country. There are three Anglo-Irish marriages at this very table—Dennis and Sally, Kevin and Helena, Julia and I. We should also include Llewellyn and Lydia which is a joining of English and Welsh. Let's pay our holiday tribute to Anglo-Celtic alliances!" Submit visibly winced and her lips tightened but she remained silent.

Julia then stood and said:

"Before we move into the living room and music room for blackberry cordial and brandy, Let and I want to thank you all most enthusiastically for contributing to such a harmonious time together today. We are so pleased you could join us to make this such a special celebration.

"We have said many an English and American prayer since I joined this family several years ago. This year, in honor of the sacred holiday of Christmas, I would like to end our dinner with an Irish prayer which has a lovely universal message." Julia gave it first in lovely, lilting Gaelic and then translated it:

> May the road rise to meet you.
> May the wind be always at your back.
> May the sun shine warm upon your face.
> May the rains fall soft upon your fields
> And, until we meet again,
> May God hold you in the palm of His hand.

CHAPTER 31

WHITE STAG

(October, 1856)

On the last afternoon of October, 1856, Julia and her mother-in-law were sewing together, this time in the beautiful music room which didn't get as much use as Julia would have liked. The children, Alice, now five, and Emma, three, were playing on the floor with their dolls. The sunlight filtered through the stained glass window nearest to Julia's chair. Julia let her mind wander to the lovely Boar's Hill above Castle Mac Sweeney on Sheepshaven Bay in Donegal. Submit's voice recalled her from her reverie.

"Are you daydreaming again, Julia? I wish I knew what you think about when your mind drifts far away. My mother taught me that daydreaming was a waste of time and interferes with getting tasks accomplished. By the way, have you heard any news of young Dr. Tom since he moved his office to New Haven?"

"Oh, yes. I forgot to tell you that he's engaged to Esther Ann Gilbert."

"Of the New Haven Gilberts?"

"Yes. I used to see him standing at the East window of their house staring at Lydia's house across the meadow. He was infatuated even though Lydia never gave him any encouragement. It was smart of him to move to New Haven and start afresh, both medically and socially, after his father died. He did a good job of luring Dr. Steudel from Hartford to take over their practice and buy their house with infirmary attached. Dr. Steudel is a good doctor."

"I thought at one time Tom was becoming interested in your sister, Maggie, in Waterbury after you introduced them."

"Something might have developed, I think, if Lydia had been out of the picture. Now we have to work on finding a husband for Maggie. She's a lovely, loving person full of common sense and laughter."

"Maybe it's time for the Irish to start marrying Irish, don't you think?"

Julia threw back her head and laughed. "Pardon my laughter, Mrs. Wooster, but the Irish like to laugh at every opportunity. As you know, it's not personal. We just think it's more fun to laugh than cry and it's good for the health."

"I used to get annoyed at all of your laughter, Julia, but I must say, once one gets used to it, it can be rather engaging."

Julia was amazed by such a positive statement but could only say, "Why, thank you Mrs. Wooster. That is music to my ears. By the way, children, this is Halloween night, when all the fairies, God bless 'em, come out to play. They're probably dancing in a circle on the hill this very minute. Let's go up to the hilltop and search for the Little Folk."

"Yes, I wanna go," said Alice. "I like fairies."

Submit said nothing. She had learned that it was useless to fight against Julia's fantasies. When the children spill milk at table and Julia refuses to sop it up from the tablecloth, saying: "Leave it for the fairies!" Submit becomes unglued but Letsome abets Julia in her Irish folkloric ways:

"Humor her, mother. Humor her. It does no harm and she's quite sure there are Little People—goblins, elves and leprechauns. They're just as likely as cherubim and seraphim which are mentioned frequently in the Old Testament and once in the New Testament. I've come half to believe in them myself."

The children had been taught to speak of the Little People as if they were real. Grandmother Submit often caught little Alice talking to these invisible creatures. She might even cry out:

"Oh, Gamma, wait! Don't sit down in your chair until Gwynn hops down. He's King of the Fairies, you know."

Submit usually responded with silence and a shaking of her head. In the presence of Alice, however, Gamma sometimes went along with the pretending and took the precaution of brushing her chair off. Once she thought she had heard a high chuckle, like three peeps of a bird, as she did so. She had looked quickly at Alice, whose eyes were wide with wonder.

Julia put green jackets on the children and took them by the hand. "Come now children to the *Mullach na Sidhe*, the Hill of the Fairies, God bless 'em!" Julia had mentioned once that it was bad luck if you didn't speak God's name in the same breath with the mention of fairies. Julia and the two children went out the back door and started up the hill.

Submit sat silently and began to sew again. It was so quiet when those three souls left the house. She realized how lonely it was without them. How lucky she was to have a family surrounding her despite being suddenly widowed at thirty-six, twelve years ago. Although Submit still didn't like the Irish or their Irishness, and still resented their intrusion into quiet, well-ordered New England communities, in her lighter moments she did appreciate the almost perpetual good mood of Julia.

There was no doubt about the profound love between Julia and Let. She had never heard a harsh word between them or anything but the most loving interaction. Let had made a good choice . . . but why did she have to be Irish? Submit still found this a deep embarrassment to herself and her heritage.

Submit put her sewing down and wondered why, for about a week, she had been having intermittent pressure-like feelings over her breast bone. Her medical books suggested an early stomach ulcer or inflammation of her lower esophagus. Drinking milk didn't help; lying down did. The pains sometimes made her face get cold with perspiration. She decided to see Dr. Steudel the next day.

She was restless so she got up and paced back and forth across the living room. The pain began again, this time moving into the left arm. She sat back down. Why, she was thinking, had she never told Julia how much she cared for her children . . . why did she find it so hard to compliment Julia despite Julia being so kind to her? . . . very hard to say in words . . . she even surprised herself when she had made the flattering comment to Julia about her laughter.

She felt cold. She lighted the fire which Julia had set for her. As she reached her chair, a severe pain went through her chest, up to her chin and down her left arm. The room seemed full of darkness stabbed with little sparkling lights like fireflies. She was so tired and light-headed. She rested her head on the back of the chair. Why won't the pain go away this time?

Julia and the children romped up the hill, stopping three times to dance hand-in-hand in a circle and sing an Irish fairy song:

The fairies are dancing
In sun and in bower.
The fairies are dancing
By rock and by flower.
Their steps are so soft,
Their robes are so bright,
As they leap and cavort
In the clear moonlight!

Julia wanted to check on her fern in the granite boulder and show it to the children so they walked past the Pavilion. She had not seen the fern for six months. When they reached the spot, Julia stopped in amazement. The fern had more than quadrupled in size, expanding the crevice and splitting the granite into two separate pieces, inches apart. How did such a gentle fern even survive in such a circumstance, much less breach the integrity of hard, virtually impregnable stone?

By the time they got back to the pavilion, the sun was about to set behind Castle Rock and there were lemon-yellow and orange clouds in the sky. "What a beautiful ending to the day!" said Julia as she and the children sat down on the Pavilion steps. "It's the way all things should end, in beauty."

As always on this summit, she felt the community of hills rippling along the world's continuum, joining this hill to the lush green hills of Ireland. Why were Aengus, God of Beauty, and Lugh, whose necklace was the Milky Way, and all the kingdoms of fairies, elves and leprechauns, not as real as these visions of beauty, as real as the Spiritual Essence, the Druids' name for God?

"Mama!" said Alice, tugging at Julia's sleeve as if she were thinking similar thoughts, "Mamma. You're thinking about fairies. Tell us a fairy story."

"Which one, darlin'?"

"The one about Niamh of the Golden Hair."

"Very well, then. There was once in olden times a prince name Oisin who was a bard, a man who goes singing lovely songs down the road of life. One day's end, at sunset time like this, Oisin was walking through a meadow singing when he came to a beautiful lake. At the lake's edge, leaning against a tree, he beheld the fairest woman he had ever seen standing next to a white horse. She had long golden hair reaching to the ground. As he approached, the woman said:

"'Good evening, Sir. You are far from home. May I give you a lift on Silverhooves? Perhaps we can stop at my home for a rest on the way.'"

"'What a lovely idea.'"

"She helped Oisin onto on her horse, then leaped up to the saddle as if she were made of petals and feathers. Then she said something to the horse in a tongue Oisin had never heard before."

"Oh, what did it sound like, Mother?" asked Alice.

"Like tiny sea waves breaking softly on a pebble shore. Silverhooves walked out onto the lake, not sinking at all, making fans of water like a skimmer on a pond. When he came to the lake's very center he stood still and the waters smoothly rose over them. Soon his hooves touched on a pale green marble floor on the lake bottom.

"Oisin found himself in a beautiful green palace all shining with a thousand jeweled lamps, with gardens all around where sea flowers of pink and blue and wondrous purple moved gently back and forth in the water. Niamh herself shone with a strange light. She held out her arms to him and said:

"'A thousand welcomes to my palace. I love you, Oisin.'"

"He replied, 'Now I know this is the land of fairies. I shall never see my own home again, yet I love you, Niamh of the golden hair.'"

The children's eyes shone in the sunset light and they clapped their hands excitedly. "Go on, Mother. Go on!" said Alice.

"So they lived happily together in Niamh's palace for three hundred years. Then one day Oisin heard Silverhooves stomping so he went to his stall. The horse was restlessly tossing his mane and pawing the stable floor. Oisin saddled him and leaped on his back but, instead of taking Oisin on a ride through the gardens of sea-flowers as was his habit, Silverhooves swam up, up, up through rainbow-colored bubbles until they came to the surface. Then they flew through the air like a flying fish until the horse's silver feet came down thud! on a little strip of shore bordered by bulrushes.

"Oisin tried to jump down from Silverhooves' back but his legs felt strange and full of aches, so he got down very slowly. As soon as he touched the ground, lo and behold, a long white beard sprouted from his chin and his hands grew old and gnarly. He turned to remount Silverhooves but there was no horse there at all.

"Oisin walked slowly along the road to the house of his father and mother. There were six strange children playing in the yard. He knocked on the door and a young man opened the door."

"'Where are my father and mother?' asked Oisin."

"'And who may you be?' asked the young man."

"'I? Why, I'm Oisin.'"

"'Oisin? Your brains must be daffy, old man. Oisin was my ancestor who disappeared many generations ago. He walked away singing one day and was never seen again. Our bards sing that Oisin was carried away by the Fairy Queen,

Niamh of the Golden Hair, on her white horse to live in her beautiful palace under the lake.'"

"'The story's true,' replied Oisin. 'Always believe what the bards say!'"

"Is that all, Mommy," cried Alice. "Did Oisin live happy ever after?"

"Yes, to the rest of his days, he was happy making other people happy, singing lovely songs about the land of fairies under the deep green waters." Julia did not have the heart to tell them of Oisin's rapid ageing and early death.

"Will I see Niamh's Fairy Lake someday, Mommy?" asked Alice.

"Of course, darling. The Fairy Lake can be anywhere you wish it to be. It can be the little brook or the meadow pond or the Naugatuck River singing down there at the foot of the hill. Fairies are everywhere. You only have to open your second pair of eyes, behind the eyes you see with, to find them."

"I think they're everywhere," said Alice.

"Me, too," said Emma.

"Let's sit very still, then," said Julia, "and see if this is their evening to appear at sunset time."

They all closed their eyes.

"M-m-m-m . . . I think I hear their wings," declared Alice.

Yes, there was magic everywhere, thought Julia, like a shimmer of ever-present beauty if only one takes the time to become aware of it, quieting one's soul and sitting very still. A minute later, through the silence came a gentle sound of breaking twigs from the little hazel thicket down the slope where Julia had discovered water. From the shadowy bushes into the scarlet twilight sprang a small white stag with a miniature but fully-formed rack of horns. Julia watched the deer in astonishment. Alice cried out, "Look, Mommy! A white deer!"

"Where? Where?" cried Emma.

The white stag turned, waited a moment, then pranced quickly down towards the house and disappeared under the apple trees. A shiver ran through Julia and she stood up. "Come, children, come quickly! We have to head back."

"Oh, but I like it here, I like it here," pleaded Alice.

"I know, darling, you're a true Celt. You have the feel."

"The what, Mommy?"

"A special fairy sense. Come, girls. Lugh's Chain will be glistering overhead soon and we must be hurrying home."

CHAPTER 32

VENOM AND LAUGHTER

(November, 1856)

Julia walked rapidly down the hill following the path of the white stag. The children had to run to keep up. A palpable shadow enfolding the house came out to meet her. She headed directly to the living room where she found Submit slumped in her chair. Her face was pale, cold and moist but she was able to respond feebly. She described the powerful pain which had subsided but left her light-headed. Julia slid her down to the floor, covered her with a blanket and called to Eliza to watch over her while she went to fetch the doctor.

Dr. Steudel followed Julia back to the house, examined Submit and said she had had a small heart attack. He didn't think it was life-threatening and he thought she would get well faster at home than in his infirmary.

Julia's mother, Mary, came up from Waterbury to help with Alice and Emma. Submit felt listless and drained of energy. Dr. Steudel was optimistic as was a New Haven Consultant, but Submit was sure she was going to die. Every day she asked Let and Julia to do little tasks for her in preparation for her imminent demise.

One week passed uneventfully. One afternoon Julia sat down in Submit's favorite chair next to the west window. As she watched the children at play outside she let her thoughts rest briefly on Seymour and its intriguing inhabitants. So many hostilities were still lurking, like spitting cobras, in this seemingly peaceful valley but she had noted a slow change in attitudes which had been claw-sharp when she arrived six years before. Even Submit was a little less acid and spiteful but she was too steeped in pride, arrogance and pervasive feelings of superiority to change much.

Although it took a lot of tenacious dredging, Julia had discovered hints of a few positive attributes in Submit—strength of character, self-control in times of stress, a tenacious work ethic. From a New England Yankee perspective, she was a solid rock of an Anglo-Saxon woman. The hate-driven denigrations occurred with lesser frequency but were still venomously anti-Irish.

Julia's mother, Mary, had been in the kitchen making tea for Submit and now walked past the living room towards Submit's room with a tray. "I'll be back in a minute, dear," she said quietly to Julia. "I'm not dressed for the ice age so I won't be staying long." They both laughed.

Mary soon returned and sat down across from Julia. She had a smile on her face and then broke out laughing.

"I can't believe what I just heard! Submit was talking to Let and several times told him she was sure she was going to die and had been reflecting on her life. She went on and on with her pre-death philosophizing. She apologized to him more than once for being so inflexible and hoped she hadn't been too unpleasant a member of the household. Then she started talking about you."

"'I wish I had been more kind to Julia,'" she said. 'I truly thought she was a barbarian, that all Irish are barbarians—unwashed, uneducated, spending their days feeding garbage to their pigs.'"

"Barbarians!" Mary said. "Can you believe it? We are uncouth barbarians!" They both broke out into loud laughter.

"She must visualize us wandering around naked eating bananas and pounding our chests like gorillas!" They laughed heartily.

"That really is quite amusing," said Mary. "I've never met a barbarian but I do know that English soldiers often behaved like primitive savages when they were trying to destroy Ireland and our wonderful culture. Perhaps we should have barbarian costumes made and, after Submit has recovered, sit down to dinner in our prehistoric attire!"

"Great idea! What kind of noises do barbarians make—grunts and groans, howls and yowls?" asked Julia. They laughed.

"Do I laugh a lot?" asked Mary.

"Yes, definitely. You earn the Laughing Trophy wherever you go."

"Then I want to be called 'The Laughing Barbarian!'" More laughter.

"There's more to tell," said Mary. "Submit kept repeating to Let how sorry she was that she had never apologized to you for her many cruel remarks and unkindnesses. She wanted to but just couldn't. 'Oh, Let,' she said. 'I feel terrible about it and now it is too late . . . I feel the scythed chariot coming for me. Be sure to tell Julia. She is so kind and patient with me and I finally see what a wonderful wife she is for you. God forgive me. I realize now what a shining personality Julia has . . . almost luminous!'"

"Did she really say 'luminous?'" asked Julia.

"Yes, 'luminous!'" They laughed.

"That makes me either a Luminous Pig or a Luminous Barbarian," said Julia. They both slapped their thighs and laughed hard.

"Since you're in such a laughing mood, Julia, I have another piece of news to give you."

"I love news . . . especially when it's juicy gossip!"

"Well, this is not gossip but it's delectable all the same. Have you found anyone to introduce as a beau to Maggie?" asked Mary.

"No, I have scoured Seymour and can't think of anyone—animal, vegetable or mineral!" They laughed.

"You can stop looking," said Mary.

"Why? Has she suddenly gotten smart and decided to stay single?"

"No, she just got engaged."

"Engaged? Without dating anyone? Did she hire an Astrologist and Marriage-Arranger from Ceylon?"

Mary smiled broadly. "No, she has been secretly dating a Waterbury widower with three children for a year and just accepted his proposal a week ago. They plan to be married on Christmas day. Then neither one can forget their anniversary!" They both laughed.

"Who? You must tell me who!"

"Horace," replied Mary.

"Horace who? Horace Ingelfinger, the milkman?"

Laughing, Mary replied, "No, Horace Wooster."

"Let's older brother? Wow! Are you kidding me?"

"It's true! They fell wildly in love almost from the beginning but decided to keep it a secret until their love had matured."

"Incredible! I'm thrilled! I love Horace! He's handsome, bright, interesting, hard-working, loyal and is certainly not made of icy granite like his mother! And he's had a difficult time for the past two years raising three children after his wife died of breast cancer."

"Yes, and like the two other Wooster boys, he's very successful in business. He's already General Manager of Waterbury Brass Mill," added Mary. "I'm sure the three Woosters will eventually own a mill together, probably right here in Seymour. It's definitely in the cards."

They both remained silent for a few seconds, then Julia started laughing louder and louder. "Oh, Mother, it's just too scrumptious." I'm going to savor this extraordinary news for a long time—a true Epicurean delight! Another paddy invasion into the Land of Woosters!" They both laughed loudly.

Julia continued. "Can you imagine Submit now having two Luminous Barbarians in her family?" They laughed without restraint.

"God must be Irish!" said Mary.

"Erin go Bragh!" added Julia.

Their laughter rocked the foundations of 28 Pearl Street and they both had tears in their eyes as Let walked into the room with a smile on his face, happy with all of the laughter resounding through the Wooster home.

APPENDIX 1

ORIGINAL 1961 PREFACE BY

JULIA COOLEY ALTROCCHI

This is the story of my Irish grandmother who married in Connecticut and lived in a difficult and tense relationship in the same house in Seymour with a viciously prejudiced and often cruel Yankee mother-in-law for decades. She eventually made an honored place for herself in an exceedingly narrow-minded and intolerant community. She lived in such extraordinary affection with my grandfather, Letsome Terrell Wooster, that, when he died In 1908 at the age of seventy-eight, she died only a few days later of a broken heart.

As in a painting, landscapes and features of this historical novel are slightly altered for flow of story but most of the material is completely true. I have tried to be attentive to historical accuracy of content and calendar. I am deeply indebted to the scholarly material of two books by the dear, silver-haired friend of my childhood—author and publisher William C. Sharpe who wrote *Seymour Past and Present*, and *History of Seymour, Connecticut.* These books authenticated many of my own recollections and supplied invaluable background material.

Although I was brought up in Chicago by my Yale father and Vassar mother, Helen, the third daughter of Letsome and Julia Wooster, I was born in Seymour and spent every summer there up to the age of fifteen living in the home of my grandparents. So I am intimately familiar not only with Wooster household interactions but also with Seymour and its intriguing cast of characters, some of whose names I have changed because of the negative details involved, particularly with regard to severe racial prejudice against the Irish, recent foreign immigrants and blacks.

I have used the actual names of non-controversial persons as in the case of Dr. Abiram Stoddard, of whom a hundred dramatic tales were still told in the Naugatuck Valley in my childhood. Also, because my grandfather, Letsome Wooster, was an innovative and prominent metals manufacturer, I use the real names of other Naugatuck Valley manufacturers whom I often met as a child.

Eunice Mauwehu, the Indian woman, was a real person as were "Pitchfork" Sanford, father of the blacksmith, and the rabble-rousing "Angel Gabriel". William Hull, grandson of the illustrious Commodore Isaac Hull of *Old Ironsides* fame, was my grandfather's hired man, and Tribulation Cumming did indeed go through life with that flavorful name.

Seymour was a community I deeply loved and many of its people, good and bad, were my own kinsmen. Seymour and its lovely environs still shine for me with the glow of morning and all its hills remain enchanted in my memories, particularly the hill above the Wooster home.

If some feel that I have over-dramatized racial prejudice in a small New England town, I haven't. I lived those prejudices, saw them first hand and felt them intimately. Close family friends and members of my own family were some of the perpetrators, others the victims.

If some think I have exaggerated certain aspects of the Irish character, for instance their abundant laughter, their ability to laugh at life's ironies, good and bad, and their mystical sense,

I plead innocent. All those qualities are abundantly present in Irish citizens, Irish friends, and members of my family as observed personally by this one-quarter Irish author both in Ireland and the United States.

Little needed to be invented when there was so much nativist, anti-foreign clash and clangor up and down the valleys of New England in the mid-1800s. There was certainly ample drama, often unpleasant, surrounding my Irish grandmother trying to live in harmony with icy cold, arrogant, prejudiced Yankees into whose eminent domain she had intruded by marriage. The story of her life illustrates what may be accomplished by patience, understanding and love doing battle with battalions of adversaries harboring inbred hate.

I wish to acknowledge gratitude to my cherished mother, Nellie Wooster Cooley who, while loving her own mother dearly, was deeply embarrassed by her Irish origin. Throughout her life, she suffered a profound ignominy of being half-Irish. This was an internal trauma needlessly inflicted by years of brain-washing during childhood and adolescence by her proud, full-of-hate grandmother, Submit Swayne Chatfield Wooster, who lived in the house of Letsome and Julia Wooster for almost fifty years spewing forth her venom.

The power of Submit's poison lessened somewhat over time but it was a powerful, insidious influence over all of her descendents to the end of her days in 1898 at age ninety-two. My mother wasn't born until nine years following events described at the end of this book and yet she was deeply anti-Irish all her life. She never spontaneously told me that my wonderful grandmother was Irish. It was a dark family secret. After the hush-hush truth finally emerged, it was many years before she gave me permission to write this book about her mother.

I wish to render thanks to Mr. A. G. Wentworth, former President of the Seymour Manufacturing Company, of which my grandfather, L.T. Wooster, became owner along with his two brothers, Horace and Henry. He gave me much valuable information and hosted my visit to the factory in November, 1955. He also gave me a very helpful book, *The Brass Industry* in the United States by William G. Lathrop. I have also been helped by several librarians and archivists of Yale University, Yale Law School and the City of New Haven.

With gratitude and laughter I thank Patrick Mc Sweeney of Coolea, County Cork, Ireland, Head of Clan Mac Sweeney, and Patrick Mac Sweeney of Macroom, County Cork, for abundant fascinating material about the family and ancestors of my grandmother, most graciously given to me in 1956 when I visited all the houses and castles in Donegal and Cork connected with the family.

I am also grateful to Ruth Wooster of Seymour, the charming cousin of my mother, for many letters containing her recollections of the family. Finally, I greatly appreciate the help of my own valued cousin, retired Waterbury manufacturer, Wooster Canfield, for his contributive recollections concerning the golden summer days of our childhood spent at the Seymour home of our grandparents and great-grandmother, the protagonists of this book.

Julia Cooley Altrocchi
Berkeley, California,

1961

APPENDIX 2

A Connecticut Lady and Her Irish Daughter-in-Law in the 1870s

by Nellie Wooster Cooley

Preface to Nellie's Notes by
Julia Cooley Altrocchi (1961)

I recently found among some family papers this sketch written in the form of penciled notes by my mother (Helen; Nellie) in 1945 when she was eighty years-old. The subjects of the sketch were:

1. Submit Swayne Chatfield Wooster, a major protagonist of this historical novel, whose virulent anti-Irish prejudice had a major influence on the next three generations of her descendents including one of her granddaughters, Nellie Wooster Cooley. This book ends in November, 1856. Nellie was born nine years later, in 1865. The striking anti-Irish prejudice of Submit was in full force throughout Nellie's childhood and young adulthood.

2. Julia Adelaide Sweeney Wooster, Nellie's mother, the other protagonist of this novel, who was forced into intimate contact with the malignantly prejudiced Submit Wooster from the moment Julia married

Letsome Terrell Wooster in 1850 until Submit's death in 1898—forty-eight years of persistent, in-house, hateful verbal abuse.

Because of her penetrating hatred of the Irish and Ireland, instilled by her Yankee grandmother's frequent venomous comments, Nellie could not force herself *ever in her life* to write out the words "Irish" or "Ireland". She always wrote or typed these words: "I . . . ." and "I . . . . . ." For clarity, these words have been fully spelled out in the following text.

1945 Text by Nellie Wooster Cooley

The soul's tragedy which I am about to relate, which blighted the lives of four gifted girls, could have found its essential ingredients only in New England in the middle of the 19th Century. No other country, no other time, could have furnished the *dramatis personae*, the prejudice, pride, bigotry and hatred which laid their smothering hand upon what seemed to be a happy family, a family outstanding in the community, sure of its solid background.

The avenging fate was a paternal grandmother famed for her beauty and elegance. In a conspicuous degree the Puritan virtues of piety, industry and thrift were hers. She was proud of her ancestry, whose names made bright the military, political and educational history of her State of Connecticut.

Submit Chatfield's great-great grandfather, George Chatfield, was a settler of Guilford and Killingworth, Connecticut, whose ancestors were armigerous gentry of Chichester, Sussex, England. Submit was immensely proud of this family background and she always kept it in the forefront of her thinking.

Around the life of her second son, my father, Letsome Terrell Wooster of Seymour, Connecticut, this story spirals. His father, Albert Wooster, died of typhoid fever in 1844, when he was thirty-six years-old. My father, born in 1830, was fourteen at the time. His older brother Horace was seventeen, Henry was twelve and Emma was ten. Upon the two older boys fell very early the burden of supporting the family.

Having to give up the college education they both coveted, Horace and Letsome sent Henry and Emma to the best prep schools and colleges in the state. Meanwhile, by widespread reading and studying by himself at night, my father became widely informed on history, philosophy, religion and the natural sciences. He became the respected peer of his associates on the Board of Trustees of one of our great New England educational institutions, Wesleyan University in Middletown, Connecticut, on whose Board he served for many years.

He was trained in metallurgy trade schools and was a chemical engineering genius, gaining a worldwide reputation for his inventions of new metal alloys for household silverware. After many years working his way up in management of Seymour Manufacturing Company, he and his brothers, Horace and Henry fulfilled a lifelong dream of owning and operating a metal manufacturing company together by buying the company. Letsome always made money and was very generous in his monetary gifts to civic institutions.

In 1850, at the age of twenty, he married Julia Adelaide Sweeney who was fully Irish, born in Waterbury, Connecticut. He took his bride to the beautiful home he owned. Unfortunately, the other occupant was Letsome's mother, Submit, a lifelong mother-in-law arrangement which was supremely difficult for Julia until Submit died forty-eight years later.

Letsome's hobby was books and his bedroom walls were lined with bookshelves. Her major hobby was her garden. Everything grew and blossomed under her special touch.

The marital joining of Letsome and Julia was ideal. The ardent love of my Father and Mother was magical. Their romance lasted throughout their fifty-eight years together. I never heard an impatient word from either towards the other nor saw so much as the tiniest facial expression indicative of annoyance. Each had the profoundest respect for the other. My mother outlived my father by only three weeks, dying of a broken heart.

My father was tall and blonde with hazel eyes. My Mother matched him in height. Her hair was black with a blue sheen, and her eyes were the bluest I have ever seen. She was the second daughter of an Irish scholar, William Sweeney, who wrote and spoke Latin fluently. He was educated at All Hallows College in Dublin and was preparing to take an advanced degree and become a priest but broke with them because of their rigid dogma.

William had fallen in love with an attractive and witty girl, Mary Canty, of Macroom, Cork, where they both lived. They married and decided to start a new life in the United States. He worked in the textile industry as a chemical dyer, first in Hudson, New York, later in Willimantic and Waterbury. They had three daughters and a son. This grandfather of mine died before I was born in 1865. My father greatly respected him for his character, intellectual strength and scholarship. The positive things he had to say about William constitute one of the pervasive memories of my childhood.

From my mother's mother, Mary Canty Sweeney, I learned the stories of *The Arabian Nights;* the tales of

Haroun-al-Raschid, the Great Caliph of Bagdad; the wonderful tales of King Arthur, Sir Launcelot and Guinevere and Sir Galahad; the sad and thrilling account of Roland at the Pass of Roncesvalles that always made me cry; the true story of Charlemagne; and of the great services of the Irish monks in helping establish his schools and keep alive the spark of learning in Europe during the Dark Ages. From her I learned all the fairy stories I know. I learned of the ways of reason and the dear joys of unreason. No wonder the Irish see leprechauns!

My completely Irish grandmother died when I was seven years old. I was desolate. Now, so many decades later, I still feel the world is despoiled of some of its rare poetry-of-life and happiness because of her passing. She was beautiful and her daughter, Julia, inherited her beauty. The memory of Mary Canty Sweeney's larkspur-blue eyes and merry smile-crinkles about her mouth is vivid and ever-close to the surface of my mind and my soul. Of what clothes she wore I have no recollection, only of her lovely laughing personality and loving nature.

The picture of my austere and proud New England grandmother is a colorful but distressing portrait of detail, more negative than positive. She wore black silk, poplin, bombazine or alpaca, voluminous skirted dresses, a black onyx cameo brooch wet with pearls, lace shawls over which lace-mitted hands were piously folded, lace bonnet with string tied under the chin, and roses half hidden with lace tucked under the brim. Sometimes she wore a Persian shawl with black center and elaborate border. All these fancy trappings were accessories of decorum and dignity, austere symbols of importance calculated to inspire reverence and awe in the younger generation. Even the masterful lifting of a petticoat or the graceful wielding of a fan put a self-installed halo about her.

After years of study of human beings, I realize now that this grandmother not only had pride of race but personal vanity and arrogance in a high degree. Grandchildren, however, were not supposed to follow suit. When I tapped on her door one church-day in my Sunday Finest, to show her my new dress and hat, she instantly replied with a frozen hostile face: "Handsome is as handsome does." How one acts is more important than how one looks. I felt cruelly rebuked and the hurt of that rebuke has not yet healed.

I did not love my grandmother, Submit Chatfield Wooster. It was very hard for anyone to do so. Yet she dominated me and my sisters, implanting in all of us a life-long hatred of our half-Irish ancestry, an embarrassment which reason, study and experience have never expunged.

I thought my baby sister, Theresa (Tessie), was the most beautiful child in the world. I remember asking my father once, "What would you do, Daddy, if she should grow up to be *Irish?*" He just laughed and laughed. I couldn't understand how he could be so flip over such an important question.

How was this prejudice implanted in my childish mind? By endless, never-sleeping hostile innuendoes and spiteful criticism of my mother by my Father's mother. Was there no offsetting testimony? Plenty but it carried no weight against the constant barrage of slings and arrows of outrageous anti-Irish fortune.

My mother's older sister, Mary, also lived in Connecticut. She manifested every adjective characteristic of the Celtic race—happy, charming, laughing, mercurial, full of imagination and delightful fancy. She was proud of the great stone Canty family house in Macroom on the River Lee in County Cork, which included a number of cottages and retainers. She had inherited that small estate which became presided over by her aristocratic unmarried daughter. Mary was the repository of family tradition. The original name was "Mac Sweeney". The family descended from ancient Irish kings, particularly the royal O'Neills, the ancient lords of Donegal.

Although Aunt Mary lived in an imposing Connecticut house, and although her husband, John Cowell, had represented their Democratic constituency many times in the Connecticut Senate, her influence bore no constructive weight against the constant anti-Irish attacks of my relentless New England grandmother. The deeper my mortification grew, the more passionately became my devotion to my mother. Of her beauty and grace and graciousness I was extravagantly proud.

Is there no other testimony in favor of that despised drop of Irish blood? Yes, one intriguing item. My father's older brother, Horace, married, for his second wife, my mother's younger sister, Margaret (Maggie). They had one child, Walter Wooster, a mathematical genius despite his half-Irishness, who worked out problems in college in new ways unknown to his professors. He himself became a teacher and tutor, preparing boys for college, and was enthusiastically admired by generations of grateful pupils. His two half-sisters and half-brother, 100% Anglo-Saxons, were of ordinary intelligence and lived the commonplace, conventional lives of well-born New Englanders.

I well remember the supercilious way in which my grandmother, Submit Chatfield Wooster, in the course of a Saturday drive, called Tessie's and my attention to a group of Irishmen working on the railroad tracks which skirted the Naugatuck River. "Look at those dirty Irishmen digging the railroad," exclaimed Grandmother, pointing with a mitted hand. "*Our* people won't do that kind of low-down work! And they live in shacks down by the river, just like pigs!"

A whole race, with all its history and culture, was discounted in that gesture and comment, revealing not only her immense ingrained prejudice but also the ignorance of the commentator. Similar anti-Irish comments by Submit had to be endured by my beautiful Irish mother on a constant basis for forty-eight years, most of her adult life.

Tessie and I were preparing ourselves for Vassar at the Birmingham (now Derby) High School ten miles from our home, whither we were driven by carriage each morning with our lunch baskets. On my return home one afternoon I discovered that my precious mother was depressed. I rightly surmised that she had been once again subjected to verbal attack by her mother-in-law. As I left for school the following morning, I went to my grandmother and said:

"I want you to make my mother *happy* today."

"Miss Impertinence!" said she, with the cold blue ice of her glacial eyes penetrating me.

From that day we were enemies. She, the aristocrat, was afraid of her twelve year-old grandchild! How she hated me . . . and how proud I was to be hated by her! And yet she had successfully instilled in me a lifelong hatred of the Irish and my own half-Irish blood, a hatred I have never been able to shed.

Additional Commentary by Julia Cooley Altrocchi

Submit Chatfield Wooster was inordinately focused and proud of her "armigerous gentry" ancestors. I have checked her genealogy and, indeed, her great great grandfather, George Chatfield, an immigrant settler of Guilford and Killingworth, Connecticut, had distinguished noble ancestors from Chichester, Sussex, England. How Submit became so incredibly obsessed with her supposed pure, upper class ancestors has never been clear to her descendents.

Those who concentrate so intensely on their esteemed upper class pedigree often are quite blind to those of their remote ancestors or current relatives who don't live up to their desired heraldic standards. Submit was no exception to this "rule of selective genealogy" which demands, when one doesn't know which Robert Taylor was a direct ancestor, that one always choose the castle-owner on the hill rather than the peasant farmer in the valley who scratched a meager livelihood from the rocky soil.

Submit was widowed at the age of thirty-six. After their deaths, Submit was never heard to mention either of these two men:

(1) Her father, Joseph Chatfield, who was a full-time farmer.
(2) Her husband, Albert Wooster, a shoemaker.

Both Joseph and Albert were wise, able, successful and philosophical men, but their occupations, which Submit felt were lower-class, precluded each of them from conversational inclusion by Submit ever again after their deaths.

The extent of Nellie's anti-Irish conditioning by her New England Yankee grandmother was made manifest in many ways, chiefly, perhaps, by her determination to rise above "the ignominy", as she regarded it, of her half-Irish ancestry by achieving social distinction, which she did:

(1) She never mentioned her Irish background at Vassar and became President of her Class of 1886 for life.

(2) At the 50th Anniversary Celebration, in 1911, of the Founding of Vassar College in 1861, she was chosen to lead the Parade of Distinguished Alumnae through the campus, an honor which would have been impossible if her half-Irishness had been known.

(3) She became President of every one of Chicago's municipal and social clubs of which she became a member, e.g., the Chicago Woman's Club and the Chicago College Club. She was frequently written about in local magazines and newspapers which featured her photo and background, never mentioning her half-Irishness.

(4) She was appointed by several Governors of Illinois to chair important committees to improve the city of Chicago and its citizens. Her biographies never included her Irish background.

Her horror at being half-Irish was manifested in other ways. For instance, in forty-nine years of a very happy, successful marriage, Nellie never told her husband that she was half-Irish.

In the obituary for Julia Adelaide Sweeney Wooster written by her four daughters who loved her dearly, they completely suppressed her Irish background, referring to her only as "Mrs. L. T. Wooster". Even in death she was not allowed to revert to her origins and be her wonderful Irish self.

My Aunt Emma, Nellie's older sister, falsely told me that my grandmother's name was Julia Adelaide Smith. I wrote it that way when I paid tribute to her in the preface of my book, *Snow Covered Wagons*, published by Macmillan in 1936.

My own mother never told me that I was one-quarter Irish until one day I learned the secret during conversation with her in 1938 when I was forty-five and she was seventy-three.

While sewing and chatting with her at her summer cottage in Harbert, Michigan, I happened to remark:

"It's strange that I have *never* felt totally at home in New England, not even during my four years at Vassar or the year in Providence when Rudolph was teaching at Brown. There's something in me that admires New England and something that just does not respond, that seems *different*. Could it be the touch of French Huguenot that we have in our ancestry?"

I can still vividly recall my Mother sitting quietly, dropping her sewing limply in her lap, closing her eyes for a few moments as if to shut out an unwelcome vision, and finally saying:

"Well, Julia, I guess the time has come to tell you that you are a quarter I . . . rish." (How reluctantly and painfully she spoke the awful word!)

I exclaimed: "Good heavens! Praise God! How *wonderful!*" I felt like standing up and immediately dancing an Irish jig on the cottage porch! "All that culture and laughter and beauty! That explains so *much!* Why, *why*, didn't you tell me before?!"

"You have no idea, my child, of the agony of growing up in a New England town knowing that you are half-Irish." Then she told me the story of her New England Grandmother, Submit Chatfield Wooster, and Submit's long-duration persecution of her Irish daughter-in-law.

For me the episode was the happiest, most fabulous discovery of my life. I tremble to think that I might never have known this secret of my own Irish inheritance, that I never would have visited over and over again my beautiful, beloved Ireland!

My mother was strongly Methodist Episcopalian and Puritan in her ethic but she was, oh, so Hibernian in other respects about which she could do absolutely nothing and of which, I believe, she was quite unaware.

In appearance she had a definite but light olive cast to her skin. Having done thorough genealogical and historical studies of Ireland, I believe her olive skin came from intermixture with centuries of Spanish traders in the Galway or Kinsale regions, so near Macroom, rather than any West Coast Spanish Armada commixture. Most of those poor Armada men from storm-wrecked ships in 1588 who made it to shore were bashed on the head by British avengers or Irish plunderers, or were held captive for ransom.

Nellie's complexion was pure colleen, the rose-on-cream of the misty Irish hills plus the definite touch of olive. Her voice was the sheer melody of singing Celtic speech. She had all the towardliness, amiability, loquacity and wit of the Irish which made her very popular socially throughout her life. She had none of the stern, rigid, self-withheld qualities of her proud and arrogant grandmother, Submit Chatfield Wooster, whom she thoroughly disliked. She had an innate romanticism and exuded an intrinsic essence and spirit which can only be called poetry—and Irish poetry at that. I never pointed this out to her. I suspect she would have shuddered at the thought.

She had a passionate love of Nature and, as was *Mullach na Sidhe* so characteristic of her Irish mother, everything grew and blossomed under her magical touch. The phlox and peonies that brightened her Chicago and Michigan gardens derived from plants which flourished in Julia Sweeney Wooster's garden in Seymour ninety years before.

Without realizing it, my mother, Nellie Wooster Cooley, was a living paradox—hating everything Irish, especially her own Irish half, because she had been taught to do so since earliest childhood by her bigoted, venomous, prejudiced New England grandmother, yet manifesting in her lovely appearance and endearing personality so many wonderful Irish qualities and virtues.